The
MISSING
years of
Jesus

The
MISSING
years of
Jesus

The Greatest Story Never Told

DENNIS PRICE

HAY HOUSE

Australia • Canada • Hong Kong • India
South Africa • United Kingdom • United States

First published and distributed in the United Kingdom by:
Hay House UK Ltd, 292B Kensal Rd, London W10 5BE.
Tel.: (44) 20 8962 1230; Fax: (44) 20 8962 1239. www.hayhouse.co.uk

Published and distributed in the United States of America by:
Hay House, Inc., PO Box 5100, Carlsbad, CA 92018-5100. Tel.: (1) 760 431 7695
or (800) 654 5126; Fax: (1) 760 431 6948 or (800) 650 5115. www.hayhouse.com

Published and distributed in Australia by:
Hay House Australia Ltd, 18/36 Ralph St, Alexandria NSW 2015.
Tel.: (61) 2 9669 4299; Fax: (61) 2 9669 4144. www.hayhouse.com.au

Published and distributed in the Republic of South Africa by:
Hay House SA (Pty), Ltd, PO Box 990, Witkoppen 2068.
Tel./Fax: (27) 11 467 8904. www.hayhouse.co.za

Published and distributed in India by:
Hay House Publishers India, Muskaan Complex, Plot No.3, B-2, Vasant Kunj, New
Delhi – 110 070. Tel.: (91) 11 4176 1620; Fax: (91) 11 4176 1630. www.hayhouse.co.in

Distributed in Canada by:
Raincoast, 9050 Shaughnessy St, Vancouver, BC V6P 6E5.
Tel.: (1) 604 323 7100; Fax: (1) 604 323 2600

A catalogue record for this book is available
from the British Library.

ISBN 978-1-84850-033-4

Printed in the UK by
CPI William Clowes Beccles NR34 7TL

For my wonderful mother, Iris

And there are also many other things which Jesus did, the which, if they should be written every one, I suppose that even the world itself could not contain the books that should be written.

John 21, verses 24–5

CONTENTS

FOREWORD

You are holding a remarkable book; indeed, there is no other quite like it.

Dennis Price has audaciously tackled a question that has been bafflingly neglected for almost 2,000 years – *where was Jesus for most of His life?* The life of every other major religious figure has been documented and subjected to intense scrutiny, but there is a huge and apparently unfathomable gap of 18 years in our knowledge of the most famous human being who has ever lived.

From his experience as an archaeologist and his extraordinarily wide-ranging book learning, Price has approached the sources for the life of Jesus from a fresh and highly perceptive angle, and has ruthlessly applied logic and reasoning to establish a series of likelihoods regarding the defining characteristics of Jesus as an animated, historical individual of flesh and blood.

Having presented a series of propositions regarding Jesus's background, Price has tracked down folklore and traditions in the West Country and in his native Wales to make a powerful case for the presence of Jesus in late Iron Age Britain, prior to embarking on His public ministry in the Holy Land. Price has used his encyclopaedic knowledge of archaeology, particularly of Stonehenge and its environs, to buttress his propositions. In the course of his argument and reasoning, Price draws in parallels and case studies, and he invites us to consider, for instance, otherwise neglected matters such as the significance of pyramids in the life of Jesus. He likewise investigates subjects as diverse as Knossos, Beelzebub, William Blake, the ancient British druids, Winston Churchill, the Cathars and diabolical possession, all of which have their part to play in this methodical investigation.

Dennis Price is an archaeologist, a writer, a mystic and an acute observer of life. In the course of his minutely detailed yet eminently readable book, he has harsh words for those who have wilfully or ignorantly distorted evidence, particularly archaeological evidence, and for those who fear re-examination of religious beliefs. He has amassed an extraordinary collection of archaeological, historical and religious material for his thesis. His final conclusions are gripping and compelling.

Having known Dennis Price for more than a quarter of a century, I am honoured to introduce this text and I recommend it to you. If you are browsing – buy this book. If you have already bought it, then relish the intellectual adventure awaiting you.

Peter Mills
Clerkenwell, London
January 2009

Peter Mills is a senior archaeologist who has directed excavations at some of the most important and prestigious sites in Britain, which include Westminster Abbey, the Royal Mint, the Preceptory of the Knights of St John of Jerusalem, the Palace of Westminster and the Tower of London. He is a Director of the Mills Whipp Archaeological Consultancy based in central London.

ACKNOWLEDGEMENTS

Everyone I've named here has many admirable qualities, but I've been particularly struck by their independence of thought, their generosity of spirit, their encouragement and the fact that they possess the courage of their convictions. I've benefited immensely from the company of such people ever since I was a child and they've each contributed in their own individual way to this book ultimately being written, so it's merely justice for me to try to give them their due.

So, a warm thank you to Michelle Pilley, to Lizzie Hutchins and to everyone at Hay House for their patience, and for transforming some lengthy documents and even lengthier soliloquies into something of beauty that will hopefully be of interest and value to others. As for my friend Keith Bishop, it was a lucky day indeed for me when I met him.

Thank you to Ian Hambelton for accompanying me by the dead of night, for introducing me to the world of 21st-century technology and for *always* being there to help, in good times and in bad. Thank you to George Salim Khalaf (Encyclopedia Phoeniciana: http://phoenicia.org) for his near-infinite patience and for his constant willingness to help.

Thank you to Juris Ozols, a gentleman and another 'watcher of the skies'.

From the 1960s: A belated thank you to Miss Phillips, Mr Jack Roberts, Mr Thomas, Mrs Thomas, Miss Thomas and Mrs Evans for teaching me to value learning over ignorance.

From the 1970s: Thank you to Ralph, Sabina and Jenny for their patience and for giving me my start in archaeology all those years ago in Usk. Thank you to my classics teachers, A. L. Sockett, H. E. Phillips, Reg Hall, D. J. R. Jenkins and George Glover, and thank you also to Peter Anthony and to my friend Rufus Evill.

More recently, my grateful appreciation goes to: my sister Carol, Shirley and David, Satchi, Kumari, John, Cyrus Saifolahi, Dave Bunce, Alison and Chris, Richard and Marise, Neil Pym, Neil Jeffries, Patsy O'Hagan, Tim Jones, Deborah Lane, Alex Down, Aynslie Hanna, Jim Dowdall, Mörat, Anette Viberg, John Freeman, Barry Stephens, David Croft, Glyn Jones, Lorraine Spalding, Morna Simpson, John Witts, Hugo Jenks, Andy Marlow, Matt Rous and to Bryan and Heather, and I'm indebted to Jasmine Gould for reminding me of 'The power of thought! The magic of the mind!' A particularly big thank you, for all manner of reasons, to Gill, Jack, Tanith and Blueboy.

And finally, my belated thanks to: the late Robert Graves, for capturing my imagination with his ingenious solution to DCLXVI; Heinrich Schliemann, for discovering the fabled city of Troy by choosing to believe every word of what others at the time thought of as fairy tales.

And my Dad.

INTRODUCTION

'Somewhere, something wonderful is waiting to be discovered.' These words of joyful anticipation were written by the late Carl Sagan, the gifted astronomer who brought the swirling cosmos to vivid and unforgettable life in a series of books and television programmes throughout the 1980s. I don't know what he had in mind when he made his optimistic prophecy; perhaps, as 'some watcher of the skies', he was trying to conjure up the image of some as yet undiscovered celestial phenomenon or an abandoned alien artefact gathering cosmic dust in a cave on a distant planet in our solar system. On the other hand, he may have been thinking of more earthly treasures, or of information that has yet to come to light; and the most striking and apparently mystifying example of such lost knowledge occurs in the life of the most famous person in human history, Jesus Christ. While the Bible goes into great detail about his early childhood and the adult years of his famous ministry, it tells us precious little about the 18 years in between, stating only, 'Jesus increased in wisdom, in stature and in favour with God and men.'[1]

These years are a mystery to us now, but at one time there were surely a great many people who knew *precisely* where Jesus was and what he was doing between the ages of 12 and 30. Somewhere along the line, this knowledge was either carelessly lost or carefully concealed – but not so carelessly or carefully that a great many clues weren't left behind.

Has anyone tried to follow these up and learn what physically happened to Jesus during this time? Well, at least one person has made the attempt. In 1908 Levi H. Dowling published *The Aquarian Age Gospel of Jesus the Christ*, in which he claimed that Jesus travelled and taught in India, Tibet, Persia, Assyria, Greece and Egypt. Dowling claimed to have gained his unique insight into the 'missing years' of Jesus by consulting the Akashik Records, a collection of the sum total of human knowledge and experience that is said to exist on another plane of existence, accessible only to occult adepts. I wouldn't dismiss or deny the existence of these records, nor would I rule out the possibility that it's somehow possible to read them, but it seems that only a select few are able to gaze upon them with their own eyes. By way of contrast, the evidence that I have to present concerning the missing years of Jesus exists in tangible form and is freely available to anyone who chooses to visit the locations in question or to inspect the documentation for themselves.

I've spent years working as an archaeologist and far longer studying a range of historical mysteries for my own enjoyment and satisfaction. My interest in such things began a long time ago, when I was a young boy and my mother bought me a mesmerizing book called *Gods, Graves and Scholars*. Originally published in 1949, it's a history of archaeology up to that date and it concentrates on the efforts of remarkable men such as Howard Carter, who refused to give in to bitter disappointment and hardship in his quest for Tutankhamen's tomb, and the truly inspirational Heinrich Schliemann, who struggled against the accepted wisdom of the time to eventually locate and unearth the fabled city of Troy in 1871.[2] Some years later, as part of my Latin studies, I was similarly captivated by the enthralling tale of the descent to the underworld undertaken by Aeneas, one of the survivors of Troy after the city had been sacked by the rampaging Greeks.

In the course of his wanderings after fleeing the burning ruins of Troy, Aeneas reluctantly ventured down into the terrifying realms of the dead to consult the spirit of his father Anchises and to learn something of what Destiny had in store for him, being guided through the gloomy regions of Hell by a Sybil, or priestess. This enchanting and extremely detailed vision of the Roman afterlife was part of a much longer epic poem called the *Aeneid*, written in the latter part of the first century BC by a Roman poet named Virgil. Later, it made such a huge impression on mediaeval minds that Virgil became one of the most venerated figures of the ancient world. He was particularly admired by the Christian writers who lived after him because his poem described the founding of Rome, the Holy City. As a result, the four-teenth-century Italian poet Dante chose Virgil as his guide in his epic poem *The Divine Comedy*, better known as 'Dante's Inferno', in which Dante and Virgil travelled around the infernal regions in a vision of the Christian afterlife that's come to be regarded as one of the greatest works of literature the world's ever seen.

Just as Aeneas and Dante were led by their guides through a fearful and confusing underworld, now it falls to me to take on the mantle of guide myself. However, instead of taking a tour through the ghostly surroundings of a spiritual afterlife, we'll be wandering through the very real ancient landscapes of the Middle East and the west of England as they were in the early years of the first century BC, when Jesus was a young man. We will not be consulting directly with spectres, as Aeneas did, but we'll certainly be looking closely at certain aspects of the lives and works of men who lived long ago, men such as William Blake, the visionary poet and painter, William Stukeley, the famous antiquarian, King James I of England, Joseph of Arimathea, Pontius Pilate and, of course, Jesus himself, to see if we can encounter anything at all that can throw some light, one way or another, on what happened to Jesus in those missing years.

Our investigation will be divided into three broad parts. The first will take a close look at certain passages and words in the New Testament, the primary source of information on the life of Jesus, for anything that might indicate what he did during those years. The second part will concentrate on the physical landscape and archaeological features of the west of England, as legend has it that Jesus lived there for several years, while the third part will deal with prominent individuals or groups of people whose lives may hold something of value for us in our search for the truth.

It might seem a daunting prospect to look into a book such as the Bible, which has been pored over by scholars of repute throughout the ages, in search of something new *and* valid, but, as we'll see soon enough, many highly significant features have been discovered by

3

amateurs. Nor should we be overawed by the thought of trying to make sense of the findings of archaeologists, especially as far as certain discoveries in the west of England are concerned. We might assume that Biblical scholars and archaeologists enjoy a monopoly on insight and wisdom in their respective fields of study, but the blunt truth is that there are wildly differing interpretations of the Bible throughout the Christian world, and as far as archaeology is concerned, I know from long personal experience that some practitioners are just as likely to make hideous mistakes and indeed *lie* about their discoveries as people in another profession; in any event, archaeologists are neither infallible nor beyond reproach. So, we'll be scouring every available source for relevant information, impartially looking at whatever material may present itself and constantly querying the validity of our discoveries, but one thing we *won't* be doing is automatically deferring to the judgements of others. If those judgements still hold firm after detailed examination, that is another matter.

When embarking on a quest such as this, I'm inclined to think it wise to follow the advice of Doctor Joseph Bell, the nineteenth-century physician who was the direct inspiration for Sir Arthur Conan Doyle's fictional detective, Sherlock Holmes. Dr Bell was able to ascertain the life histories of complete strangers by doing nothing more than observe them as they entered a room, and he always stressed to his students that they should take into account the 'vast importance of little distinctions, the endless significance of trifles'.

If we, too, pay the closest possible attention to the myriad details that appear before us, we may ultimately be rewarded with a meaningful glimpse into a mysterious period in the life of the most famous man who has ever lived.

Ask, and it shall be given you; seek, and ye shall find…
Matthew 7, verse 7

PART I

VOYAGE

...Voyaging through strange seas of Thought, alone...

Wordsworth, *The Prelude*, Book iii, 1.61

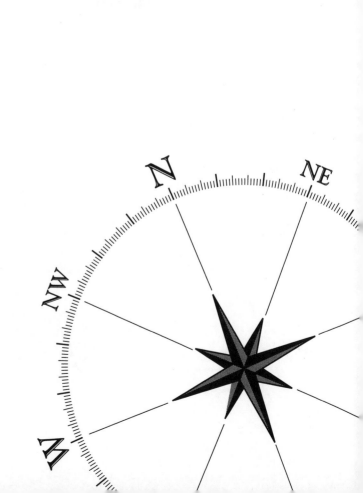

Britain and the Mediterranean Around the Ti...

Oceanus
Germanicus

Hibernia

Britannia

Germania

Oceanus
Atlanticus

Et

Gallia

Corsica

Sardinia

Italia

Hispania

Balearic
Islands

Sicilia

Pillars of
Hercules

Ir

200 Miles

Africa

Jesus

The Landscape of the Holy Land

Mediterranean
Sea

Sidon

Tyre

Capernaum
Sea
of
Galilee

Nazareth

Caesarea
Maritima

Detail of
Holy Land

Jerusalem

Bethlehem
Dead
Sea

20 Miles

ropa

Pontus
Euxinus

Asia
Minor

Graecia

Creta
Cyprus

Holy
Land

um

Arabia
Deserta

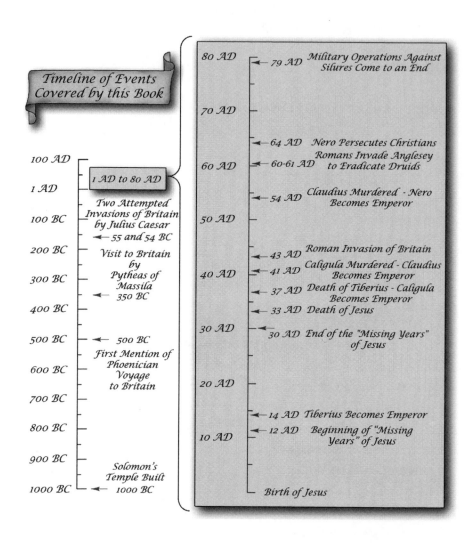

Timeline of Events Covered by this Book

1 AD to 80 AD

100 AD	
1 AD	
100 BC	Two Attempted Invasions of Britain by Julius Caesar ← 55 and 54 BC
200 BC	Visit to Britain by Pytheas of Massila
300 BC	
400 BC	← 350 BC
500 BC	← 500 BC
600 BC	First Mention of Phoenician Voyage to Britain
700 BC	
800 BC	
900 BC	
1000 BC	Solomon's Temple Built ← 1000 BC

80 AD	← 79 AD	Military Operations Against Silures Come to an End
70 AD		
60 AD	← 64 AD	Nero Persecutes Christians
	← 60-61 AD	Romans Invade Anglesey to Eradicate Druids
	← 54 AD	Claudius Murdered - Nero Becomes Emperor
50 AD		
40 AD	← 43 AD	Roman Invasion of Britain
	← 41 AD	Caligula Murdered - Claudius Becomes Emperor
	← 37 AD	Death of Tiberius - Caligula Becomes Emperor
	← 33 AD	Death of Jesus
30 AD	← 30 AD	End of the "Missing Years" of Jesus
20 AD		
10 AD	← 14 AD	Tiberius Becomes Emperor
	← 12 AD	Beginning of "Missing Years" of Jesus
		Birth of Jesus

(This and previous figure ©Juris Ozols)

CHAPTER ONE

The Undiscovered Country

And did those feet in ancient time walk upon
England's mountains green?
William Blake

There are numerous legends and traditions suggesting that Jesus once visited Britain as a young man, and in the early part of the last century three British churchmen painstakingly collected this body of folklore together in a series of books that we'll look into in due course. However, the concept of Jesus visiting Britain finds its most famous expression in a short verse entitled 'And did those feet in ancient time?' written in 1805 by William Blake as a preface to his epic poem *Milton*. The words were set to music in 1916 by C. Hubert H. Parry and the uplifting combination, now known simply as 'Jerusalem', has long been Britain's most popular patriotic song, to the extent that it's regarded as an unofficial national anthem. The first verse reads:

> *And did those feet in ancient time*
> *Walk upon England's mountains green?*
> *And was the Holy Lamb of God*
> *On England's pleasant pastures seen?*
> *And did the Countenance Divine*

Shine forth upon our clouded hills?
And was Jerusalem builded here
Among these dark, satanic mills?

There's no doubt that Blake was referring to Jesus, because in John 1, verse 29, John the Baptist specifically refers to Jesus as the Lamb of God – 'The next day John seeth Jesus coming unto him, and saith, "Behold the Lamb of God, which taketh away the sin of the world"' – and he repeats this observation a few verses later.

As well as being a highly regarded poet and painter, Blake was also a visionary and a mystic who had an intense interest in ancient Britain, and the first woodcut that he executed was called 'Joseph of Arimathea on the rocky shores of Albion'. Albion is the oldest name that we know of for the islands of Britain and it was recorded as far back as the fifth century BC, so it's hard to avoid the conclusion that Blake's woodcut reflected the widespread belief that Joseph of Arimathea, the mysterious figure who took down the body of Jesus from the cross, once visited Britain. Some of the legends state that he brought Jesus with him as a young man, and it may be this particular visit to which the first verse of 'Jerusalem' refers.

The first two lines are clear enough, suggesting that in ancient times Jesus walked on England's green mountains. Strictly speaking, unlike Wales or Scotland, England doesn't *have* mountains, but we must bear in mind that Blake was composing a poem, not compiling a detailed geographical study.

In the third and fourth lines, Blake refers to the 'Lamb of God' possibly being seen on England's 'pleasant pastures', or meadows. This might seem a very general description of the landscape, but Blake had a number of realistic options available to him, because Britain possesses a surprisingly broad range of natural features for such a small island: mountain ranges, hills, moors, plains, valleys, gently rolling downs, bogs, fens, marshes, quicksands and even a landscape resembling desert in the sand dunes of northern Cornwall and Devon. There are also hot springs, streams, brooks, rivers, lakes, ponds, steep cliffs, sandy beaches, shingle beaches, estuaries, mudflats, woods, forests, copses or groves, but

Blake wrote of Jesus being seen on 'pleasant pastures'. In the two great epic poems I mentioned in the introduction, both Dante and Aeneas descended to the underworld through gloomy woods, so if Blake had wished to follow an established literary tradition and somehow mirror these journeys to dark, godless regions, he could have simply written about Jesus wandering through the many woods, forests, copses or groves that were once part of the British landscape, but he did not.

Blake goes on to ask if the 'Countenance Divine' once shone forth on 'our clouded hills', which brings to mind Matthew 17, verses 1 and 2, where Jesus became transformed while on a mountaintop in front of Peter, James and John: 'And [he] was transfigured before them: and his face did shine as the sun, and his raiment was white as the light.' This transformation was one of the more notable events in the life of Jesus, so there's no doubt that 'the Holy Lamb of God' and 'the Countenance Divine' refer to the same person.

This brings us to the final couplet, where Blake asks if Jerusalem was built 'among these dark, satanic mills'? It's unthinkable that he was referring to a physical city replicating Jerusalem that had been built in Britain 2,000 years ago and somehow avoided detection up to 1805, when he was writing his poem. However, the Book of Revelation speaks of the Second Coming of Jesus and of the founding of the City of God, or New Jerusalem, so Jerusalem became a metaphor for heaven, or the heavenly repose of the blessed. As for the 'dark, satanic mills', it's not immediately clear what Blake was referring to, but as he was writing about ancient times, these were presumably some foreboding structures that were in existence in Britain at the time of the visit by Jesus.

Without looking any more deeply than this, the verse tells us that Blake was writing about a visit made by a young Jesus to the shores of Britain. Logic dictates that he must have been between the ages of 12 and 30 at this point, because that is the period of his life about which the Bible has little to say and there's no known mention of such a visit in the pages of the New Testament that cover the other periods in his life. It seems that he visited a region with grass-covered hills that resembled mountains and was also seen in beautiful pastures or meadows; judging from the reference to the 'Countenance Divine', some transformation occurred which *preceded* the famous event in the Book of Matthew and this event took place in a setting of clouded hills and among 'satanic mills', whatever they may have been. The result of this transformation in this infernal setting was that Jerusalem was briefly established in England in the early years of the first century AD in the form of some triumph of love or goodness over strife or evil.

Let's see if there's any evidence that this legend could be based on a historical reality.

CHAPTER TWO

Stranger in a Strange Land

But the stranger that dwelleth with you shall be unto
you as one born among you, and thou shalt love him as
thyself; for ye were strangers in the land of Egypt.
Leviticus 19, verse 34

What does the Bible tell us of Jesus's early life? In Luke, chapter 2, verses 41–2, we read: 'Every year [Christ's] parents used to go to Jerusalem for the feast of the Passover. When he was twelve years old, they went up for the feast as usual.' In verses 51–2, we learn that '[Christ] then went down with them and came to Nazareth and lived under their authority. His mother stored up all these things in her heart. And Jesus increased in wisdom, in stature and in favour with God and men.' There's nothing unusual there, but the next mention we have of Jesus comes in chapter 3, verse 23, which states, 'When he started to teach, Jesus was about thirty years old,' which makes clear that there's a gap of roughly 18 years in his life that's unaccounted for.

Most people are inclined to think that Jesus spent his formative years working as a carpenter in Nazareth, but it's surely reasonable to consider that while he may have returned to Nazareth at the age of 12, he didn't necessarily remain there for the next 18 years. It's also reasonable to suppose that the Bible is strangely silent about this period because Jesus was not in the area for anyone to record details of his daily life, something that is in fact plainly spelled out in the gospels. In Luke, chapter 4, verses 16–22, we read:

> So he came to Nazareth, where he had been brought up. And as his custom was, he went into the synagogue on the Sabbath day, and stood up to read... And the eyes of all who were in the synagogue were fixed on him... So all bore witness to him, and marvelled at the gracious words which proceeded out of his mouth. And they said, 'Is this not Joseph's son?'

The words 'where he *had* been brought up' are of immediate interest, because they tell us that although Jesus had spent his childhood in Nazareth, he had lived elsewhere for a notable period of time. This is further strengthened by the words, 'So He came to Nazareth' – to go there, he must have been somewhere else first. There's no logical alternative.

This passage also informs us that Jesus habitually went into the synagogue on the Sabbath day, but it doesn't specify that he habitually went into the synagogue at *Nazareth*. If this was what Luke had intended to convey, he could have easily put the matter beyond doubt by writing, 'And as His custom was, He went into the synagogue *there...*'

Further confirmation that Jesus had been away from Nazareth for a very long time appears when we learn that the people in the synagogue listened to Jesus reading, then asked one another, 'Is this not Joseph's son?' Now, why should they even contemplate posing such a question? If Jesus had been resident in Nazareth since his birth, he would have been a familiar figure, but even the people who knew Joseph were doubtful as to whether the person they saw before them was in fact his son. With this in mind, it's not going too far to state that Jesus had changed out of all recognition since they'd last seen him, which in turn implies an extremely long absence from the place of his childhood. It also implies that he'd left the area not long after the age of 12, as the marked physical change and growth from a boy to a man would explain this confusion. Had Jesus left the area when he was in his late teens or early twenties, there was likely to have been a less dramatic physical difference between the person who had left and the man aged 30 or thereabouts who had returned. In this technological age, it's a matter that we can easily judge for ourselves by the simple expedient of studying photographs and film of our own friends and family, then comparing their appearances at the ages in question.

The Gospel of Matthew echoes Luke's account, but provides some intriguing additional details. Let's look at chapter 13, verses 53 to 58, which read:

> …Coming to his home town, [Jesus] taught the people in their synagogue in such a way that they were astonished and said, 'Where did the man get this wisdom and these miraculous powers? This is the carpenter's son, surely? Is not his mother the woman called Mary, and his brothers James and Joseph and Simon and Jude? His sisters too, are they not all here with us? So where did the man get it all?' And they would not accept him. But Jesus said to them, 'A prophet is only despised in his own country and in his own house,' and he did not work many miracles there because of their lack of faith.

First, we're told that Jesus went to his hometown, so it's beyond question that he'd been away, albeit for an unspecified period of time. Secondly, whatever he said and however he said it, his teachings clearly astonished the people in the synagogue enough for them to ask, 'Where did the man get this wisdom and these miraculous powers?' There's no answer to this perfectly reasonable question in any of the gospels.

Next, just as we're told in Luke's gospel, the people asked, 'This is the carpenter's son, surely?' This could be taken to mean, 'Because this man has spoken in such a way, he can only be the son of the carpenter,' the implication being that the people were familiar with Jesus, but were astounded by his sudden powers of oratory. Moreover, it could mean that while they may have doubted the identity of Jesus at that time, they were expecting to be astonished by him at some point. However, the following verses contradict this. When we read that they exclaimed, 'Is not his mother the woman called Mary, and his brothers James and Joseph and Simon and Jude? His sisters too, are they not all here with us?' it's clear that while the immediate family of Jesus were instantly recognizable and were furthermore living among the people in the synagogue, Jesus himself was physically unfamiliar to them. The most logical explanation is that he had been absent for many years. The following sentence – 'So where did the man get it all?' – puts the matter beyond doubt.

Finally, Matthew's gospel relates that the people of Nazareth wouldn't accept Jesus because of the confusion over his identity and the source of his powers, so Jesus said to them, 'A prophet is only despised in his own country and in his own house.' It's hard to see how this is an abstract statement, because the sense is of historical fact; furthermore, it implies that by the age of 30, Jesus had already had experience of being revered as a prophet in a different country from the land of his birth.

ANOTHER TAXING QUESTION

There's no shortage of references to Jesus being an unfamiliar figure at the start of his ministry. In Matthew 17, we read of Jesus journeying around Caesarea Philippi and to Galilee, then we come to verses 24–7 and the curious matter of Jesus and the temple tax:

> When they reached Capernaum, the collectors of the half-shekel[1] (temple tax)[2] came to Peter and said, 'Does your master not pay the half-shekel?' 'Yes,' he replied, and went into the house. But before he could speak, Jesus said, 'Simon, what is your opinion? From whom do the kings of the Earth take toll or tribute? From their sons or from foreigners?'[3] And when he replied, 'From foreigners,' Jesus said, 'Well then, the sons are exempt. However, so as not to offend these people, go to the lake and cast a hook; take the first fish that bites, open its mouth and there you will find a shekel;[4] take it and give it to them for me and for you.'

Simon and Peter were one and the same person, as we know from Matthew 4, verse 18, 'As [Jesus] walked by the Sea of Galilee, he saw two brothers, Simon who is called Peter and his brother Andrew...' The temple tax was a levy imposed for the upkeep of the synagogue, but it's not necessary for us to be familiar with details of ancient administrative history to understand the full implications of this passage.

Capernaum was a city close to where the River Jordan flowed into the Sea of Galilee, an area where Jesus was frequently seen in his later years, and Nazareth was in the same region. If Jesus had lived in this area all his life, he'd have been a familiar figure to the tax collector, particularly as he was already famous by the age of 12 for his command of the scriptures. However, the man did not know him, so Jesus good-humouredly resigned himself to being regarded as a foreigner in his own land.

STRANGERS ON THE SHORE

If further proof were needed that Jesus returned to the land of his birth a virtual stranger, there are some telling episodes in the Gospel according to St John, chapter 1, verses 29–34, which describe an event at Bethany, on the far side of the River Jordan, involving John the Baptist:

> The next day, seeing Jesus coming towards him, John said, 'Look, there is the Lamb of God that takes away the sin of the world. This is the one I spoke of when I said: "A man is coming after me who ranks before me because he existed before me." *I did not know him myself,* and yet it was to reveal him to Israel that I came baptising with water... I saw the Spirit coming down on him from heaven like a dove and resting on him. *I did not know him myself,* but he who sent me to baptise with water had said to me, "The man on whom you see the Holy Spirit come down and rest is the one who is going to baptise with the Holy Spirit."' [My italics.]

John the Baptist and Jesus were first cousins, because Mary, the mother of Jesus, was the sister of Elizabeth, John's mother. Furthermore, John and Jesus were occupied with very similar business in spreading the word of God and, as already noted, Jesus was famous by the age of 12 for his knowledge of the scriptures. John should have known him intimately, but he twice announces in unambiguous terms that he *didn't* know him.

Now, we might consider that John was maintaining that he didn't recognize Jesus as the Messiah, rather than not recognizing him as his cousin, but there's further proof of the uncertainty surrounding the identity of Jesus in verses 35 to 39:

On the following day as John stood there again with two of his disciples, Jesus passed, and John stared hard at him and said, 'Look, there is the Lamb of God.' Hearing this, the two disciples followed Jesus. Jesus turned round, saw them following and said, 'What do you want?' They answered, 'Rabbi [which means 'teacher'], where do you live?'

Why should John 'stare hard' at Jesus the *next* day, other than to be sure of his identity? Why should the two disciples not know where Jesus lived? Why couldn't John have told them himself? If Jesus had been a familiar figure in the region, then John would have recognized him and the two disciples would certainly have known where he lived, but the gospels tell us otherwise.

In verses 45 to 48, we read of further confusion:

Philip found Nathanael and said to him, 'We have found the one Moses wrote about in the Law, the one about whom the prophets wrote: he is Jesus son of Joseph from Nazareth.' 'From Nazareth?' said Nathanael. 'Can anything good come from that place?' 'Come and see,' replied Philip. When Jesus saw Nathanael coming he said of him, 'There is an Israelite who deserves the name, incapable of deceit.' 'How do you know me?' said Nathanael.

We know from John chapter 21, verse 2, that this Nathanael was from Cana, which was only four miles north of Nazareth. If Jesus had remained in his hometown throughout his life, particularly given his early fame in the synagogue, it's simply irrational to believe that a man from a town a mere four miles away should be in any doubt about his identity. However, not only does Nathanael seem to be unaware of Jesus and the fact that he came from Nazareth, but his question 'How do you know me?' makes it clear that their paths had never crossed in 30 years or so.

LOST IN TRANSLATION?

The blunt fact is that whichever translation of the Bible we read, there's simply no doubt that Jesus was absent from his homeland for such a prolonged period of time that he was physically unrecognizable upon his return. The evidence is plain to see:

- So he came to Nazareth, where he had been brought up.
- And they said, 'Is this not Joseph's son?'
- ...Coming to his home town, he taught the people in their synagogue in such a way that they were astonished...
- 'Where did the man get this wisdom and these miraculous powers?'
- 'This is the carpenter's son, surely?'
- 'Is not his mother the woman called Mary?'
- 'His sisters too, are they not all here with us?'
- 'So where did the man get it all?'
- But Jesus said to them, 'A prophet is only despised in his own country and in his own house.'
- When they reached Capernaum, the collectors of the half-shekel (temple tax) came to Peter and said, 'Does your master not pay the half-shekel?'
- 'A man is coming after me who ranks before me because he existed before me. I did not know him myself...'
- 'I saw the Spirit coming down on him from heaven like a dove and resting on him. I did not know him myself...'
- On the following day as John stood there again with two of his

disciples, Jesus passed, and John stared hard at him…

- Jesus turned round, saw them following and said, 'What do you want?' They answered, 'Rabbi, where do you live?'
- When Jesus saw Nathanael coming he said of him, 'There is an Israelite who deserves the name, incapable of deceit.' 'How do you know me?' said Nathanael.

If one of these examples existed in isolation, then we could perhaps dismiss it as a curiosity, but it's hard to argue with the gospel truth of 18 missing years. What are we to make of this?

CHAPTER THREE

Behold the Man

'I dare do all that may become a man…'
William Shakespeare, *Macbeth*, **Act I, Scene VII**

In our search for a solution to the mystery of the missing years of Jesus, it's as well to bear in mind that the vast majority of the New Testament deals with his teachings, his birth and his death. There's almost no information about his physical appearance and there's a negligible amount of detail about any personal habits or idiosyncrasies that would distinguish him from anyone else, apart of course from his ability to perform miracles. As a result, we must minutely inspect what little is available, for if we study what we are told of the character and humanity of Jesus, as well as his cultural background and upbringing, it's bound to be of some assistance when we try to discover what he did during the missing years.

We'd also do well to bear in mind that at the time he went 'missing', Jesus was a young man, and it's in the nature of teenage men of every creed and colour to be impetuous, to believe they can change the world, to believe that they're invincible, to be curious, to be daring, to be exuberant and to yearn for new horizons. In the words of *Gaudeamus Igitur*, a mediaeval song:

Let us rejoice, therefore, while we are young.
After the joys of youth
And the tiresomeness of old age
The earth will hold us.

As we're specifically told that Jesus came to Earth to learn what it was like to be human, it seems only natural to credit him with the characteristics of millions of other male adolescents, but what else do we know about him?

I may be alone in this, but I can't help noticing a faint trace of humour in the way Jesus dealt with the tax collector. Is this important? I believe so. Jesus was patently capable of displaying a variety of emotions, such as joy, sorrow, anger, defiance and even despair, as shown when he cried out, 'My God, my God, why have you forsaken me?' just before he died. But the Bible also holds other, more telling clues to his character.

LORD OF THE HIGH PLACE

When we search the New Testament for details that might throw some light on the personal disposition, habits and idiosyncrasies of Jesus, we cannot help but be struck by his inclination to visit remote high places, especially for the spiritual purposes of prayer, exorcism, solitude and retreat.

In Matthew's gospel, we read that after sending the crowds away, '[Jesus] went up into the hills by himself to pray.'[1] This took place directly after the miracle of the feeding of the 5,000 at an otherwise undefined 'lonely place'[2] after Jesus had stepped ashore from a boat. We also learn that 'Jesus took with him Peter and James and his brother John and led them up a high mountain where they could be alone.'[3] What followed brings to mind William Blake's reference to the 'Countenance Divine' and 'clouded hills', because directly after the four men had ascended this mountain, an astonishing phenomenon occurred whereby Jesus's face shone like the sun, his clothes became white and the phantom forms of Moses and Elijah appeared.[4]

In Mark's gospel, we read of Jesus visiting the lakeside town of Capernaum, where he cured the sick and cast out many devils. After this, he travelled to another undefined 'lonely place'[5] long before dawn. We later read of another episode where he successfully cast out many unclean spirits on the shores of the Sea of Galilee, after which we're told, 'He now went up into the hills and summoned those he wanted.'[6]

Luke writes of Jesus going into the hills to spend a whole night in prayer[7] after what appears to be the same event, this time involving the cure of a man with a withered hand. Luke also tells us the famous story of the Gadarene swine, in which Jesus encounters a madman possessed by demons living among the tombs. This naked creature routinely broke the chains and fetters used in a futile attempt to restrain him and he chillingly supplied his name as 'Legion' on account of the sheer quantity of unclean spirits infesting his person. As for the geographical location, Jesus exorcised this swarm of demons on a mountainside,[8] after which they rushed into a large herd of pigs that charged over a cliff and drowned themselves in the waters of the Sea of Galilee.[9]

John's gospel speaks of Jesus ascending hillsides[10] prior to the first miracle of the loaves, and also of him going to the Mount of Olives, a rocky outcrop whose summit stands 300 feet higher than Jerusalem, while Matthew gives us details of the famous Sermon on the Mount[12] overlooking the Sea of Galilee.

But these aren't the only occasions where Jesus visited 'high places' in conjunction with dramatic mystical episodes in his life. All four gospels speak of the temptation of Christ in the wilderness, an event that took place prior to the start of his ministry, and Matthew's gospel supplies us with the greatest detail. We learn that the Devil took Jesus to the holy city, or Jerusalem, and made him stand on the parapet of the temple, urging him to throw himself down because the scriptures wrote that angels would support him. Jesus rebuked him, quoting another scripture warning that God was not to be put to the test. Immediately afterwards:

Again, the Devil taketh him up into an exceeding high mountain, and sheweth him all the kingdoms of the world, and the glory of them; and saith unto him, 'All these things will I give thee, if thou wilt fall down and worship me.'[13]

Once more Jesus rebuked his adversary with a scriptural quotation and the Devil departed, so here was yet another mystical occurrence of great consequence in the life of Jesus, this time taking place at the summit of 'an exceeding high mountain'.

Now we may consider that there's nothing so very strange about all these journeys to high places and we may also suppose it was inevitable that a man who lived in such a locality would occasionally choose to wander to high places during his ministry. To find out if this was really the case, we must ask if there was any realistic and obvious alternative.

John the Baptist, as already noted, was a cousin of Jesus who had a similar calling at around the same time. The two men were roughly the same age and had much in common. Mary, the mother of Jesus, came to be with child through the Holy Spirit, while her barren sister Elizabeth came to bear a child as a direct result of the earnest prayers of her husband Zechariah.[14] The fathers of both Jesus and John received visits from angels to tell them of the pregnancy and of the impending birth of a son who would be special in some way.

We've already noted the silence that surrounds the adolescence and early adult years of Jesus, but there's an equal vagueness about the early life of John the Baptist. We're simply told that he grew up, that his spirit matured and that he lived in the desert until he appeared openly preaching the Word of God.

Jesus and John apparently lived in the same locality and when the ministry of Jesus began, the two men were often confused with each other. Luke's gospel tells us of the Gadarene swine, of the exorcism of the man named Legion and of a young girl being brought back from the dead,[15] events that excited great interest elsewhere:

Meanwhile, Herod the tetrarch had heard about all that was going on; and he was puzzled, because some people were saying that John had risen from the dead,[16] others that Elijah had appeared, still others that one of the ancient prophets had come back to life...[17]

In chapter 16 of Matthew's gospel, we also read:

When Jesus came to the region of Caesarea Philippi, he put this question to his disciples, 'Who do you think the Son of Man is?' And they said, 'Some say he is John the Baptist...'[18]

Despite the similarities between the two men, however, each chose a very different environment in which to operate. In Luke's gospel, we read of John the Baptist:

Meanwhile the child grew up and his spirit matured. And he lived out in the wilderness until the day he appeared openly to Israel.[19]

Matthew has much more to say, telling us that John preached in the wilderness, wore a garment of camel-hair with a leather belt around his waist and lived off locusts and wild honey.[20] It's reasonable to expect that two virtually identical prophets would have chosen similar lifestyles as a path to enlightenment, yet Jesus displayed a marked preference for the hills.

If any doubt remains that Jesus shunned the desert lifestyle, there was a notable occasion when he warned his disciples that at the end of the world there would be those who would impersonate him:

For there shall arise False Christs and False Messiahs and shall show great signs and wonders, insomuch that it if were possible, they shall deceive the very elect. Wherefore, if they say unto you, 'Behold, he is in the *desert*,' go not forth [my italics].[21]

Why, apart from the brief interlude of 40 days in the wilderness, was Jesus not drawn towards the desert as place of contemplation and preparation? Why did such a location suit John, but not Jesus? Why did Jesus prefer high places as locations for prayer and miracles? Did he acquire these habits during the years prior to his ministry? If so, where, and how did Jesus get to these places?

The New Testament tells us of a number of means by which Jesus made his way around, but his main mode of transport was walking. There are some striking examples of this; for instance, the occasion when Jesus spoke at the synagogue at Nazareth and enraged the people there:

> They sprang to their feet and hustled him out of the town; and they took him up to the brow of the hill their town was built on, intending to throw him down the cliff, but he slipped through the crowd and walked away.[22]

This episode is remarkable inasmuch as it's an attempt to lynch Jesus at a high place early in his ministry; it also demonstrates that he possessed an almost supernatural calm, for he was able to slip through a furious crowd intent on murder, then simply walk away, rather than run. In fact, there's no Biblical mention of Jesus running or marching at all; he apparently walked or wandered up to the crest of hills and mountains rather than climbed them, but throughout the gospels, he also employed a far more striking mode of transport.

THE ANCIENT MARINER

> *They that go down to the sea in ships:*
> *And occupy their business in great waters;*
> *These men see the works of the Lord:*
> *And his wonders in the deep.*
> **Psalm 107, verses 23–4**

Matthew informs us that early in his ministry, directly after the temptation in the wilderness, Jesus chose to settle near the sea:

> Now when Jesus had heard that John was cast into prison, he departed into Galilee; and leaving Nazareth, he came and dwelt in

Capernaum, which is upon the sea coast, in the borders of Zabulon and Nephthalim…[23]

After this, there are innumerable references to Jesus and boats, so many that it would be tedious to list them all. We're used to reading of Jesus gathering fishermen, telling them that he'd make them 'fishers of men',[24] and going out on the Sea of Galilee; in fact we're *so* familiar with these stories that it's easy to overlook the obvious fact that Jesus was a highly accomplished seafarer.

In Matthew 13, verses 1–2, for example, we read that Jesus was sitting on the shore when a huge crowd gathered around him. Rather than slip through them, as he'd done when the lynch mob tried to throw him over a cliff, he waded out to a boat and sat there while the crowd stood on the shore listening to his parables.

After hearing of the beheading of John the Baptist, we read: 'When Jesus heard of it, he departed thence by ship into a desert place apart: and when the people had heard thereof, they followed him on foot out of the cities.'[25]

Mark speaks of Jesus crossing the Sea of Galilee, going to the far side of the River Jordan and setting out for the territory of Tyre,[26] one of the most famous ports in the ancient world, while Matthew observes that Jesus travelled to Sidon,[27] another renowned Phoenician port on the Mediterranean coast. Luke tells us that Jesus directed some skilled but despondent fishermen to pay out their nets at a deep point of the Sea of Galilee, with amazing results,[28] something that suggests that he possessed a more than passing familiarity with marine conditions, and the same gospel also observes that many people came from the coastal region of Tyre and Sidon to hear Jesus preach.[29]

John's gospel contains few explicit references to Jesus and water crossings, although he does speak of Jesus frightening the disciples in a boat by walking on water four miles out from the coast during a storm on the Sea of Galilee.[30] Be that as it may, the most striking reference to Jesus as a hardened mariner comes during the calming of the storm, an episode recounted in the gospels of Matthew,[31] Mark[32] and Luke:

Now it came to pass on a certain day, that he went into a ship with his disciples: and he said unto them, 'Let us go over unto the other side of the lake.' And they launched forth. But as they sailed he fell asleep: and there came down a storm of wind on the lake; and they were filled with water, and were in jeopardy. And they came to him, and awoke him, saying, 'Master, master, we perish.' Then he arose, and rebuked the wind and the raging of the water: and they ceased, and there was a calm.[33]

When we look closely at this passage, we see that it contains two principal elements, one of which is Jesus performing a miracle by calming a storm. There's no doubt about it, but neither is there any doubt that the passage also tells us of a man who, by the end of his missing years, was so thoroughly accustomed to long voyages and to sailing in stormy seas that he could sleep through a tempest of such savagery that it threatened to swamp his boat.

Quite simply, Jesus reappears from out of nowhere with several prominent characteristics, one being a disposition toward visiting high places for spiritual purposes and another being a noted ability as a seafarer. With these two qualities in mind, the mysterious but constant figure of Joseph of Arimathea looms up at us from out of the mists as the sole person mentioned in the Bible who was realistically in a position to familiarize a young Jesus both with sea travel and with a country, or a *region* of a country, notable for its high places.

CHAPTER FOUR

A Siren Song

Stabant orantes primi transmittere cursum
Tendebantque manus ripae ulterioris amore.
(They stood begging to be the first to make the voyage over
And they reached out their hands in longing for the further shore.)
Virgil, *The Aeneid*, Book VI

The shadowy figure of Joseph of Arimathea long ago assumed legendary proportions in the story of Jesus, and rightly so. It's virtually certain that by the time Jesus began his ministry his father Joseph was dead, because there are many references to his mother Mary during this period but none at all to her husband, although none of the gospels see fit to actually mention Joseph's death.

More surprising is how the Biblical accounts either do not or cannot agree on the last words that Jesus uttered before he died. Given his huge importance and that there were so many witnesses to his crucifixion, it'd be logical to expect that if the gospels agreed on *anything*, it would be on those words, but this isn't the case. Matthew tells us that Jesus called out, '*Eloi, Eloi, lama sabachthani?*' or 'My God, my God, why have you forsaken me?'[1] Admittedly, he adds that Jesus later 'cried out in a loud voice' before giving up his spirit,[2] but no words are provided. Mark gives an identical account, but in Luke's gospel, we read, '[Jesus] said, "Father, into your hands I commend my spirit." With these words he breathed his last.'[3] John tells us that Jesus said, 'I am thirsty,'[4] in order to fulfil a scriptural prophecy, but then he records his last words as being, 'It is accomplished.'[5]

Despite marked discrepancies such as these, all four gospels unambiguously speak of Joseph of Arimathea, so we're forced to wonder at the enormous significance of a man whose existence is of greater importance than the last words of Jesus or the death of his father.

Joseph of Arimathea appears after the crucifixion to ask Pontius Pilate, the Roman governor, for the body of Jesus, and Matthew describes him as a rich man who had become a disciple of Jesus.[6] Mark says that he was a prominent member of the council who lived in hope of seeing the Kingdom of God,[7] while Luke describes him in virtually identical terms.[8] John concurs, but adds a statement to the effect that Joseph was a secret disciple of Jesus because he feared the Jews.[9]

Arimathea, the town that is assumed to be the birthplace of Joseph, is similar in a number of ways to Camelot, the British domain of the renowned King Arthur during the Dark Ages. Both places acquired an alluring, mystical fame as the centuries passed and both became known as a kind of sanctuary or preserve of valour, especially in mediaeval times. Both locations are now lost to us. Some people equate Arimathea with the Rama or Ramathaim-zophim mentioned in the Book of Samuel,[10] while the Aramaic translation of the Hebrew Bible[11] describes the place as 'Ramata, where the pupils of the prophets reside'.

We may not know the setting of Arimathea, other than it was somewhere in Judea,[12] but the enigmatic Joseph of Arimathea is pivotal to our understanding of where Jesus spent his 'missing years'. Many legends place him in Britain early in the first century AD and some also maintain that he brought a young Jesus to Britain with him. All these stories specify that he visited the west of Britain and we need only glance at a map to see that while the east of the island is largely flat, the west is composed of highlands, mountains and hills, or high places.

The legends state that Joseph was involved in the mining trade and it's a historical fact that the western peninsula of England was particularly rich in tin. This metal was highly prized in the ancient world but was in short supply, apart from in the west of England, where it was easily mined in large quantities.[13] By contrast, copper was abundant in the ancient world, but was a soft metal unsuitable for making durable weapons or tools. However, when the correct proportion of tin was added to copper, the resulting alloy was bronze, a far tougher metal that blazed like the sun when forged and polished and would hold a sharp blade for far longer than a copper implement. All the immortal heroes in Homer's *Iliad* and *Odyssey* were equipped with bronze weapons, while King Solomon's fabulous Temple in Jerusalem was bedecked with a huge array of stunning bronze treasures fashioned by the incomparable craftsman Hiram of Tyre.[14]

However, it's not necessary to trawl through mediaeval legends to find substantiation that Joseph of Arimathea was involved in the mining trade, because there's compelling evidence in the Bible itself:

When the even was come, there came a rich man of Arimathaea, named Joseph, who also himself was Jesus's disciple: He went to Pilate, and begged the body of Jesus. Then Pilate commanded the body to be delivered. And when Joseph had taken the body, he wrapped it in a clean linen cloth, and laid it in his own new tomb, which he had hewn out in the rock: and he rolled a great stone to the door of the sepulchre, and departed.[15]

The Greek text clearly states: '[Joseph] placed [the body of Jesus] in his own new tomb, which he had hewn out of the rock.'[16] The gospels of Mark, Luke and John[17] simply refer to a sepulchre or tomb, but Matthew specifies that Joseph *himself* had hewn this tomb out of the rock.

What are we to make of this? As we've been told, Joseph was a rich man, so why should he be personally engaged in such arduous and dangerous labour as quarrying? This was no small cavity or recess in a boulder either, because Mark tells us that after the Sabbath was over, Mary of Magdala, Mary the mother of James, and Salome, all went to the tomb,[18] where they were amazed to see the heavy stone that had previously blocked the entrance rolled away:

> And entering into the sepulchre, they saw a young man sitting on the right side, clothed in a long white garment; and they were affrighted. And he saith unto them, 'Be not affrighted: Ye seek Jesus of Nazareth, which was crucified: he is risen; he is not here: behold the place where they laid him.'[19]

The tomb that Joseph had hewn was therefore big enough for three women to enter comfortably without stooping and was also spacious enough to seat another figure, presumably an angel. Furthermore, we get some idea of its size when the youth invited the women to look around so as to be *certain* that the body of Jesus was gone.

The Gospel of Luke echoes this, informing us that when Mary of Magdala, Joanna and Mary the mother of James went into the tomb, two men in shining garments appeared by their side, telling them that Jesus was alive.[20] More surprising still, Luke adds that: 'It was Mary Magdalene, and Joanna, and Mary the mother of James, and other women that were with them, which told these things unto the apostles.'[21] So, as well as two grown men and three women carrying spices and ointments, this tomb was large enough to accommodate an additional unspecified number of women, as well as sufficient space for the body of Jesus to be laid to rest in a dignified fashion. A sepulchre of a substantial size is clearly indicated.

We must also remember that this cavity went sideways into the rock, not down like a grave. Whoever built it was certainly familiar with the principles and practice of mining, as it requires little skill to safely dig a hole downwards, but greater expertise to quarry rock from the side of a hill. If the excavators wish to divide the stone into blocks for later use as statues or pillars, they don't want to have their exertions wasted by the mineral fragmenting, nor do they have any desire to cause a fatal landslide. This exercise in itself requires considerable skill, but it's another matter altogether for a man to dig or quarry sideways *into* rock so as to leave a stable ceiling above him. First, he must ensure that the surrounding material doesn't shatter as he chisels an entrance, because then he'll simply be eroding the rock or moving its face back, rather than boring into it. Once he has constructed an entrance, it then requires some degree of expertise to ensure that a few badly chosen strikes don't cause the vault to collapse. With this alone in mind, it's undeniable that the Gospel of Matthew credits Joseph of Arimathea with an impressive mining exploit.

Now, this might not be so remarkable if Joseph of Arimathea had been a simple labourer, because this tomb seems to have been nothing unusual; the implication in the gospels is that there were others of its kind. However, we're specifically told that Joseph was a rich man, so unless he was quarrying a sepulchre for himself as a hobby or as a labour of love, which seems unlikely, it would seem reasonable to suppose that his wealth and his undoubted ability to mine a good-sized tomb by himself from solid rock were somehow connected.

Matthew also informs us that the tomb was new, which implies that Joseph had constructed it during the years of Jesus' ministry. It further implies that Joseph must have been younger rather than older and also extremely able-bodied, as there's no suggestion of any miracle being involved in the construction.

There's further evidence of just how robust Joseph of Arimathea was, as both Matthew and Mark tell us that he single-handedly rolled a great stone across the entrance of the tomb after he'd laid the body of Jesus inside. We learn just *how* large this stone was when the women come to anoint Jesus's body:

And when the sabbath was past, Mary Magdalene, and Mary the mother of James, and Salome, had bought sweet spices, that they might come and anoint him. And very early in the morning the first day of the week, they came unto the sepulchre at the rising of the sun. And they said among themselves, 'Who shall roll us away the stone from the door of the sepulchre?' And when they looked, they saw that the stone was rolled away: for it was very great.[22]

As well as rolling into place a 'megalith' or a stone of considerable size, it was no mean feat to take the body of Jesus down from a cross and carry the dead weight to the tomb. John tells us that a man named Nicodemus assisted Joseph, but he adds that Nicodemus was carrying 100 pounds of myrrh and aloes.[23]

Whichever way we look at it, Joseph of Arimathea was clearly capable of notable feats of endurance and strength. After the crucifixion, the chief priests and Pharisees went to Pilate to ask for a guard to be put on the tomb,[24] because they were worried that *the disciples* (plural) of Jesus would steal his body so as to fake his resurrection, but Joseph of Arimathea was capable of carrying a dead body and moving a huge stone unassisted.

A SECRET DISCIPLE

As well as his undoubted importance to the authors of all four gospels, Joseph of Arimathea has another distinction: he's the only person described in the Bible as a *secret* disciple of Jesus. Most translations of John's description of Joseph tell us that this was because he was afraid of the Jews. There's something very strange going on, however, because the fact that Joseph of Arimathea 'went in *boldly* unto Pilate, and craved the body of Jesus'[25] doesn't readily bring to mind a man who was frightened of Jews, or Romans for that matter, but the translation isn't entirely accurate. The actual words that John used are:

μαθητης του 'Ιεσου κεκρυμμενος δε δια τον φοβον των 'Ιουδιαων
Mathetes tou Iesou kekrummenos de dia ton phobon tohn Ioudiaohn'.[26]

This literally means 'a disciple or learner of the Jesus having been hidden because of *the* fear of the Jews'. The word *kekrummenos* means 'someone who has been hidden away', the strict sense being that someone else did the hiding away or concealing, rather than the person themselves, because the passive voice is used. There's no specific reference to Joseph of Arimathea actually fearing the Jews, rather having been hidden away because of the fear of the Jews, a fear whose owner-ship could be ascribed to either Joseph or the Jews themselves. Looking at the common translation followed by a more elegant version of the literal translation, the contrast is clear:

> Joseph of Arimathea was a secret disciple of Jesus because he was afraid of the Jews…
> Joseph of Arimathea was a disciple of Jesus who had been hidden away because of the fear of the Jews…

In the final analysis, however, it doesn't really matter whether it was Joseph or the Jews who were afraid, nor does it make any difference if Joseph chose to keep his allegiance secret or if someone else deliber-ately 'hid him away', because there's a simple explanation that covers both eventualities.

If there was one thing that the Jews feared above all else, it was conta-gion or corruption of their religion from outside sources. A perfect example of this is provided in the accounts of the first-century Jewish historian Josephus, when he describes how the Jews reacted to Pontius Pilate ordering his men to bring Roman standards into Jerusalem:

> On one occasion, when the soldiers under his command came to Jerusalem, he made them bring their ensigns with them, upon which were the usual images of the emperor. Roman battle standards were considered idolatrous by the Jews. The ensigns were brought in secretly by night, but their presence was soon discovered. Immediately multitudes of excited Jews rushed to Caesarea to petition him for the removal of the obnoxious ensigns. He ignored them for five days, but the next day he admitted the Jews to hear their complaint. He had them surrounded with soldiers and threatened them with instant death unless they ceased to trouble him with the matter. The Jews then threw themselves to the ground and bared their necks, declaring that they preferred death to the violation of their laws. Pilate, unwilling to kill so many, succumbed and removed the ensigns.[27]

It already seems overwhelmingly likely that Jesus spent his formative years preparing for his controversial ministry in a country that wasn't the Jews' sacred homeland. Likewise, it also seems beyond doubt that Joseph of Arimathea played a pivotal part in helping Jesus travel to this other country, so when faced with the prospect of deliberately enraging people who readily chose death before dishonour, it's little wonder that he kept quiet about the whole affair.

We don't know how long this state of secrecy had lasted for, but the implication is that it was at least as long as the ministry of Jesus, i.e. roughly three years, which brings us to another apparent mystery.

We know that Joseph was an 'honourable councillor',[28] apparently one of the Sanhedrin.[29] Mark, Luke and John all *imply* that he was wealthy, as he owned a tomb and was able to provide fine linen and costly spices in which to wrap the body of Jesus, but Matthew specifically describes him as rich. We already know that he was a secret disciple of Jesus who waited for the Kingdom of God, according to Mark, so it's fair to assume that he had been a disciple for some time before the death of Jesus and it's not at all unlikely that he'd been a disciple from the start, whenever that may have been. With all this in mind, it's absolutely certain that he'd have heard the story of the rich young man:

And, behold, one came and said unto him, 'Good Master, what good thing shall I do, that I may have eternal life?' And he said unto him, 'Why callest thou me good? There is none good but one, that is, God: but if thou wilt enter into life, keep the commandments.'

He saith unto him, 'Which?' Jesus said, 'Thou shalt do no murder, Thou shalt not commit adultery, Thou shalt not steal, Thou shalt not bear false witness, Honour thy father and thy mother: and, Thou shalt love thy neighbour as thyself.'

The young man saith unto him, 'All these things have I kept from my youth up: what lack I yet?' Jesus said unto him, 'If thou wilt be perfect, go and sell that thou hast, and give to the poor, and thou shalt have treasure in heaven: and come and follow me.' But when the young man heard that saying, he went away sorrowful: for he had great possessions.

Then said Jesus unto his disciples, 'Verily I say unto you, That a rich man shall hardly enter into the kingdom of heaven. And again I say unto you, It is easier for a camel to go through the eye of a needle, than for a rich man to enter into the kingdom of God.'

When his disciples heard it, they were exceedingly amazed, saying, 'Who then can be saved?'[30]

So, Joseph must have known that there was more chance of a camel passing through the eye of a needle than there was of him entering the Kingdom of Heaven, yet none of the gospels makes anything of this blatant contradiction. What are *we* to make of this? What's the most likely explanation for this apparent paradox? Why are we told that this rich man was actively anticipating[31] the Kingdom of God, when as a disciple of Jesus he must have known that such a thing was unthinkable because of his wealth?

When the young man of the story had gone away, Jesus explained to his loyal disciples that as they'd given away all their wealth, the day would come when they would sit on 12 thrones to judge the 12 tribes of Israel, adding:

'And every one that hath forsaken houses, or brethren, or sisters, or father, or mother, or wife, or children, or lands, for my name's sake, shall receive an hundredfold, and shall inherit everlasting life.'[32]

And he adds a mysterious footnote to this that goes unquestioned: 'But many that are first shall be last; and the last shall be first.'[33]

In the light of this, it is interesting that a number of legends tell us that after the crucifixion Joseph of Arimathea fled to Britain and established Christianity there. This would inevitably mean that he had given up his belongings and family for Jesus's name's sake and so would inherit everlasting life. And if he were the last of the disciples to renounce worldly wealth, it wouldn't have mattered in the least, because of what Jesus had said about the last being first.

Is there a parallel elsewhere in the gospels for a hidden and seemingly contradictory function on the part of one of Jesus's disciples? Certainly there is, because Judas Iscariot is virtually the mirror image of Joseph of Arimathea.

During the course of the Last Supper, Jesus announced to his assembled disciples that one of them was about to betray him. They all expressed disbelief and horror at this, but Jesus assured them that it was nonetheless true:

> Now when the even was come, he sat down with the twelve. And as they did eat, he said, 'Verily I say unto you, that one of you shall betray me.' And they were exceeding sorrowful, and began every one of them to say unto him, 'Lord, is it I?'
>
> And he answered and said, 'He that dippeth his hand with me in the dish, the same shall betray me. The Son of Man goeth as it is written of him: but woe unto that man by whom the Son of Man is betrayed! It had been good for that man if he had not been born.'[34]

For Jesus to fulfil his life's mission and his part in the scriptural prophecies, it was vital that Judas betray him, but unfortunately for Judas, his pivotal role in history was rewarded with eternal damnation rather than everlasting life.

Joseph of Arimathea was a secret disciple, while Judas Iscariot was a 'secret' traitor, but what Judas and Joseph had in common was that they both played a major role in the great scheme of things as far as Jesus's destiny was concerned. Without the treachery and betrayal of Judas, Jesus couldn't have fulfilled the scriptural prophecies, as Jesus himself admitted. Joseph of Arimathea seems to have played a similar role in helping Jesus fulfil a scriptural prophecy, in this case the famous 'man of sorrows' passage from the prophecies of Isaiah: 'And he made his grave with the wicked, and with the rich in his death...'[35]

We're left to wonder if Joseph of Arimathea *had* to be rich so as to allow a prophecy concerning the Son of God being buried in a rich man's grave to be fulfilled, or was there a further part that Joseph played in this matter?

Whether or not it is strictly true that he feared the Jews, it's certain that the high priests, scribes, elders and Pharisees were intent on having Jesus put to death and that they succeeded in this. If a disciple were then to break cover, so to speak, and incur the murderous wrath of the elders by reverentially placing Jesus's body in a rich man's tomb rather than leaving it to be unceremoniously disposed of by his enemies, then it would make sound sense for that disciple to possess sufficient wealth to be able to leave the region immediately and depart for new shores, preferably taking a fast ship to a distant land with which he was intimately familiar. Many later legends maintain that Joseph of Arimathea did precisely this; in any event, he disappears from the gospels just as soon as he's arrived, yet that's far from being the end of his story.

HALF-HIDDEN FROM THE EYE

It's hard to avoid the conclusion that Joseph of Arimathea knew a very great deal about Jesus and had an extremely close relationship with him, despite the brief mention he's accorded in the gospels. We must also ask how it was that John could possibly have known that Joseph of Arimathea was a secret disciple and how he could have known that the specific *reason* why he was hidden away was the apparent fear of the Jews. There has been a lot of speculation about the authorship of the Gospel of St John, but certainly whoever wrote it was somehow in on the secret himself; he stops short of providing us with any further details about the mysterious Joseph of Arimathea, but he does conclude his gospel with the highly telling observation:

> This is the disciple which testifieth of these things, and wrote these things: and we know that his testimony is true. And there are also many other things which Jesus did, the which, if they should be written every one, I suppose that even the world itself could not contain the books that should be written.[36]

Even if John became slightly carried away with his estimate of the number of accounts that could be presented, could we possibly ask for more categorical proof that there's at the very least *one* major untold story from the life of Jesus? The answer must be 'no'.

A wealth of engaging material has been brought to light fairly recently. A manuscript that's come to be known as 'The Gospel of Judas' surfaced in the 1970s, but it wasn't until April 2006 that a completion of the restoration and a translation was announced by the National Geographic Society. This manuscript is genuine inasmuch as it's been dated to the second or third centuries AD, so it's not a mediaeval or modern forgery. However, its content is highly contentious because the text maintains that Jesus taught only Judas Iscariot the truth about the Kingdom of Heaven, while being critical of the other disciples.

The publicity surrounding the presentation of this gospel drew a response from the Vatican, where Pope Benedict XVI disagreed with the content but didn't contest the provenance. A similar response came from Rowan Williams, the Archbishop of Canterbury, who said in his 2006 Easter sermon: 'This is a demonstrably late text which simply parallels a large number of quite well-known works from the more eccentric fringes of the early century Church.'[37]

The Archbishop went on to comment in detail on the popular appeal of works such as *The Da Vinci Code* which offer alternative and sometimes appealing explanations for Biblical mysteries and contradictions:

> We are instantly fascinated by the suggestion of conspiracies and cover-ups; this has become so much the stuff of our imagination these days that it is only natural, it seems, to expect it when we turn to ancient texts, especially biblical texts. We treat them as if they were unconvincing press releases from some official source, whose intention is to conceal the real story; and that real story waits for the intrepid investigator to uncover it and share it with the waiting world. Anything that looks like the official version is automatically suspect.[38]

The Archbishop may well have a valid point, but the blunt fact remains that everything we've learned in our investigation so far has been gleaned from a painstaking and entirely reasonable study of the gospels in the official New Testament. It's ironic that the Archbishop should observe that 'We are instantly fascinated by the suggestions of conspiracies and cover-ups' and that he should speak of 'unconvincing press releases… whose intention is to conceal the real story' when the original Greek in the Gospel of St John describes Joseph of Arimathea as κεκρυμμενος (kekrummenos) or 'a man who has been hidden or concealed by others'. It's more ironic still that, in direct connection with a mysterious man who single-handedly quarried a tomb, this word should have as its root the verb κρύπτω (krupto), from which we get our words 'cryptic' and 'crypt'.

Furthermore, we have not treated the accounts in the New Testament as 'unconvincing press releases' – on the contrary, we've treated them as the gospel truth, and we've been rewarded with a wealth of original and intriguing information. Simply by attending to every minute detail contained in the accounts of Matthew, Mark, Luke and John, we find ourselves in a position where all the evidence suggests that:

- Jesus was absent from his homeland for a prolonged period between the ages of 12 and 30.
- His father Joseph died during this time.
- He returned to his homeland a virtual stranger to those who should have known him intimately.
- He returned as a highly experienced mariner or seafarer.
- He returned with a marked disposition for visiting high places for spiritual purposes.
- He returned with the ability to perform a variety of miracles.
- He returned with the ability to project his voice and amaze audiences with his powers of oratory and delivery, as opposed to simply impressing people with his knowledge of scriptures.[39]
- He had a longstanding and intimate connection with Joseph of Arimathea.
- There was something sufficiently strong or meaningful in this relationship, or there existed some clearly defined and vital objective for Joseph of Arimathea to achieve, and this was something that

completely exempted him from the otherwise rigid restriction on rich men entering the Kingdom of Heaven.

- Joseph of Arimathea had at least one and possibly more connections with mining or quarrying.
- On a strict interpretation of the original Greek wording, Joseph of Arimathea was a man 'who had been hidden or concealed by others'.
- Joseph of Arimathea was a man of great physical strength.
- It's far from certain that Joseph of Arimathea was afraid of the Jews, as all the translations suggest; his bold actions in publicly petitioning Pilate for the body of Jesus in the face of the proven homicidal fury of the elders or Sanhedrin strongly suggest otherwise.
- Immediately after placing the body of Jesus in a sepulchre, Joseph of Arimathea left his homeland by sea for a distant destination with which he was familiar.
- The 'secret' part played by Joseph of Arimathea in the destiny of Jesus was extremely important and was known by at least three people at the time, these being Joseph himself, Jesus and Nicodemus, the man who assisted Joseph in laying the body of Jesus in the tomb.

And this is merely the tip of the iceberg, because we've far from exhausted our lines of enquiry concerning Joseph of Arimathea. For example, we noted earlier that the Gospel of Matthew made clear that Joseph himself had dug the tomb in the rock, as shown to us by the use of the word 'ελατομηοεν, or *elatomesen*.[40] This word for mining or quarrying is directly related to the word λατομος, or *latomos*, which specifically means 'a worker in rock or stone' or 'a stonemason'. As such, we needn't rely on mediaeval accounts of the mining exploits of Joseph of Arimathea as our only evidence, as others have, because we've found ample confirmation in the Bible itself. Furthermore, there are other suggestions in the New Testament that the story of Jesus visiting Britain is nowhere near as outlandish as it might initially appear.

TO BOLDLY GO

> *'Boldness, be my friend!*
> *Arm me, audacity.'*
> **William Shakespeare, *Cymbeline***

The Gospel according to St Mark provides us with the following account:

> Joseph of Arimathaea, an honourable counsellor, which also waited for the kingdom of God, came, and went in boldly unto Pilate, and craved the body of Jesus. And Pilate marvelled if he were already dead: and calling unto him the centurion, he asked him whether he had been any while dead. And when he knew it of the centurion, he gave the body to Joseph.[41]

Mark's use of the word 'boldly'[42] is curious; what was 'bold' about approaching Pontius Pilate and asking for the body of Jesus? And does it supply us with any further clues about Joseph of Arimathea?

John's gospel tells us that Nicodemus assisted in embalming the body of Jesus and that he was a Pharisee who came to Jesus by night to proclaim his faith that Jesus was a teacher sent by God.[43] This clandestine activity, coupled with the assistance he later provided to Joseph of Arimathea, strongly suggests that Nicodemus was *also* a 'secret disciple'. It's possible, therefore, to infer that Joseph was bold to approach Pilate because Nicodemus didn't accompany him when he made this request. But as Nicodemus openly helped to remove the body, entomb it and embalm it afterwards, this also implies some boldness or daring worthy of comment, especially when we consider the tensions surrounding the crucifixion, yet the gospel merely states that *Joseph's manner in approaching Pilate* was 'bold'.

It might be argued that approaching Pilate was in itself an audacious act, but nothing in the gospels suggests that it took bravery to speak to the Roman governor on the subject of Jesus. On the contrary, Matthew's gospel spells out that Pilate was extremely reluctant to have

Jesus crucified, offering him every chance to answer the charges brought against him and expressing amazement when Jesus remained silent.[44] Pilate also asked the crowd if they wanted either Jesus or a notorious prisoner named Barabbas released and John's gospel adds that he knew full well that Jesus had been handed over out of jealousy.[45] Furthermore, when the crowd called for the release of Barabbas, Pilate despairingly asked what was to be done with Jesus. When the reply came for him to be crucified, Pilate asked, 'Why? What harm has he done?' Seeing that he was making no impression and that a riot was imminent, he notoriously washed his hands in front of the crowd, announcing, 'I am innocent of this man's blood. It is your concern.'[46]

Given that the gospels of Mark, Luke and John provide virtually identical accounts of how Pilate was very unwilling to condemn Jesus because he could find no case against him, it seems unlikely that Joseph of Arimathea would have anything to fear from the Roman governor, even if he were directly associated with a man who'd just been crucified.

Would he have had anything to fear from another quarter? If he was a member of the Sanhedrin, he'd have been facing considerable hostility in asking for the body of a condemned criminal who'd aroused such fierce passions in such an influential group of men. However, as he was a *secret* disciple, then this wouldn't apply, because the Sanhedrin wouldn't have known about his association with Jesus.

Given the hostility of the Sanhedrin, why was Joseph openly asking Pilate for the body in the first place? In both Roman and Jewish law, a family member could request the body of an executed criminal, something that in and of itself spells out that Joseph of Arimathea was directly related to Jesus. Jesus's father Joseph wasn't around to collect his body, nor were any of his brothers, so everything points towards Joseph of Arimathea being a close relative of the crucified man. Jesus's mother Mary was still alive and the Gospel of John specifically states that she witnessed the crucifixion of her son,[47] so it's impossible to see how Joseph of Arimathea could have taken the body in the face of opposition from the Sanhedrin unless he'd received Mary's consent and was furthermore directly related to both Mary and Jesus.

However, even if Joseph of Arimathea were legally entitled to claim the body, this still doesn't entirely explain why he went 'boldly' to Pilate. You could perhaps argue that this boldness was a conviction that no one could possibly contest his case, something that bolsters the claim that Jesus was his nephew, but there's another distinct possibility and it adds considerable weight to the notion that Jesus visited the west of England early in the first century AD with a rich uncle who was a miner.

We are told that Joseph was a wealthy man of good standing; the original Greek word is 'ευσχημον, or *euschemon*, meaning 'well figured', 'respectable' or 'presentable', so it wasn't as if an ill-tempered Pilate was being approached by a criminal, slave or other social inferior. In fact, Joseph's boldness may well have been borne of personal familiarity, something that would make perfect sense of the context.

If this were the case, then how could Pilate and Joseph of Arimathea have known each other? Pilate spent the majority of his time in Caesarea Maritima, the flourishing port built by Herod the Great. We have archaeological confirmation of his residency there from an inscription unearthed[48] in the ruins. We'd also reasonably expect to find an affluent man connected with the mining trade frequenting such a place. King Solomon's fabulous Temple in Jerusalem was bedecked with bronze treasures fashioned by Hiram of the city of Tyre,[49] yet another notable port renowned for millennia for the skills of its Phoenician sailors, while the tin used to make these rich adornments most likely came from mines in the west of England, on account of its sheer abundance there and what we know of early Phoenician voyages. The first *recorded* visit of a Phoenician[50] to Britain occurred sometime around 500 BC, or five centuries before Jesus, showing beyond doubt that the trade routes from the Middle East to the west of England had long been established by the time of Joseph of Arimathea; we know from the Greek historian Diodorus Siculus, for example, that the tin trade in Cornwall was flourishing in the first century BC.

Everything points toward Joseph of Arimathea being an uncle of Jesus and a wealthy man associated with mining. As Jesus's father had died some years before, Joseph may well have become the guardian or mentor of a young Jesus and it's entirely predictable that they'd both have spent a great deal of time at one or more of the many ports on the coast of a land that had already had a link of at least five centuries' standing with the western part of the British Isles.

SITTING ON THE DOCK OF THE BAY

None climbs so high as he who knows not whither he is going.
Oliver Cromwell, 1599–1658

In an age before air travel or mass communications, ports were the focal points for the dissemination of news about other countries. It's not difficult to picture Jesus as a young man wandering the docks and quays of a bustling centre of commerce such as Tyre, Sidon or Caesarea Maritima, avidly listening to mariners' tales while his uncle was engaged in official business with other merchants and ships' captains. It stands to reason that he'd have been excited, curious and inquisitive about the weathered mariners, the creaking boats and their exotic destinations; if we attempt to deny Jesus these entirely natural and understandable characteristics, we deny him his humanity. So, which foreign land would have intrigued this young man most? Without a doubt, he'd have been captivated by virtually anything he heard about the British Isles, and the evidence in favour of this is so overwhelming and compelling that it's difficult to know where to start.

When Jesus was a youth, Britain lay at the furthermost northwestern reaches of the Roman Empire, or at the edge of the known world, which would have made it of intense interest to a young man gazing out over the familiar waters of the sea at the *centre* of the world, the Mediterranean. The Romans described the remote island as Britannia, a name that Jesus would certainly have heard at some point.

He may also have heard Britain described as Albion, or the Land of the Albiones, a description that in all probability meant 'Whiteland' or 'the Land of the White Ones'.[51] Yet another ancient name for Britain was Hyperborea or 'the Land beyond the North Wind'. He may have known Britain as Barr Tannic, from the Semitic words for 'Land of Tin'; Herodotus, the Greek historian, had referred to the Scilly Isles and the west of England as the Cassiterides, 'Isles of Tin', as far back as 445 BC.

All these names are evocative enough, but the fact that they belonged to a distant island beyond the grasp of even the mighty Roman Empire would have bestowed an added glamour on the place. Jesus had grown up in a land that had been under Roman occupation for around half a century by the time of his birth. In his later years, he was widely thought of as the Messiah or 'Anointed One',[52] a figure prophesied by the scriptures that the Jews believed would arrive as a king or liberator to deliver them from the oppressive yoke of the hated Romans, but any member of a race under Roman occupation would have been fascinated and heartened to learn that the heroic inhabitants of Britannia had successfully resisted not one, but *two* invasions led by Julius Caesar in 55 and 54 BC.

Caesar wrote extensively of the invasion of Britain in his book *De Bello Gallico* ('Concerning the Gallic Wars') in which he conveyed the impression that he had defeated the native forces of Britannia but had had to put off a more comprehensive invasion because of unrest in Gaul. However, Tacitus, a later Roman historian (AD 56–117), made an intriguing observation about the ancient Britons driving back Caesar. The passage concerns Caratacus (also known as Caractacus), a British leader who fought the legions sent by Claudius in AD 43, addressing his men prior to the Battle of Caer Caradoc in AD 51:

As for Caractacus, he flew hither and thither, protesting that that day and that battle would be the beginning of the recovery of their freedom, or of everlasting bondage. He appealed, by name, to their forefathers who had driven back the dictator Caesar, [and] by whose valour they were free from the Roman axe and tribute, and still preserved inviolate the persons of their wives and of their children.[53]

Celtic
Mediterranean

Ynys
Mon
or
Anglesey

Holy
Island

Menai
Straits

Caer Caradoc

Preseli Mountains
or
The Kingdom of Heaven

Realm of
the
Silures

Mary's
Spring

Clearwell
Caves

Realm of
the
Dubunni

Llanmelin
Hill Fort

Usk

Caerleon

Mendip
Hills

Bath

Silbury

Lundy Island

Priddy

Stonehenge

Burnham
on-Sea

Glastonbury

Quantock
Hills

Wick
Moor

Tor

Bowerchalke

Watchet

Hangley Cleave
Barrows

Bridgwater

Pilton

Bottlebush
Down

50 Miles

Isles of
Scilly

St. Michael's
Mount

Walsingham

The Landscape of the Holy Legend

Location associated with the legend of Jesus visiting the area as a young man in the early years of the first century.

(©Juris Ozols)

Caesar was widely acknowledged as one of the greatest generals that Rome had ever produced and it's certain that Jesus would have heard of him. It's equally certain that the mariners of the Mediterranean would have been familiar with these events, so it's not difficult to envisage an adolescent Jesus becoming consumed with admiration and curiosity when he heard about the valiant Britons or Albiones, a fierce and free people who were nonetheless well-disposed towards those living in the eastern Mediterranean and who'd already traded peacefully with them for centuries, if not longer.

Jesus may also have heard of the hot springs of the southwest of England. The city of Bath lies just a few miles away from the Mendip Hills, one of the locations specified in later traditions as being a place that Jesus visited. Bath is famous for its hydrothermal vents or hot springs and the Romans constructed an impressive complex there to allow them to enjoy the waters in luxury shortly after their arrival in Britain in AD 43. However, we know that the ancient Britons revered the site long before then, because the Romans named the place Aquae Sulis, or 'the Waters of Sulis', and Sulis was a Celtic goddess who predated the arrival of the Romans.

The Romans habitually immersed themselves in the springs for relaxation and because they believed that the waters possessed health-giving properties. As the ancient Britons venerated the place and as it was the only location in Britain where such hot springs existed, it's highly likely that the native peoples had also ritually immersed themselves there. The site was in the same region as the mines on the Mendips that had been visited for centuries by foreign visitors, so it'd be very surprising indeed if it didn't warrant at least an occasional mention in accounts passed on by mariners.

What would Jesus have made of this? Here we have a young man so thoroughly conversant with Jewish law that by the age of 12 he was able to astonish audiences with the breadth and depth of his knowledge, part of which would have included the Jewish bathing rites that were essential for a condition of ritual purity. The Book of Leviticus contains at least 15 detailed references to ritual bathing,[54] so any passing mention of similar actions in far-off Britain would have captured Jesus's attention, especially if they were connected with some religious ceremony.

Of course, the ancient world was almost literally awash with sacred springs, such as the pagan site that Jesus visited at Caesarea Philippi. However, Aquae Sulis was unique in Britain, so it may well have been mentioned in travellers' tales and it's at least possible that it came to the attention of Jesus.

THE DRUIDS

Another feature that was likely to have increased Jesus's interest in the land that's now England was the existence of the Druids. These priests or magicians were known in the Mediterranean world at least as far back as the fifth century BC and probably much further. The Greek historian Herodotus speaks of a Druid by name, Abaris the Hyperborean, telling us that he travelled the world with an arrow and ate no food during this time.[55] A young man who was later to spend 40 days and 40 nights fasting in the wilderness would have been intrigued by the story of this abstemious travelling priest, but there was far more information available about the Druids after Caesar's two abortive invasions of Britain, and this would have been widespread among the mariners that Jesus encountered. The people at the time would have known far more about the Druids than *we* do, as very little written information about them has survived, but there's more than enough to tell us that they would have immediately caught the attention of a young Jesus.

Why? Caesar wrote:

The two privileged classes are the Druids and the knights. The Druids officiate at the worship of the gods, regulate public and private sacrifices, and give rulings on all religious questions. Large numbers of young men flock to them for instruction, and they are held in great honour by the people. They act as judges in practically all disputes, whether between tribes or between individuals; when any crime is committed, or a murder takes place, or a dispute arises about an inheritance or a boundary, it is they who adjudicate the matter and appoint the compensation to be paid and received by the parties concerned.[56]

This description of a powerful officiating priesthood shows that the Druids bore more than a passing resemblance to the Sanhedrin, the body that met in the Hall of Hewn Stones in the Temple in Jerusalem. However, there's more:

> ...Many present themselves of their own accord to become students of Druidism, and others are sent by their parents or relatives. It is said that these pupils have to memorize a great number of verses – so many that some of them spend twenty years at their studies.[57]

We must ask what impression this could have made on a young man who by the age of 12 was already regarded as a prodigy concerning the scriptures.

Caesar also wrote that:

> They believe that the only way of saving a man's life is to propitiate the god's wrath by rendering another life in its place, and they have regular state sacrifices of the same kind. Some tribes have colossal images made of wickerwork, the limbs of which they fill with living men; they are then set on fire, and the victims burnt to death.[58]

Aside from this passing description of the famous 'wicker man' conflagrations, there's no mention of idols of any kind, nor does any other writer in antiquity speak of the British Druids worshipping graven images. Jesus's religious and cultural background, with its loathing of idols, is famously demonstrated by the following passage:

> 'Thou shalt have no other gods before me. Thou shalt not make unto thee any graven image, or any likeness of any thing that is in heaven above, or that is in the earth beneath, or that is in the water under

the earth: Thou shalt not bow down thyself to them, nor serve them: for I the LORD thy God am a jealous God…'[59]

The scriptures contained damning references to golden calves[60] and idols of Philistine deities such as Dagon,[61] so it must have been strange for people in Judea to hear of seemingly barbarous priests at the ends of the Earth who did *not* worship idols. More striking still, we know from Caesar's accounts that the Druids claimed descent from a single god they called Dis Pater, or Father Dis, which certainly isn't a million miles away from the notion of a Heavenly Father creating Adam and Eve.

The Greek historian Diodorus Siculus recorded another aspect of the Druids that might well have struck a profound chord with a young Jesus:

> It is not only in times of peace, but in war also, that these seers have authority, and the incantations of the bards have effect on friends and foes alike. Often when the combatants are ranged face to face, and swords are drawn and spears bristling, these men come between the armies and stay the battle, just as wild beasts are sometimes held spellbound.[62]

Jesus was later to announce to the world, 'Blessed are the peacemakers, for they shall be called the Sons of God,'[63] so the effect that news of this pacifying aspect of Druidic culture would have made upon him is obvious. Whether he'd have regarded the Druids as the 'Sons of God' is another question, but the description of Druids wandering unharmed through fired-up armies ready to do battle is eerily familiar when we recall how Jesus somehow managed to walk through a furious mob intent on murdering him by throwing him over a cliff. Are these two near-miracles merely a coincidence, or is it possible that Jesus somehow acquired this singular ability from the Druids?

It's crucial to bear in mind that while we possess detailed yet tantalizing fragments of the Druids, a great deal more would have been known of them throughout the Roman Empire in the early first century, especially by mariners who had regular cause to visit Britain.

Furthermore, the Druids were still so influential by the time Emperor Claudius invaded Britain in AD 43 that a genocidal war was ultimately waged against them in their stronghold of the Isle of Anglesey in Wales in AD 60, something we'll look into in detail later.

Aside from shunning idol worship, memorizing huge swathes of verse, being a powerful, officiating priesthood, resisting Roman rule, being monotheistic, claiming descent from a divine Father and walking unharmed through men about to fight, there are other aspects of the Druids that would have resonated with a young man in Jesus's position. The Roman writer Pliny wrote of the Druids:

Having made preparation for sacrifice and a banquet beneath the trees, they bring thither two white bulls, whose horns are bound then for the first time. Clad in a white robe, the priest ascends the tree and cuts the mistletoe with a golden sickle, and it is received by others in a white cloak. Then they kill the victims, praying that God will render this gift of his propitious to those to whom he has granted it.[64]

As a visitor to the temple in Jerusalem and as an expert on the scriptures, Jesus would have been familiar with the many Biblical accounts of the sacrifice of oxen, the most notable being:

And Solomon offered a sacrifice of peace offerings, which he offered unto the LORD, two and twenty thousand oxen, and an hundred and twenty thousand sheep. So the king and all the children of Israel dedicated the house of the LORD.[65]

It's hard to believe that over the centuries, news of the Druids *wouldn't* have reached the ports of a country with a long history of seafaring and it's equally clear that these subjects would have intrigued the general population and not just young Jews such as Jesus. Caesar also took pains to record that:

The Druids believe that their religion forbids them to commit their teachings to writing, although for most other purposes, such as public and private accounts, the Gauls use the Greek alphabet.[66]

Ever since the region where Jesus grew up had been invaded by Alexander the Great in 333 BC, Greek had been the common language for all the people living, trading and visiting there. Excavations at Sepphoris, a city just four miles away from Nazareth, have revealed a Greek amphitheatre, Greek coins, Greek mosaics and Greek inscriptions. There's little doubt that Jesus preached in Greek, even if he spoke his native Aramaic in private, and the evidence for this comes squarely from the gospels. Two of his disciples, Andrew and Philip, had Greek names and the gospels provide examples such as these:

- And he took the damsel by the hand, and said unto her, '*Talitha cumi*'; which is, being interpreted, 'Damsel, I say unto thee, arise.'[67]
- And at the ninth hour Jesus cried with a loud voice, saying, '*Eloi, Eloi, lama sabachthani?*' which is, being interpreted, 'My God, my God, why have you forsaken me?'[68]
- And he brought him to Jesus. And when Jesus beheld him, he said, 'Thou art Simon the son of Jona: thou shalt be called Cephas, which is by interpretation, a stone.'[69]

As the gospels were written in Greek, why were some words preserved or deliberately translated into Aramaic? If Jesus had *always* spoken in Aramaic, then it would seem reasonable for the authors to translate *all* the words he uttered into Greek, but as a few Aramaic words are carefully recorded, then it'd seem that Jesus habitually preached in Greek so as to make himself understood by as wide an audience as possible, speaking only occasionally in Aramaic.

Whether the Druids actually spoke Greek or not, their familiarity with the letters alone may have been yet another aspect of the strange island of Britain that intrigued a young Jesus.

THE PILLARS OF HERCULES

> *And I have felt*
> *A presence that disturbs me with the joy*
> *Of elevated thoughts; a sense sublime*
> *Of something far more deeply interfused,*
> *Whose dwelling is the light of setting suns,*
> *And the round ocean and the living air...*
> **Wordsworth, *Lines Composed a***
> ***Few Miles above Tintern Abbey***

In ancient times, the entrance to the Atlantic Ocean from the Mediterranean Sea at the place we now call the Straits of Gibraltar was known as the Pillars of Hercules. This mythical hero, known to the Greeks as Heracles, was said to have broken a mountain in two with his club to form two new peaks or 'pillars' as a gateway to the ocean, a body of water believed to be a vast stream or river encircling the known world. The ancients held the immense watery wastes beyond the otherwise land-encircled confines of the Mediterranean Sea in such awe that Hercules was said to have inscribed the ominous words *Non plus ultra*, 'Nothing lies beyond', at the feet of these towering crags.

As time went on and intrepid Phoenician navigators came to venture through this narrow portal, the sight of the twin peaks rising up on either side of the 12-mile wide strait would still have had a profound effect on anyone passing through them and would have served as a stark visual reminder that the voyagers were leaving behind the safe, familiar environment of their homelands to venture into literally uncharted waters.

If we were ancient Phoenician mariners sailing out of the Mediterranean through the Pillars of Hercules into the Atlantic Ocean, the pillar on our right, or to the north, would have been what we now know as the Rock of Gibraltar, a limestone block 1,380 feet high and two miles long. The other pillar, to the left or the south, may have been the modern Mount Acho, which overlooks the Spanish enclave of Ceuta. Twelve miles south of Gibraltar, this mountain is 669 feet high. However, there's another mountain in north Morocco called Jebel

Musa, which is 3,000 feet high, so this is just as likely to have been considered the other Pillar of Hercules by the ancients.

There's another way of looking at these ominous columns. For 150 days of the year, the Rock of Gibraltar gathers a cloud from the east wind that condenses along two-thirds of its length, while Mount Acho, opposite, is green all the year round with yellow flowers appearing on its slopes from January to April. As such, it's possible to view one pillar as being a 'pillar of smoke' and the other, alive with yellow flowers, as being a 'pillar of fire'.[70]

What would a young Jesus have made of such landmarks? For someone so steeped in the traditions and history of the Jews, an integral part of his psyche would have been the story of when the Jews left Egypt and the tyrannical rule of the Pharaoh to be led by God Himself into the Promised Land:

And the LORD went before them by day in a pillar of a cloud, to lead them the way; and by night in a pillar of fire, to give them light; to go by day and night: He took not away the pillar of the cloud by day, nor the pillar of fire by night, from before the people.[71]

It's possible that mariners such as Joseph of Arimathea viewed these landmarks in a Biblical light because of billowing mist and vivid yellow flowers, but the simple reference to the Pillars of Hercules was universal at the time. On top of all the other elements that called Jesus to Britain, I suspect that the mere mention of the Pillars of Hercules would have resonated with him and he couldn't help but have viewed them as a gateway beckoning him on to another mysterious Promised Land.

This idea's intriguing enough, but while the Exodus from Egypt in earlier times was certainly a profound matter for the Jews, we should remember that Mary and Joseph later sought sanctuary in Egypt with their young son to escape King Herod, having been warned by an angel sent by the Lord:

And when they were departed, behold, the angel of the Lord appeareth to Joseph in a dream, saying, 'Arise, and take the young child and his mother, and flee into Egypt, and be thou there until I bring thee word: for Herod will seek the young child to destroy him.'[72]

If, as he grew older, Jesus was made conscious of Egypt with its prominent pyramids, then it's entirely possible that a similar structure in Britain may have come to his attention via the sailors' stories. In the West Country of England, just 30 miles east of Bath with its famous springs, stands an immense earthwork known as Silbury Hill. Despite its sheer size and unique design, it's comparatively little known, but the fact remains that it's Britain's only official pyramid and was built at around the same time as its Egyptian counterparts, around 4,400 years ago.

With the passage of time, this vast enigmatic mound has lost some of its defining contours, but 2,000 years ago it would have appeared closer to its original design than it does now. It stands 130 feet high and covers five acres at its base, so it's little wonder that one eighteenth-century observer described it as a mountain, albeit a green one covered in grass and other plants.

Silbury Hill was constructed in remote prehistory; was it of any interest to anyone around the time of Christ? Most certainly; English Heritage recently discovered a vast Roman settlement, the size of 24 football pitches, at the base of the hill. It was put in place around 2,000 years ago and it's thought that the hill was a site of sacred pilgrimage, although we don't know precisely why. What we *do* know, however, from the records of an eighteenth-century antiquarian named Stukeley, was that local people would celebrate a fair on top of the hill every Palm Sunday, a Christian festival that celebrates the triumphant entry of Jesus as a king into Jerusalem.

Would Jesus have heard of the place? Would he have heard it described as a sacred site? Would he have heard it described as a pyramid? Would this physical link with Egypt, a country that figured prominently in his cultural background and his personal history, have intrigued him?

Let's try to imagine ourselves in this young man's place as he reclined against a wall in some ancient harbour, with the invigorating tang of the salt sea in his nostrils. Eyes hooded against the sun's harsh glare, the insistent pounding of the surf in his ears, surrounded by weather-beaten ships, strange cargoes, foreign sailors and arrogant Roman legionaries, he cast his mind beyond the ocean swell to contemplate the voyage of discovery awaiting him in the land beyond the Pillars of Hercules. With his mind teeming with tales of Britain, of her curiously familiar priests and of a people who'd twice successfully fought off the otherwise invincible Roman legions, with a rich uncle as his guardian who was habitually bound for Britain and with the evocative twin pillars at the ends of the Earth beckoning him on, it's very hard indeed to see how a young Jesus could have resisted. Every element of his cultural tradition, background, upbringing, family circumstances and daily life beneath Roman rule would have drawn him inexorably to the island in the north.

CHAPTER FIVE

'And There's Another Country
I've Heard of Long Ago'

And there's another country I've heard of long ago,
Most dear to those that love her, most great
to them that know.
Cecil Spring-Rice, *Urbs Dei*, 1908

So far, we have looked into the New Testament and examined some of the aspects of the Holy Land, its people, its culture and its history. As a result, we've learned of Jesus' absence from the Biblical record for 18 years and also of many persuasive elements that would have made him intensely curious about the ancient Britons. It would be deeply gratifying if we were to come upon as much as a single corroborating whisper that he'd visited the British Isles – but we already know that there are many of them.

Before we proceed to examine these legends, it's important to bear in mind that the question of *why* Jesus would have travelled to Britain is a different one altogether from *how* he could have travelled there. The means of transport was in all likelihood furnished by his uncle, Joseph of Arimathea, but what was the ultimate goal of his journey? For now, we can be satisfied that it was straightforward curiosity on the part of a scriptural prodigy, a desire to see for himself a remote island with an influential hierarchy that possessed extraordinary similarities to the Jewish priesthood. To this we can reasonably add simple admiration on the part of a youthful Messiah-to-be for the inhabitants and spiritual leaders of a small island that had twice repelled the otherwise all-conquering legions under Caesar.

This matter is certainly worth looking into in greater depth, because it caught the attention of no less a person than Winston Churchill, a one-time member of a British Druid lodge. Churchill had this to say:

> The unnatural principle of human sacrifice was carried by the British Druids to a ruthless pitch. The mysterious priesthoods of the forests bound themselves and their votaries together by the most deadly sacrament that man can take. Here, perhaps, upon these wooden altars of a sullen island, there lay one of the secrets, awful, inflaming, unifying, of the tribes of Gaul.[1]

When we bear in mind the sheer savagery of the three Jewish revolts against Roman rule in antiquity[2] and the curious fact that Jesus once stated, 'Think not that I am come to send peace on earth: I came not to send peace, but a sword,'[3] it's impossible to dismiss this matter of Jesus's passionate interest in the island that was the prime centre of the Druid religion.

MYTHS AND LEGENDS

Of all the legends concerning Jesus in Britain, two are particularly striking. The first concerns the Sack Stone in Fonaby in Lincolnshire and is a story that simply explains how the stone came to be in existence. It seems that Jesus was riding through the fields on an ass when he met some men sowing corn, so he asked them if his ass could eat some of the grain. The men didn't recognize him and refused, saying they had no grain, so Jesus asked them what the sack in the middle of the field was for. The men denied that the distant object was a sack, assuring him it was only a stone, so he replied, 'Stone be it!' and in an echo of what befell Lot's wife, the sack turned to stone.

The other legend concerns Christchurch Priory in the New Forest, whose foundations date back to around AD 800. An unknown workman who refused food and pay joined the builders, but when a huge wooden beam was cut too short, he touched it and it miraculously became the right length. After this, the strange man disappeared, but everyone realized that the miracle worker could only have been Jesus, son of a carpenter.

What do these legends have in common? Well, both involve what appears to be a grown man performing a miracle, but the legend of the Fonaby Stone has a version that states that St Paulinus was responsible for turning the sack to stone in AD 627, and as Christchurch Priory was first built around AD 800, it's pretty obvious that both stories refer to events that took place many centuries after the 'missing years' of Jesus. By way of stark contrast, the overwhelming majority of the other legends are remarkable because what they consistently describe are mundane and predictable activities, not miracles, and the people they mention are far from home.

On some old mining maps of Cornwall, there's a place named Corpus Christi or 'the Body of Christ', and another called 'the Wheel of Jesus', 'wheel' being an old Cornish name for a mine. It's difficult to see why anyone should choose to name a feature of the Cornish landscape after a distant Messiah, let alone a feature so seemingly unlikely as a mine. However, as we've seen, there are abundant suggestions that Jesus was somehow connected with mining through Joseph of Arimathea and there's also an intriguing passage from the Old Testament prophet Malachi[4] foretelling the coming of the Messiah:

'Behold, I will send my messenger, and he shall prepare the way before me... Behold, he shall come,' saith the LORD of hosts... 'For he is like a refiner's fire... And he shall sit as a refiner and purifier of silver: and he shall purify... and purge them as gold and silver...'[5]

Malachi's prophecy is metaphorical in parts, but it unmistakably refers to the coming Messiah as a refiner of metals. As a boy who was renowned for his command of the scriptures, Jesus would have known of Malachi's 'metal-refining' prophecy and it may have contributed to the closeness of his relationship with Joseph of Arimathea, the tin merchant, and drawn him to Britain, consciously or otherwise.

CORNWALL

Another story states that Jesus and Joseph of Arimathea actually worked in a Cornish mine named Creeg Brawse, while yet another relates that Jesus taught some Cornish miners how to smelt tin from ore, and we're left to wonder how on Earth such tales could come into being. Why should the miners of distant Cornwall suddenly have started saying that Jesus, of *all* people, had toiled in their midst as a skilled metalworker?

There's nothing remotely unfeasible about a galley carrying a young Jesus from the eastern Mediterranean putting ashore in Cornwall at some point early in the first century. The latest evidence pointing towards early contact between the regions appeared when a hoard of 28 gold and bronze objects of Mediterranean origin, dated to between 1300 BC and 1150 BC, was discovered off Salcombe in Devon on the south coast of England in 2006. One of the objects was of a kind only found in ancient Sicily, prompting Mike Pitts, editor of *British Archaeology*, to observe that the bronze artefact 'is unique this far north, and raises the possibility, however remote, of a distant traveller reaching Britain from the Mediterranean'.[6]

There are numerous other traditions concerning Cornwall, Joseph of Arimathea, Jesus and the tin trade. Some of these speak of the town of Marazion in Cornwall being visited by Joseph of Arimathea and some commentators have noted the occurrence of the word 'Zion' in this place name and have read some significance into it.[7] The town's website[8] and other informed sources dispute the connection, suggesting that the name is a derivation of the old Cornish word *Marghaisewe*, meaning 'Thursday market', but the same site says that the town claims to be one of the oldest in Britain and that it was known as Ictis by the Romans. This in itself is remarkable, because Diodorus Siculus specifically mentions Ictis, a location that sounds very much like the world-famous St Michael's Mount that's accessible from the Cornish mainland at low tide:

> They that inhabit the British promontory of Belerium [an old name for Cornwall], by reason of their converse with merchants, are more civilized and courteous to strangers than the rest. These are the people that make the tin, which with a great deal of care and labour they dig out of the ground; and that being rocky, the metal is mixed with some veins of earth, out of which they melt the metal and then refine it. Then they beat it into four square pieces like a die and carry it to a British isle, near at hand, called Ictis. For at low tide, all being dry between them and the island, they convey over in carts abundance of tin. But there is one thing that is peculiar to these islands which lie between Britain and Europe: for at full sea they appear to be islands, but at low water for a long way they look like so many peninsulas.[9]

There are also traditions from Somerset that Joseph of Arimathea and Jesus visited the Isles of Scilly and Cornwall in search of tin before venturing further north.[10] When we study them, we learn of many visits made by men from the East to Cornwall:

> There is scarcely a spot in Cornwall where tin is at present found that has not been worked over by the 'old men', as the ancient miners are always called. Every valley has been 'streamed' – that is, the deposits have been washed for tin; over every hill where now a tin mine appears, there are evidences, many of them most extensive, of actual mining operations having been carried on to as great a depth as was possible in the days when the appliances of science were unknown. Wherever the 'streamer' has been, upon whatever spot the old miner has worked, there we are told the 'Finician' (Phoenician) has been, or the Jew has mined.[11]

There are other detailed traditions in this vein, so many that it seems highly likely that specific visits to Cornwall by men from the eastern

Mediterranean in ancient times were remembered and passed down through the generations.

Significantly, there is also frequent mention of a poem or miner's song that includes the refrain: 'Joseph was a tin man, Joseph was in the tin trade.'[12] In the village of Priddy in the Mendip Hills in Somerset, the children were also supposed to have once sung a song about Joseph of Arimathea being a tin merchant. This song also included details of Jesus accompanying his uncle and arriving in the region in a boat. There is even an old saying in the area, 'As sure as Our Lord walked in Priddy',[13] which is about as unambiguous an avowal of a visit by Jesus as it's possible to get.

The tradition is quite specific:

Our Lord when a boy came voyaging with a sailor uncle to Britain. Their trading ship put in at Watchet, and from there He walked across the Quantocks to Bridgwater where He boarded a punt and crossed the lakes and marshes to the foot of Mendip, ending His journey high up at Priddy. Here, say the miners, He walked and talked and worked with them a happy while, and then, loaded with Somerset gear, He went back to Nazareth.[14]

Nor is this the only story identifying locations visited by Jesus, as there are legends at St Just in Cornwall of Jesus stepping ashore from a boat and placing his feet on a stone. A flat stone with strange markings was apparently discovered by workmen in 1932 when they were clearing a blocked culvert, and as this stone was blocking the water from a spring known as the Christening Well, it was immediately assumed to be the same stone that Jesus had stepped onto nearly 2,000 years before. It was believed that the markings were placed on the stone later, when the identity of the visitor became known, but even before this carved stone was found, there was a potent legend in the area of Jesus arriving there as a boy with his uncle.[15]

And so it goes – whenever we consult books of folklore, we find references to Jesus in the West Country. We read of Jesus and Joseph anchoring their ship in the harbour of the mouth of the River Camel so that they could come ashore for fresh water. We learn of a nearby well called the Jesus Well that was regarded as having healing powers. We hear of supposed pictographs in a church relating the story of how Jesus and Joseph had their damaged boat driven ashore one night in a storm, after which they left behind a stone commemorating their visit.[16]

At this point, it's worth noting the scale and spread of what's come to be known as 'the Holy Legend', because in Cornwall, it's been ascribed to Marazion, Ding Dong mine in Penwith, St Day, Falmouth in Parnmarth, St Just-in-Roseland, Lammana or Looe Island in Wivelshire, Mount St Michael, the Jesus Well near Padstow, Creege Brawse, Redruth, Mount's Bay near Marazion, Talland, Polperro, Mousehole, Nancledra, Carnon Downs, Polruan, Mylor and 'the Giant's Hedge'. In Somerset, it has been ascribed to Priddy, Glastonbury, Pilton, Paradise Farm near Burnham on Sea, the Mendips, the Quantocks, Bridgwater and Watchet, and after reviewing the collections and critiques of the legend, I've also learned of stories locating Jesus in Horlde near Bournemouth and Caerleon in south Wales, on the road to Winchester and at Merchant's Point on Tresco on the Isles of Scilly.

There are all manner of other tales, but however captivating they may be, our sole interest is to establish the truth of the matter, hence we need to examine a study entitled 'And did those feet? The "legend" of Christ's visit to Britain' that was published in 1989 by A. W. Smith.[17] After 14,000 words of closely argued and intensely researched text, the author concluded that there was little reason to believe that an oral tradition concerning a visit made by Jesus to Britain existed before the early part of the twentieth century, so these objections are certainly worthy of our attention.

Smith points out that the majority of stories dealing with Jesus in the West Country seem to have been collected and recorded by people of the Church: 'Among the cited witnesses to an oral tradition there seems to be a preponderance of clergy, clergy's wives and elderly female parishioners.'[18] However, as these stories concern the central figure of the Christian religion, it's hardly surprising that Christians should have had a particular interest in them, because they of *all* people would naturally have exulted in them and been at pains to preserve them.

That aside, the author takes issue with a statement made in an undated pamphlet entitled 'The Story of Glastonbury', which claims: 'There is a strong, unvarying tradition that Joseph of Arimathea... brought the boy Jesus with him on some of his visits...' In response to this and other similar claims, Smith caustically wrote:

> Is there 'a strong, unvarying tradition'? It is not strong but weak and fugitive. Is it unvarying? Far from it. Every version is different, if only in its localisation. In Cornwall alone some fifteen 'find-spots' have been recorded. (I think we may dismiss out of hand the suggestion that Jesus made repeated visits to Britain or called at each place in turn in some elaborately conceived 'tour'; whether for tin-buying or in search of Druid wisdom.)[19]

Aside from the highly dubious scholarly method of dismissing *anything* out of hand, Smith misses the point in several respects. What's important in these stories is the consistent theme of Jesus visiting Britain in the company of the one person that we know was in a realistic position to provide him with transport to the British Isles. The central and most important element is a named individual being *out of place*, and the blunt fact that the individual was notably without a Biblical alibi for the period in question shouldn't be forgotten either.

There's also clear evidence that these stories were known outside the West Country and that a well-defined group of people had been aware of them for a very long time indeed. A letter was printed in the *Western Morning News* of Plymouth on 25 March 1933, mentioning the legend of Christ in Cornwall,[20] and a fascinating response was printed on 6 April of that same year that throws further light on the antiquity of the legend. In brief, the reply[21] was submitted by Henry Jenner, a distinguished scholar of Celtic matters and Chief Bard of Cornwall, who recalled a story he'd been told about 40 years before when he was dining with one of the masters of Harrow School. The story concerned a Mr James Baillie Hamilton, an amateur in organ building who'd just been to a workshop in London to see the process of making metal pipes. While he was there, one of the workers was heard to say in a low tone, 'Joseph was in the tin trade,' before casting the metal. The foreman in charge was eventually persuaded to explain:

> We workers in metal are a very old fraternity and, like other handicrafts, we have old traditions among us. One of these, the memory of which is preserved in this invocation, is that Joseph of Arimathea, the rich man of the Gospels, made his money in the tin trade with Cornwall. We have also a story that he made voyages to Cornwall in his own ships, and that on one occasion he brought with him the child Christ and his mother too and landed them at St. Michael's Mount.[22]

Modern masons and smiths pride themselves on being able to trace their traditions back to King Solomon, in or around 1,000 BC. As Joseph of Arimathea was born 1,000 years or so *after* this, he was a comparative newcomer, so it would not be so surprising if the fraternity had retained a memory or otherwise kept some record of his visit to Britain. In any event, it's there in black and white in Jenner's letter and in his recollection of what the foreman had to say.

✦ ✦ ✦

Does the Church have anything to say on this subject? The four Church councils of Pisa 1409, Constance 1417, Sienna 1424 and Basle 1434 mention that 'the Churches of France and Spain must yield in points of antiquity and precedence to that of Britain, as the latter Church was founded by Joseph of Arimathea immediately after the passion of Christ'.[23] We don't know precisely why these councils made the remarkable decision that Christianity had not only taken root in Britain before it had become established anywhere else, but also that Joseph of Arimathea had founded a Church in Britain shortly after the crucifixion. However, we *do* know that William of Malmesbury, a twelfth-century English historian, recorded that when St David came to Glastonbury in 540 to rededicate the new church, he had a dream that changed his mind. Jesus appeared in a vision telling David that rededication was unnecessary, saying, 'He Himself had long before dedicated the church in honour of His mother and the sacrament ought not to be profaned by human repetition.'[24]

Nor is this the only mention in ecclesiastical records of Jesus himself building a church dedicated to his mother at Glastonbury. In a letter to Pope Gregory, St Augustine wrote:

> In the western confines of Britain there is a certain royal island of large extent, abounding in all beauties of nature and necessaries of life. In it the first Neophites of Catholic Law, God hath beforehand acquainted them, found a church constructed by no human art, but divinely constructed by the hands of Christ Himself, for the salvation of his people...[25]

The sixth-century Church writer Gildas had something equally interesting to say about Britain:

> Meanwhile these islands, stiff with cold and frost, and in a distant region of the world, remote from the visible sun, received the beams of light, that is, the holy precepts of Christ, the true sun, showing to the whole world his splendour, not only from the temporal firmament, but from the height of heaven, which surpasses everything temporal, at the latter point, as we know, of the reign of Tiberius Caesar, by whom his religion was propagated without impediment, and death threatened to those who interfered with its professors.[26]

As the crucifixion took place in the seventeenth year of Tiberius, who reigned for 22 years, Gildas is speaking of Britain becoming a Christian nation as early as AD 38. The language he uses certainly brings to mind Blake's later 'Countenance Divine', and elsewhere he speaks in glowing terms of England's mountains, hills, pastures and the striking beauty of the countryside.

✦ ✦ ✦

Thus far, we can reasonably be said to have achieved one of our goals, which was to find just *one* tale of demonstrable antiquity that placed

Jesus in Britain in the early first century AD. There are many other accounts to come, but before we pursue them, it may be profitable for us to examine the physical landscape around the village that's the home of the saying 'As sure as Our Lord walked in Priddy', because this may yet be the home of something far more tangible and startling than a mere folk story.

CHAPTER SIX

The Harrowing of Hell

I dream of moor and misty hill
Where evening gathers, dark and chill…
What have those lonely mountains worth revealing?
Emily Brontë

The folklorist Ruth Tongue wrote of an aged visitor to her family home describing how to find 'the Lord's Path' at Priddy, but as this event took place in 1901 when she was a very young girl, she couldn't be entirely certain in later life as to precisely what had been said. This idea is tantalizing, especially when we bear in mind the other tales we've heard about Jesus working with the ancient miners on the Mendip Hills, so it makes sense to see if there's anything else that could validate the notion that Jesus once visited Priddy.

The village of Priddy lies in the Mendip Hills in Somerset, 15 miles southwest of the springs of Aquae Sulis at Bath and 10 miles north of Glastonbury, or less than a day's walk from the place where Jesus is said to have built a wattle and daub church and dedicated it to his mother. Far and away the most prominent feature of Glastonbury, apart from its enchanting ruined abbey and modern festival, is Glastonbury Tor, the immense, teardrop-shaped hill that dominates the surrounding landscape, towering over 500 feet above the surrounding plain known as the

Summerland Meadows. As such, it's beyond question a 'high place' like those that Jesus made a point of visiting back in his homeland during his famed ministry, and the Mendip Hills themselves are self-evidently such high places also.

The name 'Priddy' most likely derives from a Celtic word meaning 'earth', which could be a reference to the Iron Age mining activities that took place in the area. *The Oxford Dictionary of English Place-Names* tells us that it probably means 'earth house', but the other possibilities are no less curious, because it could also mean 'meadowland' or 'pasture', or else 'a flock' and, by implication, the 'flock' of a church. This word of Celtic or Welsh origin is curiously out of place in the Mendip area, as it predates the later arrival of the Saxons, so we're left to wonder about the importance of the survival of a word meaning 'earth house', 'pasture' or 'flock', all of which are directly linked to Jesus in some way. The reference to an 'earth house' brings to mind the wattle and daub church that Jesus was said to have built in nearby Glastonbury, while Blake wrote of Jesus being seen on England's 'pleasant pastures' and the word 'flock' straightaway suggests sheep, or lambs, or the Holy Lamb of God.

I've heard an accusation that the story of Jesus in Priddy was invented by a schoolteacher in the early years of the twentieth century as a play for her children, but even if this were true, it doesn't cancel out the antiquity of the name 'Priddy', nor does it account for its range of possible meanings, its uniqueness as a Celtic word in a Saxon landscape or its proximity to Glastonbury, yet another place where Jesus is said to have dwelt. Writing in 1947, the Rev. C. C. Dobson spoke of nonagenarians who learned of the story of Jesus visiting the Mendips when they were children, which would date this tradition back at least as far as the 1860s, and he also made the valid point that if a schoolteacher at Priddy *had* written a play for her children, it was far more likely that she had based it on a well-known and existing tradition in those parts than that she had conjured up such a seemingly astonishing tale from out of thin air.[1]

The Mendips themselves are thought to derive their name from the mediaeval term 'Myne-deepes' and there's evidence that mining took place in the lead- and silver-rich ground during the early Roman occupation and as long ago as the Late Bronze Age (roughly 1200 to 700 BC). As far as the stories of Jesus associating with miners are concerned, there were certainly people engaged in such activity at the time when Jesus is said to have visited the place.

The area had already had *some* connection with men from the eastern Mediterranean long before the arrival of Joseph and Jesus, as has been shown by the discovery of segmented faïence beads in a round barrow, or prehistoric burial mound, near Tyning's Farm at Priddy.[2] Faïence is a form of glaze that originated in the Near East and the technology to produce it was apparently unknown in Britain when these barrows were constructed, so logic suggests that the beads arrived there by way of someone who had some connection with the eastern Mediterranean. As formerly noted, a bronze object that originated in ancient Sicily over 1,000 years before the time of Jesus was recently found off Salcombe in Devon; it's available for inspection, as are the other bronze and gold pieces discovered with it, but, sadly, the faïence beads from the Priddy barrow were destroyed by German bombers during the Blitz of Bristol in 1941.

While these details of the origins of names and of curious beads are intriguing enough, it's now time to concentrate our attention on a set of vast prehistoric earthworks that once dominated the landscape at Priddy. In doing so, we'll have to look in some detail at a time long before Jesus arrived in the area, but it'll be more than worth the effort because it'll allow us to gain a detailed picture of what this region was like in the early years of the first century AD, which in turn may give us an unprecedented insight into one of the most baffling of Christian myths.

THE OUTER CIRCLES OF HELL

Known as the Priddy Circles, these circular earthen monuments are arranged in a line that stretches for roughly three-quarters of a mile across the Mendip Hills, and they were constructed in the Late

Neolithic period, between 3400 BC and 2300 BC.[3] The vast majority of other such prehistoric monuments, commonly referred to as henges, possess an outer bank that surrounds or encircles an inner ditch, but the Priddy Circles were built with an *outer* ditch surrounding an internal bank. Furthermore, the original builders of the Priddy Circles were at pains to create monuments that were used for ritual or ceremonial purposes rather than for defensive or domestic uses, and they chose to employ a highly unusual method of construction.

The University of Bristol Speleological Society carried out excavations at Circle 1 at Priddy, the most southerly circle, between 1956 and 1959. The archaeologists discovered that instead of simply building the internal banks with earth thrown up from an adjacent ditch, the original builders fashioned a double pair of drystone walls covered with earth and stones, and the whole arrangement had a revetment or facing of stakes, hurdles, screens and posts. Furthermore, the pollen evidence suggests that additional earth and stones were brought from a site nearby to supplement the bank and that the area was originally grassland, which means that the wood for the posts had to be brought to the site from elsewhere. The archaeologists calculated that 320 posts were required just to complete Circle 1, so if this figure applied to the other circles as well, then 1,280 posts and an equal number of stakes, as well as many other materials, would have been needed to complete the whole site. The archaeologists estimated that a minimum of 160 mature trees would have had to be cut down just for Circle 1 and the whole site would have needed between 600 and 700 trees, a stupendous undertaking for men wielding wooden axes tipped with flint. Furthermore, judging from the depth and diameter of the postholes, it seems that the wooden posts at Circle 1 were large enough to protrude over the top of a bank that stood as high as six feet.

So what do the archaeologists make of all this concentrated effort?

The complex arrangement of timbers, stakes and screens, with possible cross-bracing and a lower stone bank in between, would not only have prevented glimpses of the interior from the circumference, it would also have *prevented people from accessing the tops of the banks* [my italics]. Whilst the banks of some henges could have been 'viewing platforms', this was not the case at the Priddy Circles. This suggests an extremely strict division between those who could watch the rituals and those who could not. The presence of external ditches at the circles also amplifies this effect, as external ditches are a classic feature at sites designed to keep people out (cf. defensive sites). These features – stone banks, timbers, screens, external ditches – suggest that the Priddy Circles exaggerated and manipulated principles of exclusion and unequal access to ritual knowledge in a manner that as yet has few precedents.[4]

In other words, the prehistoric earthworks at Priddy were constructed like precious few others in the whole British Isles. Not only did the ancient builders go to strenuous efforts to construct four huge circles with banks made of stone walls, posts, and screens, but they did so in such a way as to make their ceremonial purpose unmistakable. Furthermore, the mysterious rites that took place inside those forbidding earthen ramparts on the lonely plateau in the Mendip Hills were so potent and unique that the original builders went out of their way to ensure that they *remained* a secret, not only from later generations, but from the vast majority of their contemporaries as well.

Are these strange prehistoric monuments the *only* things of archaeological and religious interest in the immediate vicinity? No. The archaeologist and Neolithic specialist Jodie Lewis describes the area as 'a landscape full of special and somewhat mysterious places'. One of its unusual features is that it has an extraordinarily high concentration of swallets, otherwise known as dolines or sinkholes, which are vertical shafts in the ground formed either by limestone being dissolved by water or collapsing into a cave system beneath. These holes can appear almost overnight, while strange noises can often be heard emanating from them on account of subterranean water echoing around the cave systems, gurgling and groaning as it flows through the crooked bowels of the earth. Modern cavers attest to the hypnotic powers of these underground streams, because the sound made by gently flowing water in the darkness can seem like distant voices or unearthly music after a time and cause the imagination to run riot. Writing in the second century AD, St Clement of Alexandria recorded that German priestesses used to divine the future from noises they heard coming from streams and other bodies of water[5] and it's likely that something very similar took place on the Mendip Hills in ancient times.

As for the age of these strange sinkholes, an archaeological and geological study of the swallets at Priddy conducted in 1986 showed that many of these natural shafts are considerably *older* than the man-made prehistoric monuments that now enclose them. As Jodie Lewis observes, the implications of this are astounding, because it clearly shows that the prodigious effort that went into constructing the Priddy Circles and excluding onlookers was centred on ceremonies conducted around and *inside* these strange shafts into the underworld.

Is the notion of our ancestors conducting subterranean ceremonies in the dangerous confines of a crumbling vertical shaft too outlandish? Apparently not, because archaeologists have investigated some of the swallets on the Mendips and have found unmistakable evidence that people deliberately made their way down into the Stygian bowels of the Earth to conduct ceremonies there. This would have required both courage *and* conviction, because it's one thing to wander or even crawl into a near-horizontal cave, for example, but to safely descend a jagged, *vertical* shaft would require ropes and ladders. The physical aspect is difficult and intimidating enough before we consider the darkness and the strange noises emanating from the depths of the Earth, but the evidence that our ancestors did precisely this is there in the form of human bone, flint tools, bone tools, pottery and animal bone, materials often found in prehistoric mortuary monuments. Furthermore, the condition of these artefacts shows that they didn't suffer damage from being thrown into these gaping pits, but were instead carefully placed there.

The most striking example so far discovered was a complete handled beaker that had been placed on a ledge in a Mendip swallet at a depth of nearly 50 feet; in other words, it had remained intact and undisturbed in the same place on a small ledge in a precipitous shaft for something in the region of 4,000 years. Alongside it were animal bones and human bones that showed unmistakable signs of the original bodies having been dismembered with knives or other sharp implements.[6]

Many of these objects date from the Late Neolithic period and the early Bronze Age, around 2300 BC, but the remains of at least 28 individuals from the Iron Age and the early Romano-British period were discovered around the entrance to a swallet at Charterhouse Farm. Sadly, these excavations in the 1970s were poorly recorded, so we know little about these remains, but their existence at the threshold of this grim cavern tells us that rituals or ceremonies connected to an underworld had been performed in that area for something like 2,000 years and were still in existence in some form as late as the Late Iron Age or the early Romano-British period, which is precisely when Jesus was said to have visited Priddy.

HAUNTERS OF THE DARK

The first person to write about the Priddy Circles in modern times[7] was the Reverend John Skinner, a Somerset vicar, who described them as 'Druidical Circles'. He may not have been completely wide of the mark, but the truth, as already admitted, is that we know precious little about the Druids. Julius Caesar left us the most detailed account of the cult, but he makes no mention of the places in which they practised their ceremonies. However, the Roman writers Lucan,[8] Pliny[9] and Tacitus[10] all write of the Druids performing their ceremonies in groves, so this argument has been presented endlessly over the years by archaeologists as a means of confining Druidic activities and the presence of Druids to the middle of forests, while totally excluding them from all other monuments or natural features. However, this is to wilfully overlook the works of Pomponius Mela, a Roman geographer who compiled his work around the time of the Roman invasion of Britain in AD 43 – before Lucan, Pliny or Tacitus were writing. In light of what we've discovered about the seclusion of the circles and the underground caves at Priddy, it's intriguing to read what Pomponius had to say about the Druids:

> There still remain traces of atrocious customs no longer practised, and although they now refrain from outright slaughter yet they still draw blood from the victims led to the altar. They have, however, their own kind of eloquence, and teachers of wisdom called Druids. These profess to know the size and shape of the world, the movements of the heavens and of the stars, and the will of the gods. They teach many things to the nobles of Gaul in a course of instruction lasting as long as twenty years, *meeting in secret either in a cave or in secluded dales*. One of their dogmas has come to common knowledge, namely, that souls are eternal and that *there is another life in the infernal regions...* [my italics].[11]

It'd be a long shot to suppose that Pomponius was specifically writing about the Priddy Circles, but the Mendip Hills are by their very nature full of dales and valleys, and the Priddy Circles themselves were secluded on a high plateau and surrounded by woodland.

Furthermore, a century or so before the time of Pomponius, Julius Caesar recorded: 'The Gauls claim all to be descended from Dis Pater, declaring that this is the tradition preserved by the Druids.'[12] Dis Pater, or Father Dis, otherwise known as Hades or Pluto, was the baleful god who ruled over Tartarus, the Realm of the Dead; by extension, he was also viewed as a god of riches, because precious gems and metals had to be mined from the Earth. As Caesar noted, the Druids not only worshipped this god, but claimed physical descent or ancestry from him as well. It's hard to think of a more fitting place for them to commune with a god of the underworld than in the catacombs at Priddy, while we've already seen evidence in the form of the 28 separate dead bodies in a swallet on the Mendips that some ritual or ceremony linking these shafts with the dead was taking place at exactly the same time that Jesus was said to be in this area. So, is there a possible connection between these Druidic 'death cults' and a visit made by Jesus?

Indeed there is, as the concept of a physical underworld was a prominent part of the Hebrew religion. Jesus would certainly have been aware of a Jewish version of hell called Gehenna, a fiery place where the souls of the wicked were sent, which furthermore had a physical reality in the Valley of Gehinnom outside Jerusalem. It's first mentioned in Joshua 15, verse 8, and there's a later reference to it as a nightmare location where children were sacrificed:

> Moreover, he burnt incense in the valley of the son of Hinnom, and burnt his children in the fire, after the abominations of the heathen whom the LORD had cast out before the children of Israel.[13]

Nonetheless, the most usual destination of the dead as far as the Jews were concerned was an underworld named Sheol, which was described as a pit or a physical place beneath the Earth.[14] Perhaps the most striking reference to Sheol, which a scriptural prodigy such as Jesus would *definitely* have known about, is the chilling account of when the Earth literally opened up to swallow the family of Korah, a man who had rebelled against the Law of Moses:

> Moses said, 'By this you will know that the Lord Himself has sent me to perform all these tasks and that this is not my doing. If these people die a natural death, such as men commonly die, then the Lord has not sent me. But if the Lord does something utterly new, if the earth should open its mouth and swallow them and all that belongs to them, so that they go down alive to Sheol, then you will know that these men have rejected the Lord.
>
> The moment he finished saying all these words, the ground split open under their feet, and the earth opened its mouth and swallowed them, their families too, and all Korah's men and all their belongings.
>
> They went down alive to Sheol, they and all their possessions. The earth closed over them and they disappeared from the midst of the assembly. At their cries, all the Israelites around them ran away. For they said, 'The earth must not swallow us.'[15]

This matter of the Earth opening up in an instant to engulf a group of people is remarkable when we consider that the catacombs at Priddy and elsewhere on the Mendips were and still *are* capable of appearing overnight.

THE GATES OF HELL

> *The Gates of Hell are open, night and day,*
> *Smooth the descent and easy is the way;*
> *But, to return and view the cheerful skies*
> *In that, the mighty task and labour lies.*
>
> **Virgil, *Aeneid*, Book VI**

With all this in mind, it becomes impossible to ignore one of the most mysterious myths concerning Jesus. It's a Christian legend known as 'the Harrowing of Hell' which states that at some point Jesus descended into hell to preach the gospel and to release souls such as Adam and Eve. The event is mentioned in the Apostles' Creed and it inspired a multitude of evocative paintings and woodcuts in mediaeval times. In the Greek version of the Apostles' Creed, the relevant words are κατελθοντα 'εις τα κατωτατα, or *katelthonta eis ta katotata*, which means 'He descended to the netherworld or underworld.' In Latin, the same passage reads *descendit ad inferos*, which has an identical meaning, while both the Latin and Greek versions are sometimes translated as 'descended to the dead'.

It's an easy matter to trace the origin of this legend, because it originates in one or possibly two verses written by St Peter, the first of which states that: 'In the body he was put to death, in the spirit he was raised to life, and in the spirit, he went to preach to the spirits in prison.'[16] This makes it clear that the descent into hell took place *after* Jesus was crucified, but a following passage is less certain: 'For this cause was the gospel preached also to them that are dead, that they might be judged according to men in the flesh, but live according to God in the spirit.'[17]

A number of other Biblical verses have been taken to refer to Jesus descending to the underworld,[18] but the timing is uncertain and no location is mentioned. However, it is clear that Jesus was perfectly capable in later years of summoning up and conversing with the spirits of the dead, for example when he ascended the mountain and the phantom forms of Moses and Elijah appeared.[19]

The Harrowing of Hell was a popular story in the West Country of England and was a major theme in the Cornish version of the Mystery Plays, the religious performances of the Middle Ages. However, despite the allure and iconic status of this legend, it appears that no one has ever thought to explore the possibility that it may have been based on an historical event.

As we've seen, the New Testament is unclear as to precisely when the Harrowing of Hell took place, but if it occurred after the crucifixion, it can't have happened at Priddy. However, if it was based on something that Jesus did during that period of his life on which the Bible is mysteriously silent, then Priddy has to be a highly likely location.

THE LORD'S WALK?

It's not been a difficult undertaking to look into one of the episodes in the life of the central figure in Christianity and a hugely revered figure in the Muslim faith, an individual worshipped by billions of people the world over. We haven't had to speculate about the contents of mysterious hidden archives in order to make headway; far from it, because the stories of Jesus visiting the West Country have always been in the public domain and experts in folklore and other interested parties have assiduously collected these tales. For something like 200 years on and off, ever since the enterprising Reverend Skinner of Somerset first investigated the 'Druidical Circles' on the Mendips in the early nineteenth century, antiquarians and archaeologists have pored over the prehistoric earthworks at Priddy, even if their record-keeping has sometimes left something to be desired. There's a wealth of legitimate and scientific information available for anyone who chooses to pursue the matter, and there's equally free access to the Bible and to the area around Priddy itself. All we've done is to look objectively at each individual subject, then compare the results and try to draw a logical conclusion from them:

- Jesus is absent from the Biblical record for 18 years, between the age of 12, when he is recognized as a prodigy, and the age of 30, when he begins his ministry.
- Numerous detailed legends place Jesus at Priddy during this time and they specify that he associated and worked with miners, i.e. he ventured underground at some point.
- This highly specific site is home to prehistoric monuments virtually without parallel in Britain.
- These same monuments were in active use as conduits to the underworld at the time when Jesus is said to have visited the area.
- There's an account in the Gospel of Matthew of Jesus speaking with the phantoms of Moses and Elijah.
- There's an enduring and highly potent legend that at some point Jesus descended into hell.

In short, the evidence points toward Jesus having visited Priddy and having physically descended to the underworld there, an exploit entirely compatible with what we know of his later life.

The last time I visited Priddy, I parked on a muddy verge at the top of the winding Nine Barrows Lane, then wandered through the adjacent field that gave the road its name, up a gentle incline towards the summit. This place is home to nine Bronze Age barrows that sweep upwards in a gentle curve from the lower reaches of the field, and while there are more barrows and higher hills elsewhere, I was content to stroll around the nine burial mounds close by. I immediately found that I was less interested in studying them from an archaeological perspective than in admiring them as a part of the ancient landscape, and after a short while, I gave in to the temptation to simply laze against one of the mounds and idly watch the world go by. It was a pleasant enough summer afternoon and considerably milder and calmer than I'd have expected atop such a range of hills, so I reclined there and relaxed, as I was in no hurry.

After a short while, I felt the curious sensation of all my aches, pains and minor anxieties draining away from me; it wasn't the lethargy that comes after a long drive with the accompanying dull ache behind the eyes, but an extraordinary feeling of tranquillity, serenity and well-being. I was raised in a rural area and have enjoyed many uplifting times since then in the beauty of the English and Welsh countryside, but this warm sense of being utterly free from care was uplifting to a degree that I'd not experienced before; furthermore, it had no identifiable source other than the beauty of the landscape and the clemency of the weather. I'm not alone in having experienced this, so could it be a tangible sign that a Messiah once walked there? Is Nine Barrows Lane the Lord's Walk? It's impossible to say, but I *do* know that there are other secrets concealed in those hills.

It's by no means unthinkable that there may be archaeological evidence of Jesus in the Mendips. We have seen that there are several stones in the West Country said to have been trodden on by Jesus or erected by him to commemorate his visits there, and he is said to have built the world's first church at Glastonbury out of wattle and daub, a building that was still standing as late as the sixth century when St David encased it in lead to preserve it. But what of the underground galleries at Priddy?

A. W. Smith's aforementioned study of the legends of Jesus in Britain was critical of most of the publications recording the tales, but it had praise for a collection entitled *Popular Romances of the West of England*, which contains the following observations concerning the contents of ancient mines in Cornwall by the men who worked in them:

They maintaine these works to have been verie auncient, and first wrought by the Jewes with Pickaxes of Holme-Boxe and Hartshorne. They prove this by the name of those places yet enduring, to wit, Attoll Sarazin, in English, the Jewes Offcast, *and by those tooles daily found amongst the rubble of such workes* [my italics].[20]

It's one thing to read the opinion of unlettered miners from centuries past, but what do today's archaeologists make of the possible contents of the shafts within the earthworks at Priddy?

> It seems very likely that the swallets would have been employed in rituals taking place within the circles, possibly used for 'hidden' ceremonies and/or deposition of artefacts. Certainly, the excavation of swallets within the Circles could well yield very interesting results.[21]

PART II

TEMPLE

Hic occultus occulto occisus est.
(Here an unknown was killed by an unknown.)

Inscription on a monument for
Kaspar Hauser, who died in 1833

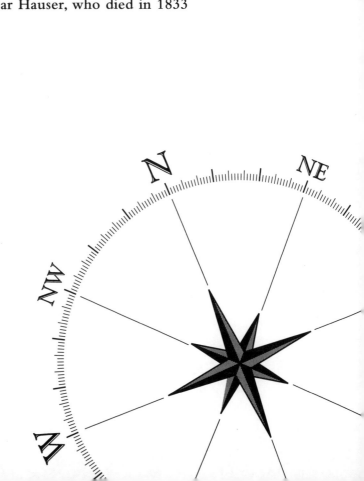

So far, we have unearthed some notable information which could indicate that during the 'missing years' of his life, Jesus visited the west of Britain. Now comes the time to break new ground by extending our search away from Cornwall, Glastonbury and Priddy, and our immediate goal will be to see if there's anything else in the landscape of the West Country that speaks of Jesus having once visited the region.

At first glance, it might seem an impossibly difficult task to retrace the footsteps of a young man who travelled to Britain 2,000 years ago. There are no written records from that time that we know of, nor were there to be any until about 30 years afterwards, when the Roman legions of the Emperor Claudius invaded in AD 43. On the other hand, even though Jesus would have been a solitary youth in a country far from home, he was already regarded as a prodigy by the age of 12 and he was a youth like no other before or since. As such, he was more likely than most to have left behind some subtle impression that we can discern, even through the intervening years.

If he did spend a lengthy period of time in Britain, then it's extremely unlikely that he'd have been a fugitive, trying to avoid contact with the native population. Reason suggests that he would have been ignored, tolerated or embraced by the people he chose to live among, so we'll have to weigh up the evidence and judge for ourselves which scenario was most likely. We'll have to ask how he sustained himself, both physically and spiritually, what factors could have induced him to stay and why he ultimately left. Was he driven away, or did he choose to leave of his own accord?

There's nothing incredible about the idea of Joseph of Arimathea and a young Jesus working in prehistoric mines in Cornwall or living and working in the region of Priddy for a number of years. However, if they did so, it seems highly likely that they would have occasionally ventured further afield, and when we glance at a map of the region, far and away the most notable structure is Stonehenge, the wonder of the world that lies a mere 30 miles to the east.

CHAPTER SEVEN

Stonehenge

The Druid's groves are gone – so much the better.
Stonehenge is not, but what the Devil is it?
Lord Byron, *Don Juan*

To get a realistic and detailed picture of the brooding ruins of Stonehenge as they would have appeared in or around AD 14, the approximate date when Jesus is said to have visited the British Isles, we'll have to travel back over 2,000 years before then to the time when the awe-inspiring megaliths were first put in place. Before we do so, however, several things are immediately apparent.

Even when the stones that make up what we recognize today as Stonehenge were being erected in or around 2300 BC, the site possessed such a potent allure that it drew visitors from as far away as the Alps. We can be sure of this because of the discovery in May 2002 of the remains of two individuals who have come to be known as the 'King' and the 'Prince' of Stonehenge, on account of the unparalleled richness of the burial of the senior figure, the proximity of the graves to Stonehenge and the facts that they were closely related and were alive in around 2300 BC, when the massive sarsen phase of Stonehenge was under construction. The king is also known as the Amesbury Archer, as his remains were unearthed at Boscombe Down, near Amesbury. I was one of the first archaeologists to see and inspect this man's mortal remains and the rich contents of his grave when they arrived at the offices of Wessex Archaeology, but it wasn't until some months later that a careful analysis of the enamel on his teeth showed that he'd originated somewhere in continental Europe.

This man wasn't the only one to have been drawn a great distance to the mysterious stone circle on Salisbury Plain, because almost exactly a year later, in May 2003, I filmed and assisted with the excavation of the men now known to us as the Boscombe Bowmen or Builders of Stonehenge. Objects found in their collective grave showed that they'd lived at around the same time as the Amesbury Archer and an analysis of their tooth enamel showed that they too had embarked on a great journey in distant prehistory, most likely from the southern part of what's now Wales. These people may have ceremonially accompanied the bluestones from the Preseli Hills when they were transported across the Severn Estuary to make up the inner sanctum at Stonehenge, or else they may have embarked on a separate pilgrimage to the site for reasons unknown to us.

The mesmerizing effect that the intricate pillars, lintels and shadows of Stonehenge had upon people from far-flung lands wasn't confined to the distant Neolithic or Bronze Ages. In 350 BC, roughly 2,000 years after the immense stones had been carefully arranged and put in place, an ancient Greek mariner named Pytheas of Massilia wrote an account of his voyage around Britain, and he was the first person that we know of to leave a written record of a visit to Stonehenge. Most of what this daring man had to say survives only in fragments quoted by other ancient authors, but something drew him inland to visit what he described as a notable temple, circular in shape, along with a city ruled by kings known as the Boreades, or 'Sons of the North Wind'. This description can only apply to Stonehenge,[1] and the city he wrote about can only be the huge Iron Age hill fort now known to us as Vespasian's Camp, situated a mile or so to the east.

It's easy to understand the fascination that the site exerted on our ancestors when we consider the sheer size of the stones and the unique way they are arranged. Today, one million visitors every year come to gaze in awe at the enigmatic ruins, so it's not difficult to envisage how two men from the East would have been drawn to travel a mere 30 miles out of sheer curiosity, if for no other reason.

There's some heated debate as to whether we could accurately describe the people who originally built Stonehenge as Druids, but it's likely that the monument would have been frequented by the Druids around the time of Jesus. The Celts had a reverence bordering on dread for the burial places of those who had preceded them and Stonehenge still lies at the centre of a vast prehistoric cemetery, even though many of the barrows or funeral mounds have been wiped off the face of the Earth over the course of time. The Druids were known to conduct their ceremonies in the presence of oak and at least one surviving stone at Stonehenge was carved so as to resemble the bark of an oak tree, while there may have been still more before the monument was vandalized and stones removed in the seventeenth and eighteenth centuries.

Furthermore, its sheer scale, unique design and setting may well have made it a focus or symbol of national resistance against the threat from the Romans, while the ceremonies of priests singing hymns of praise to Apollo as described by Pytheas of Massilia in 350 BC sound very similar to the Druids and their passion for reciting lengthy verses. Even if the Druids only gathered at Stonehenge on rare occasions, this imagery brings to mind the Jewish Sanhedrin and the courts they held in the Hall of Hewn Stones at the Temple in Jerusalem.

Finally, we've seen how Joseph of Arimathea was described in the New Testament as a man who skilfully cut into rock or stone, and it's not difficult to see how a man engaged in such a profession would have been curious about the huge, meticulously dressed stones that stood together in such a strange arrangement, the only stones on the entire island to have been fashioned in such a way.

If we simply bear in mind these aspects of Stonehenge and nothing else, then it seems inevitable that Jesus and Joseph of Arimathea would have been drawn to visit the site, as had so many others before them. When we look deeper into the matter, though, and try to picture Stonehenge exactly as it would have appeared early in the first century AD, the idea becomes far more compelling. To do this, we must first briefly travel back through the ages to a time when the imposing edifice existed only in the fevered imagination of its creator.

CONCEALED FROM SIGHT

As far as we know, Stonehenge began as a set of earthworks in or around 3200 BC, although it had certainly been a sacred site for many millennia before that, standing as it did in the centre of what was already an ancient ceremonial landscape with other huge earthworks such as long barrows carefully arranged around it. The *round* barrows are burial mounds of varying circular shapes described as bells, ponds, saucers, discs and the like, and they date from roughly when the stone monument at Stonehenge was put in place in 2300 BC; however, the *long* barrows existed well over 1,000 years before, and as their name suggests, they are often enormous elongated mounds of earth and chalk that once contained a diversity of human and animal remains.

The first structure on the site of Stonehenge was a circular ditch roughly 360 feet in diameter with an irregular, segmented internal bank, a causewayed entrance to the south and a causewayed entrance to the northeast; then 56 holes were dug in a circle inside, hugging the confines of the bank. As the centuries passed, the earthworks became more sophisticated and timber structures were added, most notably a dense, irregular arrangement in the centre with arrays of posts marking out passageways to the south and northeast.

It's interesting to see what some senior archaeologists made of this early design:

> The site has not been completely excavated, so there may well be other postholes in the north and south western quadrants, but the superimposition of possible circles on the post holes within the enclosure do not produce any completely convincing circular structures. At the north-eastern entrance and at the southern entrance, however, it is likely that there were wooden corridors in place, possibly with roofs. These corridors may have served to channel people into the

ceremonial circle, while if they were roofed and screened to either side, they would have effectively created a sense of mystery and anticipation for whatever lay ahead in the enclosure.[2]

Already, an official archaeological report has virtually spelled out one of the main reasons why the timber phase and the later stone phase of Stonehenge were built and what precise use they were put to, with the observation that the roofs, channels and screens 'would have effectively created a sense of mystery and anticipation for whatever lay ahead in the enclosure'.

Even today, for those of us fortunate enough to have been allowed into this inner sanctum on private visits, this sense of uneasy expectancy remains, not least because the narrow gaps between the outer stones, the shadows and the crowd of man-sized bluestone pillars inside constantly obscure our lines of sight, only allowing us a restricted field of vision at any one time. We can be sure that this feeling would have been tinged with awe, fear and quite possibly dread for our ancestors when they approached such a forbidding and complex structure.

CULT OF THE OX

One of the many extraordinary aspects of Stonehenge and the burial mounds in the surrounding area is the sheer quantity of ox or cattle bones that have been discovered there over the centuries. There are few long barrows in which the remains of these creatures haven't been discovered and there's good reason to believe that these bones were treated just as reverentially as the human skeletons. The cattle bones most commonly found in the long barrows were skulls that had been ceremonially placed in these ancient tombs long after the creatures had died or been killed, which suggests that they were revered in some way.

At least one ox skull and two ox jaws were carefully put in place at the bottom of the first circular ditch that was dug around Stonehenge

(© Juris Ozols)

in 3200 BC, while we know from radiocarbon dates that these bones had been kept above ground for centuries before they were laid either side of the southern entrance to Stonehenge.

Cattle skulls were also placed alongside human skeletons in the prehistoric tombs. This suggests a close link between cattle and human death in the minds of the people who went on to build the first earthen phase of Stonehenge, but human and cattle bones have also been discovered nearby in barrows of the later Bronze Age, a period that coincided with the mighty stones being put in place; in the words of Professor John North, 'It leaves little doubt as to the existence of a cattle cult of extraordinary tenacity.'[3]

HUMAN DEATH

We know from the results of archaeological excavations in the early years of the twentieth century that the cremated remains of as many as 240 individual people were buried at Stonehenge during the first 1,000 years or so of its existence, when it was an intricate set of earthworks and timber structures, although there may have been many more whose bodies weren't burnt, but disposed of in another way. Due to the abysmal records kept by the early archaeological investigations in the twentieth century, it's unlikely we'll ever know the true figure, but as Mike Pitts observed, 'We're talking big place, big events.'[4]

As far as Stonehenge and dead human beings are concerned, the figures are overwhelming and slightly disconcerting. The 15 long barrows that were carefully arranged in the immediate area around the eventual site of Stonehenge were repositories for substantial numbers of human dead, to which we can add at least 240 individuals from the early years of Stonehenge and possibly many more. In addition to this, we know that a mortuary enclosure once stood just south of Stonehenge at Normanton Down, where dead bodies were exposed to the elements, birds and wild animals until the flesh had been stripped from the bones, which were then used and moved around for a variety of unknown purposes.

The monument's intimate connection with human death is inescapable. Several human skeletons dating from prehistoric times were discovered during early twentieth-century excavations, while still more were dug up and discarded many centuries before by treasure hunters. One was discovered as recently as 1978, buried in the ditch close to the Heel Stone, prompting the authors of *Stonehenge in its Landscape* to observe that these remains 'hint at an otherwise unattested use of the monument'.[5] What could this mysterious use possibly be?

The man discovered in the ditch in 1978 died sometime around 2300 BC in a hail of arrows, but it's highly unlikely that he was the only person to meet a violent end at Stonehenge in prehistoric times. It's not currently fashionable to consider the lurid spectacle of human sacrifice at the ancient site, but everything suggests that it took place on a regular basis, and the renowned prehistorian Dr Aubrey Burl presents a great deal of evidence to this effect in his book *The Stonehenge People*.[6]

AN ARCHITECT OF GENIUS

So far, we've identified three indisputable components of Stonehenge: it was built and used by people who worshipped cattle in some way; it was a place of mystery, anticipation and concealment; and it was also intimately connected with human death. To this we can add that by *any* definition, the person responsible for building it was a genius.

To begin with, we could reasonably say that a stone structure that has survived for almost 4,500 years *has* to qualify as a wonder of the ancient world. Few would dispute this; there's nothing else like Stonehenge on Earth and its unique appearance makes it instantly recognizable, because the design of the circle of uprights surmounted by lintels is one that, once seen, is never forgotten.

These massive lintels are curved, they interlock in a ring using tongue-and-groove joints, and they're further fixed in place on top of the sarsen uprights by mortice and tenon joints. As if that weren't impressive enough, the Neolithic engineers also managed to make the whole upper surface of the lintel circle completely level despite the fact that the monument stood on a sloping hillside, and the axis of a circle of almost 2,000 tons of meticulously dressed stone is carefully aligned on the midsummer sunrise and the midwinter sunset. There are many other striking features to Stonehenge, but these alone make it a structure like no other.

The inner arrangement of massive trilithons may once have stood alone for a while as a separate monument, as logic suggests that they had to be put in place before the outer circle was completed, but everything points towards the whole arrangement as having been the product of a single creative genius. It's the only stone circle in Britain composed of carved and interlinked stones and its whole appearance strongly implies the Lovecraftian vision of a single person, rather than something that was gradually put together over the centuries as different ideas occurred to different builders.

The method of construction and the way that the monument is laid out with regard to the summer and winter solstices is undeniably a work of brilliance and outstanding ability. However, it's one thing for a lone architect to mentally picture such a finished work, but quite another for them to endow this towering vision with a physical reality, and this brings us to the final basic component of Stonehenge.

THE KINGS OF STONEHENGE

We've already seen how the ancient Greek mariner Pytheas of Massilia described Stonehenge in 350 BC, saying that there was a city nearby ruled by kings called the Boreades, or 'Sons of the North Wind'. This arrangement was likely to have existed long before Pytheas visited Britain, because the city of kings he describes, a hill fort known as Vespasian's Camp, was in use as far back as the Bronze Age and we've also found Neolithic pits there, pointing towards the place being in use before the stone phase of Stonehenge was put in place.

On the ridge to the east overlooking Stonehenge are two sets of huge Bronze Age barrows known respectively as the New King Barrows and the Old King Barrows, names that were given in previous centuries by antiquarians who decided that they must have been the graves of kings on account of their sheer size. Further afield, in nearby Boscombe, was the grave of the man archaeologists have called the King of Stonehenge, but he's not the only such person we know of.

In 1808 an antiquarian named William Cunnington dug into Bush Barrow, a large funeral mound less than a quarter of mile southwest of Stonehenge, and found the body of a tall man buried with a fantastic selection of artefacts and weapons, including a limestone mace head, a bronze axe, copper and bronze daggers, an inscribed gold plaque, a gold belt buckle and thousands of tiny gold pins. These and other similar discoveries tell us of 'dynastic tombs, the burial-places of powerful chieftains or princelings in a heroic age where authority was obtained through warfare and manifested through the display of exotic and unique regalia'.[7]

It doesn't matter whether we refer to such people as 'chieftains', 'princelings', 'a ruling élite', 'a dynasty' or 'royalty', because all these terms amount to pretty much the same thing: the presence of kings, one of whom ordered the building of Stonehenge. The most recent carbon dates and analyses of the cremated remains from the earliest phase of Stonehenge have led Professor Mike Parker-Pearson and others to conclude that the site was once some kind of royal burial place, so now we must see if we can make sense of a complex monument that was a place of concealment and anticipation built by a genius on the orders of a king, strongly connected with the worship of an ox or bull and strewn with human bones.

As Lord Byron remarked, 'What the Devil is it?'

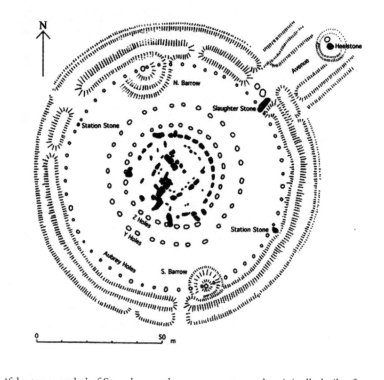

The 'false topography' of Stonehenge: the monument wasn't originally built of stone, nor
was it ever a henge in the sense that these earthworks are classified. It's extremely doubtful
that there was ever a complete circle of stone lintels supported by uprights, while it's a
glaring anachronism to describe the inner arrangements of bluestones and sarsen trilithons
as 'horseshoes'. The repeated description of this astonishing structure as a 'ritual meeting
place' adds nothing to our sum total of knowledge about the ruins, whereas all the evidence
suggests that the intricate architecture of Stonehenge represented a ceremonial dance floor,
or labyrinth. See text for fuller explanation. (Illustration from *Hengeworld* by M.W. Pitts,
published by Century. Reprinted by permission of The Random House Group Ltd.)

CHAPTER EIGHT

The Man, the Monster and the Maze

What immortal hand or eye
Could frame thy fearful symmetry?
William Blake, Tyger Tyger

One cold winter's morning, I stood on the footpath in the field to
the south of Stonehenge, trying to make out the stones through the
freezing mist that shrouded the dreary ruins. The effect was ghostly
and almost taunting, as if some supernatural force were deliberately
cloaking a secret from human eyes. My imagination in check, I asked
myself what were the most fundamental and indisputable aspects of
Stonehenge? What elements were completely beyond question?

Archaeologists, antiquarians and others have unearthed a vast amount
of information about Stonehenge over the centuries, but they've either
disagreed over what conclusions to draw from the evidence available
to them or else they've been at a complete loss as to how to make
sense of it. Stonehenge is certainly a complex and highly sophisticated
monument and could have been simultaneously used for a variety of
functions such as star-gazing and venerating the dead, yet there is more
to it than that.

It had taken many years of staring at Stonehenge before I'd recognized what I'd been looking at, but I'd eventually remembered a chilling

story about a fantastic structure of stone made by a human genius on the orders of a king. This story also told of the deliberate killing of humans, of human flesh removed from human bones, and of a bull, or rather the ghastly *form* of a bull, that was tracked down and slain in its dreadful lair by a hero.

The story has been known to humanity for thousands of years – it's the story of King Minos and the terrible Labyrinth that he ordered to be built beneath his palace in Crete by the brilliant architect Daedalus. It was to house the Minotaur, a monster that was partially a man, partially a bull, that Minos' wife, Pasiphae, had given birth to after unnatural congress with a white bull. Some accounts imply that the Labyrinth was constructed *beneath* the palace of Minos at Knossos.[1] Its winding passages were so confusing that it was supposed to be impossible to escape from it and the hero Theseus only managed to make his way out by using the golden thread supplied to him by Ariadne, daughter of Minos, which he unwound on his way in, then rolled back up on his way out, after he'd slain the Minotaur with a sword.

No one has yet found the remains of a building conforming to our modern notion of the Labyrinth built by Daedalus. However, Sir Arthur Evans, a contemporary of the great Heinrich Schliemann who discovered Troy, excavated the palace complex at Knossos in Crete in the early twentieth century and discovered many intriguing structures and artefacts that throw some light on the legend of the Minotaur. There were many frescoes of bulls and representations of bulls' horns around the palace and one fragment depicted a building with pillars inscribed with axes and decorated with horns. In the palace at Knossos was 'the Room of the Throne' in which a stone throne, believed to date to 2000 BC, backed onto a frescoed wall and overlooked one of many strange rectangular pits which Evans described as 'lustral pits', all of which were elaborately built and approached by pillared staircases. After studying the seismic activity or earthquakes in Crete, Evans concluded that these pits were constructed to provide an entrance to the underworld, and ceremonies to appease some powerful deity might have been conducted there.

Evans also discovered what he termed 'pillar crypts', which were dark subterranean chambers that sometimes lay beneath other rooms but at other times had no building above them. Nonetheless, the central feature of each crypt was always a massive stone pillar, so it was clear that these huge stone columns hadn't been put in place to support a heavy roof. Most pillars were inscribed with the sign of a double axe, the Minoan sign denoting royalty, while in some cases there were drains or vats nearby to receive the blood of sacrifices in these sinister windowless rooms.

Aside from the archaeological evidence, there are further clues in the writings of ancient authors. In a fragment of Sophocles, the Labyrinth is described as 'αχανης – *achanes*, or 'roofless'.[2] The earliest reference to Daedalus and Ariadne comes in Homer's *Iliad*, where we read, 'Next the god depicted a dancing-floor like the one that Daedalus designed in the spacious town of Cnossos for Ariadne of the lovely locks.'[3] The god in question is Vulcan, or as the Greeks knew him, Hephaestus, the metalworker or blacksmith of the gods, and in the passage quoted above he's making new armour for Achilles during the siege of Troy at the request of Achilles's mother, Thetis.

The word that Homer uses for dancing-floor is *choros*, otherwise known to us as the chorus, which was originally the band of singers, dancers, musicians and performers at the Dionysiac festivals in Athens. The term is still familiar to us in terms of musical theatre, where members of the chorus support the principal performers. However, to the ancient Greeks, the chorus was the activity, the performers and the place as well. We learn this once more from Homer, when King Alcinous orders a feast to celebrate the visit by Odysseus to his enchanted island, then commands the young men to mark out a chorus so that they may dance upon it.[4] Plutarch also tells us that a complicated dance to celebrate the death of the Minotaur and the safe return of the Athenian hostages was performed at Delos in imitation of the Labyrinth.[5]

With its winding passageways, pillars, pits, columns, windowless crypts, staircases and varied levels, the entire palace complex at Knossos is often reasonably described as labyrinthine in itself, without having to pinpoint a single separate structure that could have been the Labyrinth of Daedalus. The dominant motifs throughout the royal palace are bulls' horns and the royal double axe, so for our purposes it only remains to add three further details.

First, King Minos was said to have imprisoned Daedalus in the Labyrinth with his son, Icarus, because Daedalus had supplied Ariadne with the reel of golden thread that enabled Theseus to escape after slaying the Minotaur. Most people are familiar with the story of how Daedalus built two pairs of wings, one for himself and one for his son, in order to escape, which would seem to be further confirmation that the Cretan labyrinth was indeed *achanes*, or roofless, as Sophocles described it.

Secondly, at the palace of Knossos, Evans discovered that the royal apartments had been dug out of the eastern part of the hillside on which the complex was situated. This appears to have been done so that the royal rooms would stand on a platform and thus catch the rays of the sun at specific times. What Evans termed 'the Grand Staircase', an impressive five-flight construction of stairs and pillars, led to these royal apartments.

Finally, it remains to explain the precise meaning and origin of the word 'labyrinth', which derives from a pre-Greek word λαβρυς, or *labrus*, meaning 'a double axe'. The double axe long ago became the defining symbol for Minoan or Cretan royalty, so the name 'Labyrinth' in and of itself does not mean a maze, or anything like. It simply means 'royal place', 'king's place' or 'the royal building', and this is precisely what Daedalus constructed on the orders of King Minos to imprison the Minotaur or the Bull of Minos.

STONEHENGE V THE LABYRINTH

Now that we've assembled virtually everything that's known about the Labyrinth, let's compare it with what we know of Stonehenge:

• Surviving fragments of frescoes from Knossos depict a structure of pillars. Stonehenge was built in the same way.

- The Labyrinth was described as roofless. There's no evidence that Stonehenge ever possessed a roof.
- Knossos, home of the Labyrinth, was conspicuously adorned with axes. Notable engravings of axes at Stonehenge were discovered in the 1950s and still more were uncovered in 2002 when one of the stones was scanned using lasers.
- Knossos was adorned with horns. Ox skulls and horns were buried around Stonehenge and others may have been attached to the stones or fixed atop poles.
- The Labyrinth may well have been a dance floor or *chorus*. Stonehenge was described by Geoffrey of Monmouth in mediaeval times as being the *Chorea Gigantum,* or Giants' Dance.
- Both structures had unique and innovative designs.
- Both structures were located in easily accessible locations amid large populations.
- Both structures had some function that required that they be approached via water: the Avenue to Stonehenge led from the nearby River Avon, while the Athenian youths sent as tribute or victims of the Minotaur arrived at a port and were led to the Labyrinth.
- Both structures had a particular connection with the sky, celestial objects and the sun, Stonehenge on account of its open top and orientation towards the midsummer sunrise and the midwinter sunset, among others; the Labyrinth because its creator Daedalus escaped from the structure with his son, Icarus, who flew too close to the sun and perished.
- The palace of Knossos, home to the Labyrinth, had a carefully engineered eastern section designed to catch the sun's rays in the royal apartments. Stonehenge has a carefully engineered north-eastern section that has a similar emphasis on sunrise in the form of the Avenue and the sun rising over the Heel Stone.
- Both approaches to these royal eastern sections were marked by pillars or columns. At Knossos, the Grand Staircase was lined with pillars and at Stonehenge an eighteenth-century antiquarian named Aubrey claimed to have seen holes for stones marking the

borders of the Avenue.

- Apart from man, the predominant creature at Knossos was the bull. Apart from man, the predominant creatures at Stonehenge were oxen or cattle.
- The inner part of the fearsome Labyrinth was hidden from sight and the high internal bank and timber corridors at Stonehenge, in the words of archaeologists, 'would have effectively created a sense of mystery and anticipation for whatever lay ahead in the enclosure'.

Stonehenge is always described as unique, but it's obvious from even a passing inspection that it shares a great many characteristics with the fabled Labyrinth. Nor is the idea of a labyrinth in the West Country 'in ancient time' purely hypothetical, because what's thought to be a Bronze Age carving of a labyrinth on a rock face at Tintagel, Cornwall, is an officially recognized ancient monument.[6]

Professor Richard Atkinson dug at Stonehenge from 1950 to 1964, recording some of his thoughts in his book *Stonehenge*.[7] Towards the end, he remarked on the axe carvings that had been discovered there and even went so far as to mention the Labyrinth, although he didn't pursue the matter further. If he had, he might have noticed some other links.

One of the most enigmatic discoveries at Stonehenge is referred to simply as the 'Stonehenge ceramic object' and is thought by some archaeologists to have been used as a small suspended lamp. It's a couple of inches across, circular and flattened, with three lugs set into the space between the upper and lower surface, but everyone I've shown it to thinks it resembles a reel around which thread was wrapped. Could this be linked to the legend that Theseus was given a sword and a reel of string or a *mitos* by Ariadne, daughter of King Minos?

As for the sword that Ariadne gave Theseus, there is a also a link with Stonehenge in that the most famous engraving there is one that resembles a Mycenaean dagger, carved onto the front of Stone 53 in the middle of the axe engravings.

Of all these similarities, perhaps the most astonishing of all concerns the axes and the pillars. As we've seen, the name 'Labyrinth' derives directly from the ancient pre-Greek word λαβρυς, or *labrus*, meaning a particular kind of axe denoting royalty. As such, the word 'labyrinth' meant 'royal', or 'royal place' and the huge pillars and columns engraved with axes at the labyrinthine palace physically embodied this notion. As we've seen, Stonehenge was unquestionably connected with kings and royalty throughout its history, so it follows that any prehistoric visitors to Britain from the Mediterranean region who saw (or perhaps even *carved*) the axes on the sarsen pillars at Stonehenge would have seen *literally spelled out for them* on the stones: 'This place is the Labyrinth.' This seal of unambiguous identification was discovered as far back as 1953 and remains there still. It's been staring every visitor in the face for millennia.

✦ ✦ ✦

There's also another, almost identical, way of viewing the matter. In a diary entry for 22 July 1654, John Evelyn wrote:

> Now we were arrived at Stone-henge, indeed a stupendous monu-ment, appearing at a distance like a castle... about the same hills are divers mounds raised, conceived to be ancient entrenchments, or places of burial, after bloody fights.[8]

We know from the numerous weapons and wounds found on bodies in the barrows surrounding Stonehenge that these people lived in violent times, but there's a further suggestion of organized violence and ritual-ized killing there.

Without exception, every archaeologist who has written about Stonehenge has observed that the ruins had something to do with what are broadly called 'funerary rituals' and there's a horrendous precedent for such ceremonies transforming into ritualized killing. As far back as the sixth century BC, the Etruscans of central Italy would stage ritual combat between two men at the funerals of prominent individuals. The Etruscans were an advanced and sophisticated people who were ultimately wiped out by their more aggressive southern neighbours, yet the Romans themselves adopted this foreign funerary custom with a vengeance, beginning in 264 BC. Combat between individuals at Roman funeral games became more ferocious and more highly staged, with the result that at their height, 5,000 pairs of gladiators fought on a single day in AD 107 under the emperor Trajan. Over the course of 1,000 years or so, the Etruscan funerary games had evolved into the industrialized savagery that prompted the creation of the Colosseum, a purpose-built circular monument to death that still exists today.

Could something broadly similar have taken place at Stonehenge? The evidence shows that over the course of a comparable period, it had been saturated with the odours, sounds, sights and manifestations of death in many forms, but then it all came to a very abrupt and apparently mysterious end in 1600 BC. If we establish exactly *why* this happened, we'll get a clear and compelling picture of the precise nature of the ruins of Stonehenge as they would have appeared to a visitor from the eastern Mediterranean region in the early years of the first century AD.

CHAPTER NINE

Lord of the High Place

Like one that on a lonesome road
Doth walk in fear and dread,
And having once turned round, walks on
And turns no more his head;
Because he knows a frightful fiend
Doth close behind him tread.
Samuel Taylor Coleridge,
'The Rime of the Ancient Mariner'[1]

The last building work at Stonehenge in prehistoric times that was directly related to the monument was the digging of two circles of pits around the stones in roughly 1600 BC. These pits are known as the Y and Z holes, a lacklustre name that belies their enormous significance, because they're without doubt the most mysterious aspect of an already enigmatic monument. Each circle of pits closely surrounded the stones of Stonehenge and there were 30 pits in each circle, roughly mirroring the 30 sarsen pillars and lintels opposite. The pits were a yard across and a yard deep, although their sides sloped inwards towards the bottom of the hole like a bathtub, exactly like the graves that had been dug beneath the many surrounding round barrows.

When they were excavated in the early twentieth century, the bottoms of the holes in these circles showed no signs of crushed chalk, as would have happened if the holes had once held stones or posts. The sides were similarly undamaged and some of the pits held picks made from stag horns as well as complete sets of antlers, showing that the people who dug them had thrown their tools back into the holes almost as soon as they were finished. Each hole was found to contain a fragment or two of bluestone, suggesting that they'd been deliberately placed there, but the strangest aspect of these pits was that they'd never been used or filled in, because they'd naturally silted up over the course of centuries.

What are we to make of this? The fact that these sinister pits were indistinguishable from nearby graves beneath the round barrows tells us that they hadn't been dug to receive stones or posts, but that some ceremony connected with the dead or with inhabitants of the under-world had been in the thoughts of the people who dug them. It's worth also bearing in mind what we have already learned about the precise way that the huge prehistoric earthen circles were built at Priddy, just 30 miles away, with their internal banks and external ditches like the ones at Stonehenge and ceremonial entrances to the underworld:

> This suggests an extremely strict division between those who could watch the rituals and those who could not. The presence of external ditches at the circles also amplifies this effect, as external ditches are a classic feature at sites designed to keep people out (cf. defensive sites). These features – stone banks, timbers, screens, external ditches – suggest that the Priddy Circles exaggerated and manipulated princi-ples of exclusion and unequal access to ritual knowledge in a manner that as yet has few precedents.[2]

Precious few prehistoric monuments in Britain were built in such an unusual way, so whatever dark ceremony was planned or was taking place when these ominous pits were dug was something of extraordi-nary importance and daring, while the evidence of the silting and the antlers shows that Stonehenge 'fell into disuse', as the archaeologists put it, virtually overnight, although the term 'was abandoned' seems far more appropriate, all things considered.

The aforementioned Professor Atkinson, who dug at Stonehenge from 1950 to 1964, gave a great deal of thought to the Y and Z holes. He wrote about their uniform spacing from numbers 9 around to 23, then described a marked deterioration, as though the builders had lost their sense of purpose and abandoned the work, observing:

> We shall never know what it was that induced the state of apathy, or despair, whether it was some natural calamity, such as the collapse of the stones, the death of a priest, or some portent presaging disaster and the wrath of the gods. But clearly it was something considerable, if it could lead to the abandonment of a plan projected on so large a scale.[3]

Atkinson thought that the bluestone chips had been placed in the pits to 'ward off any evil consequences...'[4] although, as was the case with the Labyrinth, he chose not to pursue the matter further. What possible calamity could have resulted in Stonehenge being abandoned overnight? And how does this give us a clearer picture of the Stonehenge that Jesus and others would have seen around 1,600 years later?

As far as archaeologists are concerned, there's no convincing reason why Stonehenge 'fell into disuse'. The only suggestion is that worship and ceremony at such a huge and already ancient monument somehow became unfashionable, but it would have been an astonishingly rapid fall from grace for it to happen overnight after a major undertaking to dig two carefully laid out circles of deep pits.

Could hordes of murderous invaders have suddenly fallen upon the people who dug the pits, or could they have been overtaken by plague, drought, famine, flood, fire, meteor strike or swarms of wild beasts? Could this be what left Stonehenge adrift and bereft of human company, like a prehistoric *Mary Celeste* on the rolling downs of Salisbury Plain? There's simply no archaeological evidence of any of this. The abandonment of Stonehenge in 1600 BC is one of the great mysteries of the site, but it receives scant mention, precisely because no one can put forward a remotely credible suggestion for why such a bizarre thing took place at all, let alone so quickly.

To my mind, the *only* disaster that could possibly explain the sudden abandonment of the site and the bluestone fragments being left in the pits 'to ward off evil' is that Stonehenge had become haunted, and terrifyingly so at that. Let's consider whether this is likely or not and what relevance it could have had for Jesus many centuries later.

THE RESONANCE OF RITUAL

If there's one solitary thing that archaeologists and other researchers agree upon, it's that Stonehenge was a 'ritual' site, which can mean everything, anything or nothing, because to describe a location as 'a ritual site' simply means that an activity of sorts was repeated on a regular, periodic basis there. As Stonehenge appears to have been in active use in one form or another for something like 2,000 years, or a duration roughly equivalent to the lifetime of the Christian papacy thus far, it's beyond question that it saw a great deal of 'ritual activity', even if comparatively few people ever frequented the site.

We simply have no choice other than to concede that Stonehenge was for many years a place of the dead, a place where religious ceremonies were conducted, a place of violent human death and a monument erected by people whose lives were dominated by their perception of occult forces and supernatural entities all around them. No prehistorian or archaeologist would dispute these points, but no one is prepared to contemplate the undeniable fact that the real or perceived existence of ghosts, demons or other supernatural entities would have had a palpable and lasting influence on the lives of the people who frequented Stonehenge when it was in active use. Pilgrims to St Peter's Square in Rome, for example, don't go there simply because it's a pleasantly decorated enclosed space; they go there because they believe in their hearts that when they receive a blessing from a pontiff, it'll make a real difference to their lives. Muslims don't go to Mecca to walk around the Kaaba for exercise; they do so because they devoutly believe that undertaking such a pilgrimage will have a profound effect upon their lives and upon their souls in the afterlife.

Of all the rituals that we perform, religious rituals seem to make the deepest and most lasting mark not only on the people involved, but also on the places where they are carried out, and this can last for centuries. Far and away the most common ghosts are those of people who had a strong ritualistic element to their lives, which appears to be the explanation behind the innumerable appearances of ghosts of nuns and monks from Land's End to John O'Groats, and the variety of places where the singing of ghostly choirs can be heard.

I've seen and heard many ghosts, but I don't claim to know what a ghost actually *is*. It has to be said that behind most sightings of phantoms, there's an explanation that doesn't involve the supernatural; however, even the most hardened sceptic would be hard pushed to deny that throughout recorded history, there have been recorded sightings of bizarre phenomena in circumstances that make it very easy to understand why witnesses claim to have seen ghosts. Many such sightings are convincing enough in our modern era, but to our prehistoric ancestors they must have been an indisputable part of the fabric of their lives.

Perhaps the matter was best described by the late Robert Graves when he wrote:

The common-sense view is, I think, that one should accept ghosts very much as one accepts fire – a more common but equally mysterious phenomenon. What is fire? It is not really an element, not a principle of motion, not a living creature – not even a disease, though a house can catch fire from its neighbours. It is an event rather than a thing or creature. Ghosts, similarly, seem to be events rather than things or creatures.[5]

If a ghost is an event, then it must have a cause, because there's no event in the known universe that doesn't have a cause behind it. When we examine accounts of hauntings, we find that a variety of reasons are given for the creation of ghosts, and one of these is a tragic or violent death, or an otherwise unjust one. On these occasions, it's not only the ghosts of the victims that seem to wander the Earth; their tormentors are often doomed to do the same thing. Where the dead are deposited also seems to be a factor; there are many cemeteries and graveyards in Britain that possess phantoms of one kind or another. Religious sites are often haunted – there are hundreds of churches, chapels and cathedrals that have well-attested stories of haunting attached to them. Ghosts also feature at many stone circles throughout Britain, as well as at other prehistoric structures such as long barrows. Hill forts such as Cadbury Castle are also reputed to be haunted by humans or by elemental creatures such as fairies, and there's scarcely a royal building in Britain that does *not* possess a ghost.

If we view Stonehenge as a place of at least *one* violent death, as demonstrated by the man killed by arrows in the ditch, then this suggests at least a likelihood of the place being haunted. If we view Stonehenge as a place where humans were buried or otherwise ritually deposited, that would also be the case. If we view Stonehenge as a religious site, it is the same. If we regard it as a royal place, through its connection with the King of Stonehenge and others, then it is hardly likely *not* to be haunted. Even if we regard Stonehenge as an astronomical observatory, there exists a precedent for a haunting at such a place; Herstmonceux Castle in East Sussex was once owned by the Royal Greenwich Observatory and phantoms were spotted near the moat by many observers over the years, while the Tower of London, one of the most haunted locations in Britain, was also once used as an observatory. On every imaginable count, Stonehenge is a place destined to give rise to a haunting; taken altogether, if ever any place in the British Isles was once haunted, it was Stonehenge.

ANCIENT HAUNTINGS

It's all very well for us to view the place in this light, but what did our ancestors think of such matters?

It seems they took them very seriously. In 470 BC the Spartans walled up their treacherous general Pausanias in the temple of Athena Chalchioikos, or Athena of the Bronze House, and Pausanias's own mother laid the first brick in place. When he was on the brink of death from starvation, two guards entered the temple and escorted him outside to unconsecrated ground, whereupon he died immediately, but his ghost appeared soon after and terrified everyone by haunting the doorway to the temple. This infestation was so dreadful that the Spartans were advised by the Delphic Oracle to send for exorcists from Italy, who constructed double bronze effigies of Pausanias and performed other rituals that eventually drew the enraged phantom away from the temple.[6] This account is no traveller's tale, because it concerns a general who was a nephew of Leonidas and a son of King Cleombrotos and who, before his treachery, had been highly regarded in Sparta for routing the invading Persians at the Battle of Plataea in 479 BC. The place of his death was the temple of one of the Spartans' most revered deities and the account has been passed down to us by reputable historians such as Thucydides.

In the first century BC Pliny the Younger wrote a letter to his friend Lucius Sura, describing a terrifying haunting in Athens:

> There was formerly at Athens a large and handsome house which none the less had acquired a reputation of being badly haunted... Some few mocking sceptics who were once bold enough to watch all night in the house had been well-nigh scared from their senses at the sight of the apparition; and what was worse: disease and even death itself proved the fate of those who after dusk had ventured within those accursed walls. The place was shunned... year succeeded year and the house fell almost to ruin and decay...[7]

If a sophisticated group of people such as first-century BC Athenians could speak of a lethal haunting in a mansion in their prosperous city and be so utterly terrified of what lurked inside that they shunned it until it fell into disrepair, what of the eventual fate of Stonehenge? The last sentence of Pliny's letter seems to describe its fate perfectly.

With this in mind, it's interesting to read an account by the Roman writer Lucan, who recorded events in the early first century and who left us with this highly emotive and detailed portrayal of a Druidic ceremony:

The pious worshippers approach not near
But shun their gods and kneel with distant fear:
The priest himself, when or the day or night
Rolling have reached their full meridian height
Refrains the gloomy paths with wary feet
Dreading the demon of the grove to meet:
Who, terrible to sight at that fixed hour
Still treads the round about his dreary bower.[8]

It's interesting that the demon is capable of appearing at noon, rather than being confined to the hours of darkness. Many sightings of ghosts in our modern age have been during the hours of daylight, while noon was traditionally a haunted time in Greece because this was when Pan slept and he'd be angry if he was woken.

The haunting of the temple of Athena by the ghost of Pausanias and the demon in the grove as described by Lucan are not by any means the only examples of supernatural manifestations in antiquity. The Roman historian Tacitus left us with a vivid and detailed account of a fearful series of events that took place at Camulodunum, the Roman capital of Britain at the time of Boudicca's rebellion in AD 60. The following passage describes what occurred in the city when the inhabitants became aware that the barbarians were at the gate:

While the Britons were preparing to throw off the yoke, the statue of victory erected at Camulodunum fell from its base, without any apparent cause, and lay extended on the ground with its face averted, as if the goddess yielded to the enemies of Rome. Women in restless ecstasy rushed among the people, and with frantic screams denounced impending ruin. In the council chamber of the Romans hideous clamours were heard in a foreign accent; savage howlings filled the theatre, and near the mouth of the Thames the image of a colony in ruins was seen in the transparent water; the sea was purpled with blood, and, at the ebb of tide, the figures of human bodies were traced in the sand. By these appearances the Romans were sunk in despair, while the Britons anticipated a glorious victory.[9]

The context makes clear that the Romans heard disembodied voices clamouring in an unknown or foreign language, an element frequently encountered in cases of demonic possession and poltergeist disturbances. These sounds have also been recorded near certain barrows in the British Isles, especially when those barrows were about to be disturbed by treasure-seekers, as well as in the vicinity of a notoriously haunted mountain in Scotland, Ben Mac Dhui.

As for apparitions, the horrified Romans saw an entire colony lying in bloody ruins beneath the waters of the Thames. If such a series of events could be recorded by a renowned historian as taking place in daylight in the prosperous and populous capital city of a new Roman province in AD 60, a city moreover largely inhabited by tough retired veterans and presumably unimaginative tax collectors, then it's not difficult to picture similar or worse events taking place at an arcane heathen temple dedicated to the dead, awash with piercing screams and spouting blood beneath the cold, unblinking stars in faraway prehistory.

Our own holy places aren't immune from such infestations. As recently as 1995, a *Sunday Times* article reported the tribulations of the Dean of Lincoln, Dr Brandon Jackson, who had found himself at the centre of a highly publicized consistory court trial before being cleared of the charges brought against him. A monk who worked at the cathedral told him:

'There are currents of conflict, hate and evil that have been swirling around your cathedral for centuries. You have disturbed them. That's why things like this court case have been flung at you. You won't change it, but God is with you.'[10]

Dr Jackson had heard the 'swirling evil' theory repeated by deans and provost at their annual conference in April. The dean of another cathedral told him that Lincoln Cathedral was one of the most evil places he'd ever been in, while yet *another* dean expressed his belief that the building had been constructed on a junction of ley lines and that this could be the cause of the evil atmosphere and disturbances. Furthermore, Dr Jackson claimed that he'd been asked by monks and nuns to close the cathedral for *six months* so that it could be exorcised with prayer.

In addition to this, many worshippers at the cathedral would like to tear down a gargoyle in the cathedral known as the Lincoln Imp. This imp is a creature that is said to have been turned to stone by angels on account of its meddlesome and frightening habits, including tripping up the lord bishop of the time, knocking down the dean and causing consternation among the worshippers and other clergy.

If such a thing can occur in one of our stone places of worship in the twentieth century, a hallowed place dedicated to prayer, peace, love and the Light of the World, then it takes little imagination to accept that something far more menacing could manifest itself in an ancient temple which was dedicated to the dead, a place which saw violent human death on a regular basis and which was strewn with iconic, fearful symbols such as ox skulls.

SURVIVAL

It's one thing to accept that Stonehenge became ferociously haunted some 1,600 years before Jesus is said to have visited the region, but is there anything to suggest that this haunting could have persisted for nearly two millennia and still been active at the time of Christ?

Close to the village of Hangley Cleave in Devon is a group of round barrows dating from the Bronze Age. In 1908, they were visited by Eric Dauncey Tongue, who went on to become a big-game hunter and a district commissioner in east Africa, and he glimpsed something near them that he described as the most terrifying sight he'd ever seen. He believed he'd encountered a 'Barrow Guardian', which he described as 'a crouching form like a rock with hair all over it, and pale, flat eyes'.[11]

There are many other examples of deeply unpleasant hauntings persisting from prehistoric times to our modern era, such as the one linked to the Bettiscombe skull that originated from a Bronze Age barrow[12] or the fatalities associated with the plundering of Castle

Neroche in Somerset in 1754,[13] so there's no good reason for thinking that a haunting at Stonehenge dating from an earlier period would have vanished by the early years of the first century AD. In addition, there's archaeological evidence that the site, while apparently little frequented, was still of immense importance after being abandoned, because radio-carbon dates show that the Avenue leading to it was extended as late as 1000 BC, six centuries afterwards. Why go to such huge efforts to construct a walkway with banks and ditches towards a set of ruins that no one seems to have been using? The only reasonable explanation seems to be that the people of the time believed that a supernatural being dwelt among the stones, so they extended the already huge cere-monial approach to the stone circle out of reverence for its demonic inhabitant and for the use of those few brave souls prepared to try to commune with the monster within.

This is all very well, but is there any evidence that anyone *could* ever confront and interact with such a malevolent entity? We can look to this account given by Dr R. C. C. Clay to L. V. Grinsell concerning a phantom he'd encountered at Bottlebush Down:

> During the winter of 1927/8 when Dr R. C. C. Clay was excavating the Pokesdown urnfield, he met with the following experience. One night he was returning from Pokesdown to his home at Fovant and proceeding in his car along the road from Cranborne to Handley, when about 150 yards past Squirrel's Corner he saw a horseman on the downs to the north-east, travelling in the same direction as himself.

> 'Thinking he was from the training stables at Nine Yews, I took very little notice of him at first. Suddenly he turned his horse's head and galloped as if to reach the road ahead, before my car arrived there. I was so interested that I changed gear to slow my car's speed in order that we should meet, and I should be able to find out why he had taken this sudden action. Before I had drawn level with him, he turned his horse's head again to the north, and galloped along parallel to me about 50 yards from the road.

I could see now that he was no ordinary horseman, for he had bare legs and wore a long, loose coat. The horse had a long mane and tail, but I could see no bridle or stirrups. The rider's face was turned towards me, but I could not see his features. He seemed to be threatening me with some implement which he waved in his right hand above his head. I tried hard to identify the weapon, for I suddenly realised that he was a prehistoric man; but I failed. It seemed to be a two-foot shaft. After travelling parallel to my car for about 100 yards, the rider and horse suddenly vanished. I noted the spot, and the next day found at the spot a low round barrow.'

A few years later, the late Alexander Keiller reported to Dr Clay that two girls, returning to Cranborne from a dance, had complained to the policeman at Handley that they had been followed and frightened by a man on horseback. Within the last 30 years [since 1958] there have been other reports, from shepherds and others, of apparitions having been seen in the vicinity of Bottlebush Down.[14]

Dr Clay was a renowned archaeologist who dug at the Stonehenge Avenue in 1927 and, as such, his account of interacting with a phantom from prehistory is bound to carry a great deal of weight, but are there any other suggestions from archaeologists that Stonehenge was once haunted?

Professor Richard Atkinson seemed to think so, because he wrote of the 'numinous principle' that inhabited the inner sanctum of the ruins. More recently, Dr Aubrey Burl wrote of Stonehenge:

The days are finished. The people are gone. Now the ring is like a broken cage around which sightseers wander as in an empty zoo, disappointedly hoping to understand, to see something, sense some presence inside the vacant circle. But there is nothing to be seen. If there were some invisible power it may have escaped between the fallen bars into its own Other-World. Or... quite possibly, it has never wished to leave.[15]

The eerie feeling seems to have persisted down the centuries, because in 1823 Thomas Stokes Salmon wrote a poem about Stonehenge that included the following lines:

> *Here oft, when Evening sheds her twilight ray,*
> *And gilds with fainter beam departing day,*
> *With breathless gaze, and cheek with terror pale,*
> *The lingering shepherd startles at the tale,*
> *How, at midnight, by the moon's chill glance*
> *Unearthly forms prolong the formless dance...*[16]

The mention of dancing at Stonehenge brings to mind the legend of the Labyrinth, which was re-enacted as a dance, and also Geoffrey of Monmouth's description of the place as the *Chorea Gigantum*, or Giants' Dance. There are also mediaeval stories connecting Stonehenge with the Devil, but is there anything sinister about the site *today* that we can point to?

Whatever the cause, whether it be poor driving, bad weather, drivers craning their necks to catch a glimpse of the ruins or sheer bad luck, the fact remains that people are killed within sight of Stonehenge every year, most often on a nearby stretch of the A303 known as 'the Devil's Batch'. I don't know of any other prehistoric structure associated with the Devil where such tragic events occur on a regular basis, and doubtless this is sheer coincidence. However, there are a number of strange phenomena that take place within the circle itself, so we'll briefly look at one of these now and we'll deal with the other in the next chapter.

In March 2007, I went to Stonehenge on a private after-hours visit as part of a group of astronomers aiming to photograph a lunar standstill there and while the others were engaged in their observations, I came across the melancholy sight of a young dead hare lying close to the southern entrance.[17] There was no sign that this creature was injured or diseased and it was just one of many such animals that are regularly and inexplicably found dead inside the ruins, either by the security guards or the English Heritage custodians, as the sun rises. Despite my best efforts, I've not been able to get anyone with the relevant expertise to look into this matter, so it must remain yet another of Stonehenge's dark mysteries for the time being.

BEELZEBUB

When we consider all the evidence, it seems inevitable that Stonehenge was haunted at some point during its grim history. Even if some fearful apparition or spectre wasn't visible or indeed audible in the early years of the first century, we know that the place was little frequented and there's little doubt that it had a baleful aura of ancient gods about it as far as the inhabitants of the time were concerned.

How would this have been described to a visitor from the East? Stonehenge stands just beneath the summit of a sloping hill, commanding a wide view over most of the surrounding countryside, and the ceremonial approach of the Avenue climbs steeply up the side of a valley before it reaches the stone circle. The stones themselves are some of the tallest in Britain, exceeded in height only by the prehistoric 'Devil's Arrows' many miles further to the north, so by *any* standards, Stonehenge would have been described most simply as 'the high place', and any resident supernatural entity would have had a title such as 'the Lord of the High Place', even it were also known by another name.

What has this to do with Jesus? In the New Testament, there's frequent mention of a pagan god or demon known as Beelzebub, a word that originally had Canaanite and Phoenician roots. While this deity is most often known as 'the Lord of the Flies', the name most likely derives from the words *Baal – zebul*, literally 'the Lord of the High Place'. Baalzebub was worshipped in the Philistine city of Ekron, which was also known as Akkaron, a name which in turn would have sounded very similar to the ancient Greek word for 'high', *akron*, as in 'acropolis' or 'acrobat', reinforcing the idea of Baalzebub as a Lord of the High Place. Regardless of which languages were spoken, any visitor from the Middle East would have recognized Stonehenge as a notable high place, so it follows that the resident deity there would have been known by a similar title.

The subject of demons, pagan gods, human sacrifice and ghosts is dark indeed, but there's no future in ignoring it, not least because these matters have a very real bearing on the life of Jesus. He was undeniably the greatest exorcist the world has ever seen, because there are frequent mentions in the gospels of him driving out unclean spirits. However, there's a particular event that may be of even greater interest to us.

Early in Jesus's ministry, just after he'd reappeared from wherever he'd spent his missing years and before he'd even gathered his disciples around him, we learn that unclean spirits immediately recognized him and obeyed him: 'And unclean spirits, when they saw him, fell down before him, and cried, saying, "Thou art the Son of God."'[18]

Now, we might reasonably view such a thing as a stunning achievement for Jesus and that he would be keen to broadcast it, but immediately afterwards, we learn that he commanded these unclean spirits to remain silent about him: 'And he straitly charged them that they should not make him known.'[19]

And immediately after *this*, Jesus headed for one of his 'high places', where he called the disciples to him and gave them power over evil or unclean spirits:

And he goeth up into a mountain, and calleth whom he would: and they came unto him. And he ordained twelve, that they should be with him and that he might send them forth to preach. And to have the power to heal sicknesses, and to cast out Devils.[20]

Shortly after this episode, we learn that Jesus is accused from out of the blue by the Pharisees of being in league with Beelzebub, the Lord of the High Place: 'And the scribes which came down from Jerusalem said, "He hath Beelzebub, and by the prince of the Devils casteth he out Devils."'[21]

What are we to make of this? As a child, Jesus shows no signs whatever of being able to cast out Devils, then he goes missing for 18 years. There's every indication that he travelled to and lived for some years in a region renowned for its high places. Moreover, according to legend, he's specifically located at *two* high places that have a connection with some form of afterlife: Priddy has its prehistoric catacombs, while Glastonbury has long been thought to have been an entrance to the underworld. Furthermore, these two ghost-infested high places are a mere 30 miles away from perhaps the most notable high place of them all and one inextricably linked with spirits and ghosts. In the words of Mike Pitts, professional archaeologist, noted expert on Stonehenge and current editor of *British Archaeology*: 'At this stage in its long history, around 4,900–4,400 years ago, Stonehenge was dedicated to funeral ceremony, the earth replete with the dead, the space above alive with spirits.'[22]

Jesus then reappears in the Holy Land and hardly has his famous ministry begun than unclean spirits are presenting themselves to him and openly acknowledging his mastery over them, but for some reason, he orders them to remain silent. He immediately travels to *another* high place, calls his disciples together and gives them power over evil spirits, and is then accused by the Pharisees of being in league with 'the Lord of the High Place'.

We can readily think of a number of reasons why Jesus didn't want these unclean spirits announcing that he was the Son of God at that point, but what it boils down to is this: he didn't accuse these entities of lying and one of the main themes of the New Testament is that Jesus *was* the Son of God. Whether we believe this or not is neither here nor there; as far as Jesus was concerned, the unclean spirits were telling the truth, but he didn't want this particular truth *known*. It's a state of affairs that has clear echoes of Joseph of Arimathea being a disciple who either *chose* to keep silent or was concealed or kept silent by others. In almost all other matters, the gospels place a high value on telling the truth, so we have to ask if these two blatant instances of deliberately *concealing* the truth were linked in any way.

The unparalleled gift that Jesus possessed for driving out demons may have manifested itself from out of the blue at the start of his ministry, but if we accept this explanation, we're restricting ourselves to viewing him as a purely divine figure who had little in common with the rest of mankind. However, if we accept the message that's repeated throughout the New Testament, that Jesus came to Earth to learn what it was like to be human, then it follows that somewhere along the line, during those years about which the Bible is mysteriously silent, he acquired his various skills and abilities as a result of trial, practice and observation.

If there was one region where Jesus could have become a supreme master at casting out unclean evil spirits, then it was in the spectre-infested landscape of the west of England during the early years of the first century AD. And if there was one specific location where he'd have been likely to have faced a formidable malevolent entity known as the Lord of the High Place, then it was at Stonehenge, a place where centuries earlier the people had been so terrified by the monstrosity they'd summoned down from the brooding constellations that they'd abandoned their ancient temple overnight.

Archaeologists and prehistorians are inordinately fond of talking about ritual monuments, ritual walkways, ritual objects and ritual land-scapes, but they lapse into sullen and uncharacteristic silence when it comes to facing up to the logical result of religious rituals such as prayer, sacrifice or summoning demons, because it stands to reason that such rituals and ceremonies often *worked*. If we're to believe the Biblical accounts of unclean spirits and other supernatural manifestations such as the raising of the ghost of the prophet Samuel by the Witch of Endor,[23] then there's no reason to doubt that such things were once a bleak reality in the gloomy precincts of Priddy and Stonehenge. If Jesus did once walk there, it's fascinating to think what he may have encountered and what that may have taught him.

CHAPTER TEN

The Doors of Perception

Star of wonder, star of night,
Star with royal beauty bright,
Westward leading, still proceeding,
Guide us to thy Perfect Light.
Reverend John Henry Hopkins,
The Quest of the Magi

We've seen how Stonehenge could have been perceived by Joseph of
Arimathea and Jesus; as the only known place of dressed and interlinking stones in Britain at that time, it would have been of far more
than passing interest to two men working in rock and stone. Had
they heard it described as a symbol of national resistance against the
Romans, this would have intrigued them as well. The same applies if it
had been described to them as a meeting place of the Druids, a Hall of
Hewn Stones or simply as the lair of the Lord of the High Place.

It doesn't matter if some of these interpretations are contradictory
as far as we're concerned; we're simply trying to see if the place would
have exercised a fascination for Jesus in one or more ways and it's abundantly clear that it would have done so. Were there any other aspects
of Stonehenge around the time that Jesus is said to have visited Britain
that would have caught his attention and drawn him there?

❖ ❖ ❖

Some years ago, when I was talking to someone who'd worked for many years as a night security guard at Stonehenge, I learned of another remarkable property the place possessed. This was confirmed by speaking to the English Heritage custodians and other security staff who regularly worked at the site, and I later went on to witness it for myself.

I was told that on certain nights, Stonehenge seemingly possessed the ability to 'draw down starlight'. Everyone I spoke to on the subject said that when they were standing inside the ruins gazing outwards into the night, they were able to see someone approaching the stones long before the person doing the approaching was able to see either the observer or the stones themselves. It was as if the person making their way towards the stone circle were somehow illuminated by starlight; this was something I was able to observe for myself on the night that I discovered the young dead hare by one of the outer stones, and the effect was startling.

I've since looked into this phenomenon by consulting experts in relevant fields such as photography and it appears that there's a straight-forward explanation, although it's not yet been conclusively proved that it is the explanation for what takes place at Stonehenge, as no one has conducted any experiments there. We know that even in very dim lighting conditions such as starlight, the human eye is able to discern shapes, but it's a great deal easier to make out the forms of people or animals moving in the open at night than it is to recognize static objects or creatures in darkness. This phenomenon is simply related to the human eye's ability to collect light and the brain's ability to make sense of the images that are illuminated, so we can be sure that our ancestors would have recognized that it was easier to see a moving form than a static one by night a very long time ago. However, Stonehenge is a unique, atmospheric and imposing monument set in the middle of a lonely plain, so it wouldn't be remotely surprising if in addition to its many other fearsome attributes, it acquired a reputation as a place that somehow 'drew down starlight', whether such a thing were scientifically true or not; after all, this is precisely what's happened in the twenty-first century. But what does all this have to do with any impression that Jesus may have formed of Stonehenge?

In the Gospel of Matthew, we're told that Magi, or wise men, came from the East to Jerusalem because they'd seen a star that they believed foretold the birth of the King of the Jews. When King Herod heard about this, he summoned the wise men to him because he was worried by this prediction, but he told them that he wanted to worship this king and asked them to find the place where he had been born. 'When [the Magi] had heard the king, they departed; and, lo, the star, which they saw in the east, went before them, till it came and stood over where the young child was.'[1]

It follows that Jesus would have been told of this astonishing story surrounding his birth, not least because his parents were forced to flee into Egypt shortly afterwards to escape Herod. If this was the case, then the young man who had been identified as the King of the Jews could hardly fail to have been fascinated by a unique structure associated with kings that was *also* said to 'draw down starlight' in some way.

I've often been asked why so many meteors, shooting stars and comets appear over Stonehenge, but the truth is that such celestial objects don't appear in the night skies above the ruins any more frequently than they do over other places in Britain. However, Stonehenge stands near the brow of a hill, so our gaze is naturally directed upwards, and all the more so because of the otherworldly silhouette that appears there. As a result, we're liable to notice shooting stars and other celestial phenomena far more often when we're in the vicinity of Stonehenge than we would elsewhere, so it's hardly surprising that we make a connection between the two things. And if *we* do so today, then we can be sure that our ancestors would have done so too. Certainly we know that there was one group of people with an obsessive interest in such things in ancient Britain, and that was the Druids.

It's one thing for Stonehenge to be closely linked with the stars because of an optical illusion and because of where it stands, but there's a more sinister possibility that might have a bearing on how Jesus may have perceived the place. The legends of Theseus and the Minotaur date back to the seventh century BC, long after Stonehenge had been built and abandoned, so as far as dates are concerned, it's possible for the story of the murderous ox-cult at Stonehenge to have become entwined with the ancient Greek legend of the Minotaur and the Labyrinth. Early historians such as Diodorus Siculus tell us that there'd been a warm relationship between the inhabitants of Greece and Hyperborea, or Britain, since 'the earliest times' and there's the engraving of what appears to be a Mycenaean dagger, as well as the numerous royal axes, in the centre of Stonehenge to reinforce this link with ancient Greece.

Be all that as it may, the most interesting thing is that some versions of the Minotaur legend actually supply the bull-headed monster with a name, 'Αστεριων, or 'Asterion', which means 'Ruler of the Stars' or something similar. We also know from the way that they sited their monuments that the builders of the long barrows that preceded Stonehenge were fascinated by the stars to the extent that they may have regarded them as their ancestors[2] and there's little doubt that 'star-gazing' in the form of astronomy or astrology took place at Stonehenge throughout its early history. So, it's a possibility that in addition to being known as 'the Lord of the High Place', whatever monstrosity lurked inside the stone circle may have been known by the evocative title of 'Star King' or something similar.

All these things are merely possibilities and some are more likely than others, but if we fail to look into even the smallest matter, it stands to reason that we're ultimately limiting our ability to make an informed judgement about what Jesus may have done in his 'missing years'. Or, as the famous Roman emperor Marcus Aurelius once observed, 'Nothing has such power to broaden the mind as the ability to investigate system-atically and truly all that comes under thy observation in life.'[3]

STAIRWAY TO HEAVEN

We've done our best to try to see the world of the early first century AD as it would have appeared to Jesus as a young man, but we have to ask if there's anything else that could assist us in this, in addition to considering factors such as his youth, his country being under Roman occupation and so forth. One obvious and highly relevant subject we've not yet looked into is the matter of his father, Joseph.

It's commonly supposed that Joseph was a carpenter, an idea that's based on the use of the Greek word τέκτων, or *tekton*, which is how Joseph is twice described in the gospels.[4] If we wish to continue believing that, 'like father, like son', Jesus also worked as a carpenter, then it'll do no harm, nor will it make any appreciable difference to our thoughts on where he spent his lost years. However, if we're to acquire as full and as detailed a picture as possible, there's certainly much of interest from even a brief look into the meaning of the word *tekton*.

In English, we recognize it as the basis of the word 'tectonic', as in 'tectonic plates', but it also forms part of the word 'architect'. It *can* mean 'carpenter', certainly, but it was also used to describe a variety of skilled craftsmen, and a great deal of study has been done on this. Several notable scholars believe that the word is best translated as 'builder' or even 'master of the craft', while another school of thought maintains that its true meaning is 'scholar'.

Does this help us better visualize Jesus as a human being? If we think of him as the son of a scholar, then it makes more sense of Luke's description of him in the temple, where 'all who heard him were amazed at his understanding and his answers'.[5] Otherwise, if we think of him as a builder, this immediately brings to mind the story that he once constructed a church at Glastonbury and dedicated it to his mother Mary. A carpenter would have been able to supply the worked timber for such an undertaking, but realistically it would have required the skills of a builder to put the whole thing together. Furthermore, we're told that it was sufficiently solid to have remained in place for some centuries, so once again, an open, enquiring mind and a minute attention to detail and to what's actually written in the gospels have provided us with further food for thought and perhaps insight, if not definitive answers.

At this stage, it's difficult to gauge whether Jesus would have been hostile, curious or well-disposed towards Stonehenge. In the Book of Judges, we read of Samson being captured by the Philistines, blinded in Gaza, then taken to the temple of their god Dagon, where the assembled crowds mocked him before he strained on the twin pillars supporting the temple and brought it crashing to the ground.[6] As a scriptural prodigy and possibly the son of a noted scholar, Jesus would certainly have been aware of the story of Samson, so he may have regarded a notable pagan temple with suspicion or dislike, but it's certain that he wouldn't have been indifferent towards it.

'A DREADFUL PLACE'

In an attempt to ascertain precisely how Jesus would have viewed Stonehenge, we'll be looking into many other aspects of his life, but for now it would be extremely helpful to possess an account of Stonehenge written from the perspective of someone who was both a Christian *and* a Druid. Amazingly enough, just such an account exists and while it doesn't date from the early first century AD, it's better than nothing and it's undoubtedly intriguing.

William Stukeley (1687–1765) was an English antiquarian who was one of the first people to take anything resembling a modern archaeological interest in Stonehenge. He immersed himself in the ruins and the surrounding landscape, and we're fortunate that he recorded a great many of his thoughts and findings in print. Stukeley became so convinced that the British Druids had built Stonehenge and so enamoured with the cult that he actually styled himself as one, calling himself Chyndonax, the Arch Druid. However, he took holy orders in 1729 and thereafter became known as the Reverend Stukeley.

Regardless of whether or not he was correct in his views about the Druids, he is unique in that he studied them at length, spent years examining Stonehenge in minute detail and then took holy orders. As such, his perception of the place is invaluable: 'Often when I have been in Stonehenge, I have been rapt up in Jacob's soliloquy, how dreadful is this place, this is none other but the House of God and this is the Gate of Heaven.'[7]

The soliloquy he refers to concerns the famous dream that Jacob had in the Book of Genesis and it's well worth looking at the words in their entirety:

> And Jacob went out from Beersheba, and went toward Haran. And he lighted upon a certain place, and tarried there all night, because the sun was set; and he took of the stones of that place, and put [them down to use as] his pillows, and lay down in that place to sleep.
>
> And he dreamed, and beheld a ladder set up on the earth, and the top of it reached to heaven: and behold, the angels of God ascending and descending on it. And, behold, the LORD stood above it, and said, 'I [am] the LORD God of Abraham thy father, and the God of Isaac: the land whereon thou liest, to thee will I give it, and to thy seed; And thy seed shall be as the dust of the earth, and thou shalt spread abroad to the west, and to the east, and to the north, and to the south: and in thee and in thy seed shall all the families of the earth be blessed.
>
> 'And, behold, I [am] with thee, and will keep thee in all [places] whither thou goest, and will bring thee again into this land; for I will not leave thee, until I have done [that] which I have spoken to thee of.'
>
> And Jacob awaked out of his sleep, and he said, 'Surely the LORD is in this place; and I knew [it] not.' And he was afraid, and said, 'How dreadful [is] this place! This [is] none other but the house of God, and this [is] the gate of heaven.'
>
> And Jacob rose up early in the morning, and took the stone that he had put [as] his pillows, and set it up [as] a pillar, and poured oil upon the top of it. And he called the name of that place Bethel: but the name of that city [was] Luz at the first.[8]

When we bear in mind all these Biblical references to angels, stones, the heavens above, pillars and anointing oil, it's little wonder that Stukeley saw Stonehenge as a dreadful place, the House of God and the Gate of Heaven. As Jesus was steeped in the scriptures, we must ask ourselves if he'd have viewed the ruins in the same way and on balance, it seems extremely likely.

IMAGINE

We'll soon be looking at other factors and influences that may have played a defining part in shaping any view that Jesus may have had of Stonehenge, but before we get to that, let's allow ourselves the luxury of physically placing him there to see if there's anything out of place, ill-fitting or unlikely about this scenario.

For the moment, let's forget that there's any controversy about the idea of Jesus and Joseph of Arimathea spending a number of years in Glastonbury and Priddy. Let's forget any relationship Jesus may have had with the natives of Britain, and let's suppose that he travelled to the imposing ruins of Stonehenge out of simple curiosity. What's the most realistic picture that emerges?

To begin with, it would have been less arduous to travel the 30 miles from Priddy or Glastonbury to Stonehenge during the summer months, and this is also the time when the most famous celestial event occurs at Stonehenge, the rising of the sun over the Heelstone on the morning of Midsummer's Day.

Let's also suppose that Jesus was accompanied by Joseph of Arimathea and possibly some other men, either natives of Britain or friends, relatives or colleagues of Joseph of Arimathea, or both, if only on the grounds that it's highly unlikely that Jesus and Joseph travelled to Britain as the sole crew and passengers of a single boat.

The sun shining down the Avenue or ceremonial approach to Stonehenge on Midsummer's Day would surely have been a notable feature of this strange temple, so it's reasonable to assume that the group made their way either on foot or on horseback the day before, camped overnight nearby, possibly at what's now known as Vespasian's Camp, then made their way to the ruins just before dawn.

Would Jesus have felt apprehensive about visiting what the Reverend Stukeley later envisaged as 'a dreadful place'? I very much doubt it, but then again, we're pondering a time before he embarked on his famous ministry. It seems likely, however, that he'd have prayed after rising and before such an undertaking as a matter of habit.

The placid River Avon snakes around the Stonehenge landscape, past the southern end of Vespasian's Camp, and the Avenue once began its course on the river's banks before it curved to the northwest up a gentle incline, then descended into a valley. From there, it made its way up another steep incline, then finally merged with the gloomy portals of what Stukeley described 17 centuries later as the Gate of Heaven. If a young Jesus had had Psalm 23 in his mind at the time, a scripture with which he was certainly familiar, it would coincidentally have matched his every step, from waking on a grassy bank to entering the temple precinct itself:

> *The Lord is my shepherd; I shall not want.*
> *He maketh me to lie down in green pastures; he leadeth me beside the still waters.*
> *He restoreth my soul: he leadeth me in the path of righteousness for his name's sake.*
> *Yea, though I walk through the Valley of the Shadow of Death, I will fear no evil: for thou art with me; thy rod and staff they comfort me.*
> *Thou preparest a table for me in the presence of mine enemies: thou anointest my head with oil; my cup runneth over.*
> *Surely goodness and mercy shall follow me all the days of my life: and I will dwell in the house of the Lord forever.*

When his short journey was completed, just before sunrise, what would the observers present have seen? Stonehenge was a place of the dead and a place of ghosts, and as we've already learned, unclean spirits readily made themselves known to Jesus at the very beginning of his ministry. Whether or not any phantoms appeared, any observers standing behind Jesus as he gazed back along the Avenue would have seen him silhouetted against the brilliance of a rising sun while standing on a high place. If this uncomplicated scenario sounds familiar, it's because it immediately brings to mind the later event when Jesus underwent a remarkable transformation on a mountaintop:

> And after six days Jesus taketh Peter, James and John his brother, and bringeth them up into a high mountain apart, and was transfigured

before them: and his face did shine as the sun, and his raiment was as white as the light. And behold, there appeared unto them Moses and Elias talking with him.[9]

In later life, Jesus famously announced: 'I am the light of the world; he who follows me will not walk in darkness, but will have the light of life.'[10] Of course, this doesn't prove anything about his supposed visit to Stonehenge, but it's another pointed reference to light.

We should perhaps also bear in mind that Gildas had something highly specific to say about Jesus, rays of sun and ancient Britain:

Meanwhile these islands, stiff with cold and frost, and in a distant region of the world, remote from the visible sun, received the beams of light, that is, the holy precepts of Christ, the true sun, showing to the whole world his splendour, not only from the temporal firmament, but from the height of heaven, which surpasses everything temporal, at the latter point, as we know, of the reign of Tiberius Caesar, by whom his religion was propagated without impediment, and death threatened to those who interfered with its professors.[11]

Gildas was speaking of events that he claimed had taken place in AD 38, some years after Jesus was said to have visited Britain, but it's interesting at least to note the specific references to Jesus as the 'true sun'.

As far as a visit to Stonehenge is concerned, it fits perfectly with everything we know of Jesus. He may well have spent the night among the ruins, as Jacob did at the place called Bethel, or the House of the Lord, when he had his famous dream of angels. The next morning, we read that Jacob set up a stone as a pillar and anointed it with oil, presumably to consecrate the place in some way, which brings to mind a famous passage from Exodus where God gives Moses explicit instructions on building an altar: 'And if thou wilt make me an altar of stone, thou shalt not build it of hewn stone: for if thou lift up thy tool upon it, thou hast polluted it.'[12]

Jesus would certainly have been aware of the Book of Exodus and its contents, so he may well have viewed Stonehenge as more pagan or heathen than any other stone circles in Britain, purely because it's the only one made of hewn or dressed stone. Whether he stayed the night there or arrived before dawn, it seems overwhelmingly likely, given what we know of his background, that he'd have consecrated one of the stones as an altar before taking his leave of the place. We might also bear in mind the occasion later in his ministry when he used a metaphor reminiscent of all these strange stones, telling Peter that '…upon this rock I will build my church.'[13]

The idea of Jesus or anyone else approaching Stonehenge as a place of communion with spirits or enlightenment might seem unlikely, but a surprising discovery was made at the Avenue approaching Stonehenge in 2008 by archaeologists working on the Stonehenge Riverside Project. They found that the original builders of the Avenue had incorporated a massive tree as large as 15 feet in circumference into the Avenue by carefully building and curving the chalk bank around the huge trunk. Further excavations might well reveal similar features. It had previously been thought that the immediate Stonehenge landscape was bare of trees when the monument was in use, but now we know that at least one such tree was deliberately incorporated into the ceremonial approach to the ruins.

We also know that the Druids had an enormous reverence for oak trees and it's clear that their forerunners had a very good reason for including either an oak or a yew in the approach to Stonehenge. We don't know precisely why they did so, but we do know that the Buddha famously found enlightenment beneath the branches of a tree, while the Norse god Woden hung himself from a tree for three days for the specific purpose of gaining wisdom. If such a tradition existed when the Avenue was built, then it's possible that something similar still existed in the early first century, not least because we know that the Avenue had been deliberately extended many centuries after Stonehenge had apparently been abandoned. With all this in mind, it's not unthinkable that Stonehenge was still regarded as a place where people sought to commune with supernatural entities or to otherwise seek enlightenment.

Of course, there will be those who react with sheer incredulity to the notion of the most famous human being who has ever lived once visiting the most famous prehistoric monument on Earth, but even a cursory study of the facts transforms this captivating image from an impossibility to pretty much a foregone conclusion. Jesus not only vanishes from the Biblical record but returns as a stranger with certain notable characteristics that we'll examine in more detail toward the end of this book. The only place where he's consistently located during his so-called 'missing years' is the west of England, approximately 30 miles from Stonehenge or whatever name the ruins were known by at that time, and we know that many others before and after his time travelled great distances to visit this place. The most fundamental aspects of Stonehenge are its unique, immense architecture and the undoubted fact that it performed a religious function, as opposed to a purely practical one, so it's no great leap of faith to picture a young man who embodied spirituality and who was involved with carpentry, stone-cutting or building of some description being drawn to the place, most likely as a mystic rather than as a sightseer. The blunt fact is that men of note were drawn to Stonehenge thousands of years before the time of Jesus, and this tradition has continued long after his time, with all manner of eminent people queuing up to gaze in awe and wonder-ment at this gift from our ancestors. To dogmatically maintain that Jesus was the exception to this rule can only be described as a particularly perverse example of Orwell's 'doublethink'.[14]

If the legends of Jesus visiting Britain and staying there for a long period of time are correct, then the idea of him visiting Stonehenge and claiming it for the Lord, so to speak, not only seems entirely predictable but could also throw an astonishing new light on another of our most popular songs, in addition to Blake's 'Jerusalem'. We've already looked in minute detail at the similarities between Stonehenge and the Labyrinth and we've seen the many references to the labyrinth also being a dance floor or a dance, and that the historian Geoffrey of Monmouth described Stonehenge as the *Chorea Gigantum*, or the Giants' Dance. In his highly detailed study entitled *Stonehenge Complete*, Christopher Chippindale expresses a firm opinion on this: "'*Chorea gigantum*", the mediaeval Latin name for Stonehenge, is generally trans-lated as "Giants' Ring" or "Giants' Dance". I prefer "Giants' Round", which expresses both its shape and the idea of dancing.'[15] If Jesus *did* go to Stonehenge and vanquish any resident demon, then consecrate the monument or otherwise claim it for his own, this would reasonably qualify as him 'the Lord of the Dance' by a number of ancient, mediaeval and modern standards.

There's a traditional carol called 'Tomorrow Shall Be My Dancing Day', which incidentally contains a reference to the Devil and stones, and the words to this song are related in the first person by Jesus, but far and away the better-known adaptation of this theme is 'Lord of the Dance', which was written in 1963 by Sydney Carter. He adapted a melody written in 1848 by Elder Joseph Brackett, who was a member of the Shakers, a religious group that acquired their originally mocking name because of their fondness for expressing their Christian beliefs through singing and dancing. The song that Elder Joseph originally wrote was called 'Simple Gifts' and the lyric contained a number of dance instructions; 150 years or so later, both this simple tune and the notion are still going strong, as can be seen from the phenomenal success of Michael Flatley's 'Lord of the Dance' touring production.

What did Sydney Carter have to say about *his* version of the song? He once stated:

> I did not think the churches would like it at all. I thought many people would find it pretty far flown, probably heretical and anyway dubiously Christian. But in fact people did sing it and, unknown to me, it touched a chord... Anyway, it's the sort of Christianity I believe in.[16]

He later explained:

> I see Christ as the incarnation of the piper who is calling us. He dances that shape and pattern which is at the heart of our reality. By Christ I mean not only Jesus; in other times and places, other planets, there may be other Lords of the Dance. But Jesus is the one I know of first and best. I sing of the dancing pattern in the life and words of Jesus.

Whether Jesus ever leaped in Galilee to the rhythm of a pipe or drum, I do not know. We are told that David danced[17] (and as an act of worship, too), so it is not impossible. The fact that many Christians have regarded dancing as a bit ungodly (in a church, at any rate) does not mean that Jesus did. The Shakers didn't...[18]

'Lord of the Dance' is an immensely popular song, despite the fact that some people view it as un-Christian. Blake's 'Jerusalem' is similarly regarded in some quarters, presumably because it contains no direct appeal to God and because if anyone stops to think of the words, they're inclined to think it unlikely that Jesus ever visited England. It would be astonishing beyond description if Carter's song also contained that suggestion; surely it's completely out of the question that Sydney Carter had anything remotely like this in mind when he wrote it?

That said, there are some curious parallels between the life of Carter and Professor Richard Atkinson, who went on to excavate Stonehenge and to compare it to the Labyrinth in the mid part of the last century. Both men were English and they were born within five years of each other. Both studied at Oxford; Carter studied history, while Atkinson went on to become a prehistorian. Both men were Quakers. Both were conscientious objectors during World War II. Both served in the ambulance service, although I don't know if they knew each other. Carter wrote his famous song in 1963, the year that Atkinson was concluding his excavations at Stonehenge. I've not been able to discover if they ever met, but their parallel lives and the fact that each devout man is best remembered for his connection with an unusual 'dance' of one form or another is far from being the last remarkable coincidence we'll encounter.

CHAPTER ELEVEN

The Pillars of Creation

*...out of the abysses between the stars swept chill currents
that made men shiver in dark and lonely places.*
H. P. Lovecraft, *Nyarlathotep*

When archaeologists dig up the remains of some nameless man, woman or child who lived in prehistory, or in an era before written records, they go to extraordinary lengths to reconstruct the life of that person, depending of course on whether or not they think it's ultimately worth the effort involved. They assess the size and condition of skeletons, they analyze tooth enamel and, on those rare occasions when they can, they examine the stomach contents of people who've been preserved in peat bogs or as mummies. When they've collected all the evidence, they try their best to bring the person to life and to endow them with a character, speculating as to what status they may have held when they were alive, where they travelled to, what their profession was and so forth, and they are often working with scant material. On occasion, they may use computer imagery and forensic expertise to try to put a digitalized face of flesh and blood to some of these ancestors, but that's about as far as they get, and the rest is often either informed guesswork or wishful thinking.

By way of complete contrast, we're not dealing with a set of bones, but with the documented history of the life of the most famous human being who has ever lived. In addition, we have at our disposal detailed legends that specify ports, mines and villages in the West Country, and these legends also speak of Jesus interacting with miners and building a church to his mother. We have the word of churchmen in ecclesiastical records, we have physical sites such as Glastonbury, Priddy and Stonehenge that are readily available for inspection and we also have the considered reports of eminent archaeologists. In many respects, we have an embarrassment of riches at our disposal and by using these, we've convincingly placed Jesus in the West Country. Furthermore, we've learned of physical artefacts that were found in tin mines in Cornwall, that a meticulous archaeological excavation could possibly reveal the foundations of the original church that Jesus built at Glastonbury and that an examination of the swallets at Priddy might well reveal surprising results. It has taken no great leap of faith to envisage Jesus at Stonehenge, so now we have to ask whether there is any indication that he really did visit the ruins?

Starting in chronological order, there's a famous letter that was written in 601 by Pope Gregory to Abbot Mellitus. It contained matters of the utmost importance that Pope Gregory wanted passed on to Bishop Augustine, who was already in Britain and who would become the first Archbishop of Canterbury. The Pope wrote:

When (by God's help) you come to our most revered brother, Bishop Augustine, I want you to tell him how earnestly I have been pondering over the affairs of the English: I have come to the conclusion that the temples of the idols in Britain should not *on any account* be destroyed. Augustine must smash the idols, but the temples themselves must be sprinkled with holy water and altars set up in them in which relics are to be enclosed. For we ought to take advantage of well-built temples by purifying them from Devil-worship and dedicating them to the service of the true God. In this way, I hope the people (seeing their temples are not destroyed) will leave their idolatry and yet continue to frequent the places as formerly, so coming to know and to revere the true God [my italics].[1]

There's a great deal of interest to us here, but we must first ask why Pope Gregory spent so much time earnestly pondering over the affairs of the English and why he was so interested in their temples. We know that the British Church had developed along different lines from the Church in Rome as far as traditions and practices were concerned, but Pope Gregory's letter seems far less concerned with ecclesiastical niceties than with what would appear to be the relatively straight-forward matter of converting the horde of pagans on the island to Christianity.

Given that he's 'come to the conclusion that the temples of the idols should not on any account be destroyed', he's clearly given the matter a lot of thought. Why? And what difference is there between smashing the idols and destroying the temples themselves? Why should he specify that 'the temples of the idols should not on any account be destroyed'? Why such a strong prohibition? What harm could possibly come to Christianity if one or two or even more pagan temples in England were to be destroyed? It's hard to imagine that the pagan populace could be provoked to any greater fury than they would be after all their idols had been pounded into gravel, so we have to ask if there was another reason behind this emphatic prohibition.

The most obvious explanation that springs to mind is that Pope Gregory was aware of the stories of Jesus and Joseph of Arimathea having once visited Britain and he may also have heard other rumours or accounts that have since vanished from the record. If this was the case, then he could have been absolutely certain that neither of these two men from the East would have erected idols of any kind, but he would naturally have wondered whether they'd visited any British temples and consecrated them while they were there.

As already noted, the twelfth-century historian William of Malmesbury recorded that when St David came to Glastonbury in 540 to rededicate the new church, Jesus himself appeared to him in a dream, pointing out that rededication was unnecessary, because 'He Himself had long before dedicated the church in honour of His mother and the sacrament ought not to be profaned by human repetition'.[2] Naturally, there's some disagreement as to whether William of Malmesbury invented this story, but if he didn't, and the event in question took place in 540, then it stands to reason that Pope Gregory, with his eagle-eyed interest in the affairs of the English, would certainly have heard it by the time he wrote to Abbot Mellitus in 601. It would go a very long way indeed towards explaining the amount of thought he'd given to British temples, because if Jesus had once stayed there long enough to build and consecrate a church of his own, then there was every chance that he'd have consecrated a few pagan temples on his travels as well. Pope Gregory would not have wanted to be responsible, even indirectly, for destroying a structure directly connected with Jesus.

So, precisely what temples did Pope Gregory have in mind? For him to have written such a considered letter in the first place, reason dictates that he wasn't blindly guessing as to the circumstances in Britain but had at least a fair idea of how things were on the island. The buildings that he was most likely considering were those temples built during Roman times. Even though Christianity had been legalized by Emperor Constantine in 313, there would have been many temples in which pagan gods such as Mithras were worshipped, while the influx of invaders from the continent after the Roman legions left Britain in 410 brought with it the worship of other gods such as Woden.

We've already seen what Professor John North had to say about 'a cattle-cult of extra-ordinary tenacity' and we've also looked closely at the connection between Stonehenge, assorted demons and Beelzebub, or 'the Lord of the High Place'. With this in mind, it's fascinating to read what else Pope Gregory had to say in his famous letter:

And because [the English] are used to slaughter many oxen in sacrifice to Devils, some solemnity must be given them in exchange for this, as that on the day of the dedication, or the nativities of the holy martyrs, whose relics are there deposited, they should build themselves huts of the boughs of trees about those churches which have been turned to that use from being temples, and celebrate the solemnity with religious feasting, and no more offer animals to the Devil...[3]

Does any of this prove that Jesus once visited Stonehenge? No, but Pope Gregory the Great was an intelligent man. He knew that the Romans had come to Britain *after* the time of Jesus and the vast majority of pagan temples would have been Roman ones with no possible connection with Jesus. He'd clearly had reports that the natives were indulging in Devil worship and this was something he wanted to stamp out. If there was a single prehistoric structure in Britain at the time that was in plain view, that utterly dominated the landscape around it and that, by virtue of its unique interlinking crown of lintels, could be described as an obviously pagan temple, then it was Stonehenge, and yet he simply couldn't let *any* of the temples be destroyed. Had he heard of St David's dream of Jesus informing him that he'd once built a church in Britain not far from Stonehenge? We'll have to decide for ourselves, but there's further surprising evidence that something strange was taking place at Stonehenge long after conventional wisdom tells us that it 'fell into disuse'.

It's always seemed blindingly obvious to me that something truly terrible happened there back in 1600 BC to cause it to be abandoned overnight, but it's also seemed equally apparent that as a result the place would have eventually been regarded with even greater awe than before. We have the evidence of the extension made to the Avenue or ceremonial way to Stonehenge many centuries after the Y and Z holes were dug, but a recent investigation there has thrown a startling new light on how the ruins continued to be used. In March 2008, Professors Darvill and Wainwright excavated a small trench within the ruins and when the various results were analyzed, they discovered that 'The later charcoal deposits are not the oak or birch of domestic hearths, but midwinter greenery, like holly, ivy and yew,' which suggested to them 'annual gatherings, perhaps for feasting and ceremony at the winter solstice, continuing as late as the 17th century'.[4]

Of course, it's possible that the locals were celebrating Christmas at Stonehenge in mediaeval times, which is an intriguing thought in itself, but otherwise, the idea of feasting and ceremonies in the midst of moonlit pagan ruins in midwinter brings to mind something altogether more malevolent, which again strongly suggests that Pope Gregory knew of 'diabolic rites' at Stonehenge. In his letter, he specifically suggests that the Devil-worshipping English 'should build themselves huts of the boughs of trees about those churches which have been turned to that use from being temples',[5] and this mention of greenery in conjunction with temples brings to mind the extraordinary charcoal deposits recently found at Stonehenge.

THE MOVING FINGER WRITES AND HAVING WRIT, MOVES ON

As well as being a self-proclaimed Arch Druid and an officially ordained Christian priest, the aforementioned William Stukeley was also a conscientious observer of Stonehenge. He wrote in bitter terms about the wanton destruction and vandalism of it and other ancient monuments that he personally witnessed, but by far the most heartbreaking and tantalizing record he left us was the following:

> Mr Camden says men's bones have been found hereabouts. He means in the barrows adjacent, and I saw such thrown out by rabbits very near the temple. But eternally to be lamented is the loss of that tablet of tin, which was found at this place, in the time of King Henry VIII (the era of restitution of learning and of pure religion) inscrib'd with many letters, but in so strange a character, that neither Sir Thomas Elliot, a learned antiquary, nor Mr Lilly, master of St Paul's school, could make any thing out of it. Mr Sammes may be in the right, who judges it to have been Punic; I imagine if we call it Irish, we shall not err much. No doubt but it was a memorial of the founders, wrote by the Druids: and had it been preserv'd till now, would have been an invaluable curiosity.[6]

What are we to make of this? We don't know how big this tablet was, or how old it was, or in which language the inscription was written, but the idea of having a written record of any kind from Stonehenge would be on a par with finding the Holy Grail – little wonder that in addition to writing 'eternally to be lamented is the loss of that tablet of tin', Stukeley also added a quote from the Book of Job to further illustrate his point: 'Oh that my words were now written! Oh that they were printed in a book! That they were graven with an iron pen and lead in the rock forever!'[7]

Elsewhere in his huge book, Stukeley writes of inscribed tablets being found in nearby barrows, but we only know of the one tablet ever being found at Stonehenge and sadly there's not a great deal to go on in Stukeley's account, because the letters inscribed on the tablet were alien to all the scholars who saw it. Stukeley supposed that it was a memorial of the original builders of Stonehenge written by the Druids, but whatever it was and whatever it contained, it's self-evident that it was thought of as being extremely important by whoever put it there, and when we see a mention of the metal it was made from, we immediately think of Joseph of Arimathea and his connection with the tin trade. Not only that, but Stukeley thought it most likely that the letters were Punic or Phoenician, which reminds us of Joseph of Arimathea living, working and trading on the coast of what was once Phoenicia.

Furthermore, when we bear in mind Stukeley's comparison of Stonehenge with the 'dreadful place' where Jacob dreamed of angels, this mention of mysterious inscribed metal plates reminds us of how the Church of Jesus Christ of Latter-day Saints came into existence. Joseph Smith, the founder of the Mormons or the Community of Christ, claimed that on 22 September 1827 he'd been given some gold plates containing ancient writings by an angel and that these plates, which had been buried at Hill Cumorah in New York, contained the writings of ancient prophets. This account has been regarded with scepticism in some quarters, but it has to be said that in light of Stukeley's recorded vision of Stonehenge as 'the house of God' and 'the Gate of Heaven' with angels ascending and descending a staircase to the skies, and his record of a strangely inscribed metal tablet being discovered there, the claims made by Joseph Smith take on an *entirely* different aspect.

Be that as it may, there are a great many other inscriptions at Stonehenge. In addition to the dagger and axes we've already seen, there are other prehistoric carvings and many more recent ones recording the visits of tourists and travellers. How likely is it that some engraved or written record of a visit by Jesus survives at the site? At first, such a thing seems completely out of the question, because it's widely assumed that every inch of Stonehenge has been scoured for clues, but this is most certainly not the case. Roughly one-third of the site of the monument has never been excavated; this area lies mainly to the north and to the west. All manner of wonders and curiosities have been brought to light from the ruins over the centuries, even though the vast majority of them have been lost, stolen, destroyed or even reburied there, so simple logic dictates that others await discovery.

As for engravings, the famous dagger carving has been in place on Stone 53 for millennia, but it wasn't noticed until 1953, when a close inspection brought many other carvings to light, including some axes. In 2002, Wessex Archaeology and a company called Archaeoptics laser-scanned a small area on some of the surviving stones at Stonehenge and immediately discovered previously unseen engravings of axes. The monument originally contained something close to 2,000 tons of stone in the form of pillars and lintels, so even though roughly half of them are now missing, it'd be extremely rash to say that nothing else awaits discovery there.

And what of the other stones, the ones that were removed from the site over the centuries? Some may have been smashed into fragments, but others will have survived and it's doubtful that they will have been taken far. Stukeley recorded that many were used to make bridges and dams in the local area and some may be buried in the vicinity. They're all out there somewhere, awaiting discovery, and if anyone in the 'ancient times' we're exploring was capable of leaving a record somewhere on these vast pillars and lintels, then it was Joseph of Arimathea, the man who single-handedly cut a sizeable tomb out of solid rock back in his native land.

Bram Stoker, the author of *Dracula*, once said, 'There are mysteries which men can only guess at, which age by age they solve only in part.' Over the ages, artefacts and manuscripts come to light, for example the famous Dead Sea Scrolls, which were unearthed by chance in 1947, and as I write this in early 2008, a manuscript has just been discovered which may prove to contain previously unseen drawings of chess pieces by Leonardo da Vinci. With these precedents in mind, it's not unthinkable that the 'eternally to be lamented' lost inscription that Stukeley described might be found again. Also, we mustn't forget that there are mines in Cornwall that may yet produce physical artefacts linked with Jesus and some of the stones he's said to have erected or stepped on in the West Country may also come to light. The foundations of the church in Glastonbury, the swallets or catacombs in Priddy, the unexcavated section of Stonehenge and the huge area of Vespasian's Camp just over the hill from Stonehenge may all produce something wonderful, not to mention all the missing stones from Stonehenge, as well as the many still standing that will certainly have something to tell us when they're finally subjected to a minute inspection.

In the meantime, there's a truly astonishing episode from nearly 400 years ago that we'd do well to consider when trying to come to an informed conclusion on the matter of Jesus visiting Britain.

SHADOWS ON A PAGAN ALTAR

As we've already seen, Stonehenge has long been a place of kings, from at least the time of the earliest burials there around 5,000 years ago to when the axes were engraved on the uprights, showing us that it was a labyrinth or king's building, and Pytheas of Massillia in 350 BC told us of the Boreades, or kings, who lived in the city nearby. As the 'King of the Jews', Jesus would have continued in this ancient royal tradition by visiting the stone circle, but we have indisputable evidence of a highly significant visit by a notable king far closer to our own time.

King James I of England (1566–1625), visited Wilton House in Wiltshire in 1620 as a guest of the Duke of Buckingham, who had tried to buy Stonehenge from its owner at the time, Robert Newdyk. Despite offering a vast sum of money, Buckingham was unsuccessful in his attempt to purchase the monument, but he nonetheless dug a large pit in the centre of Stonehenge and unearthed all manner of stag horns, bull horns, charcoal, arrowheads, clubs, rusty armour and possibly the bones of men, according to John Aubrey, an early antiquarian who wrote at great length about Stonehenge and Avebury.

Whatever it was that James I saw in that strange pit or discerned in the disturbing contours of the monument itself, he was sufficiently intrigued by Stonehenge to commission the famous architect Inigo Jones to conduct the first scientific study of the ruins. Not only that, but he also had an altar stone 'found in the middle of the area'[8] taken away to St James's Palace in Westminster in London.

Now, why on Earth would a Christian king, born around 4,000 years after this altar stone was first put in place, do such a thing? Why should a Christian king want to transport a pagan altar stone from the middle of a vast plain in Wiltshire to a royal palace in faraway London? Christopher Chippindale suggests that it was 'a royal prize for courtiers to admire',[9] but I suspect that there's a great deal more to the matter than that.

King James was a scholarly monarch who was obsessed with the supernatural and with dark tales of demons to such an extent that he personally interrogated a suspected coven of witches in North Berwick, in Scotland, because they claimed that they'd tried to raise a storm to sink a ship on which he'd been travelling with his new queen. He wrote a book on witchcraft and the occult entitled *Daemonologie*, which was published in 1597, then William Shakespeare wrote his notorious tragedy *Macbeth*, suffused with dark supernatural themes, in honour of the new king when James ascended the English throne in 1603.

We know that a folk tale telling of how the Devil built Stonehenge dates back to this period, while in the 1620s Thomas Rowley wrote a play entitled *The Birth of Merlin*, in which the magician traps the Devil in a huge stone, then says to his mother:

> *And when you die I will erect a monument*
> *Upon the verdant plains of Salisbury.*
> *No king shall have so high a sepulchre*
> *With pendulous stones that I will hang by art,*
> *Where neither lime nor mortar will be used,*
> *A dark enigma to thy memory.*

In 1673, after the fervour surrounding the witch trials had died down, a poem called 'The Description of Stonehenge' appeared in which the author spoke of the ruins as 'the Devil's Court' and included the couplet:

> *You shall have free admission to his shrine*
> *And yet Beel-zebub keeps good discipline.*[10]

These ominous ruins would therefore have inexorably drawn King James to them, but what did he and the other investigators of the time find there? William Stukeley has a number of fascinating things to say about these early excavations, one of which was:

Mr Webb tells us, the Duke of Buckingham dug about Stonehenge: I fear much to the prejudice of the work. He himself did the like, and found what he imagin'd was the cover of a thuribulum. He would have done well to have given us a drawing of it. But whatever it was, vases of incense, oil, slower, salt, wine and holy water, were used by all nations in their religious activities.[11]

A thuribulum is the ecclesiastical term for a censer, a vessel containing burning charcoal on which incense is sprinkled to produce an aromatic smoke. As we've just seen, the Duke of Buckingham dug a pit in the centre of Stonehenge, the area in which the altar stone was found, and among the other things he discovered was charcoal, so if the object that Mr Webb found there was indeed the cover of a censer, there's a chance that the censer and the charcoal were linked in some fashion. We have no way of knowing exactly how old these objects were, but we can make sense of them in a way that suggests there were may have been some very early Christian rituals taking place at Stonehenge.

King James apparently didn't know what Stonehenge was, which is why he commissioned Inigo Jones to study the place. There's always the possibility that he had his suspicions and wanted Jones to give him a second opinion, so to speak, but if there'd been any record during King James's time of Stonehenge being used, its mystery would have lessened and he probably wouldn't have commissioned a scientific examination of the ruins.

Henry of Huntingdon, an archdeacon at Lincoln in the twelfth century, left us what's supposed to be the first commentary on Stonehenge when he wrote:

> Stanenges, where stones of wonderful size have been erected after the manner of doorways, so that doorway appears to have been raised upon doorway; and no one can conceive how such great stones have been so raised aloft, or why they were built there.[12]

As these words were written in or around 1130 and as the passage makes clear that no one knew the reason for Stonehenge's existence at that time, it would suggest that the censer and the charcoal were being used long before Henry penned his description.

We've seen that Pope Gregory complained bitterly of the inhabitants of England being Devil worshippers who sacrificed cattle and we've also learned that the Duke of Buckingham discovered bulls' horns in a pit at Stonehenge close to the altar stone. If these were roughly contemporary with the censer and the charcoal, it points to a Christian ceremony taking place there at around the time that Pope Gregory wrote to Abbot Mellitus in 601. However, as we don't know exactly what the censer cover that Stukeley described *was*, there remains the possibility that it was an artefact connected with oil or holy water from an even earlier period. We don't even know if it was made of metal or of pottery, yet it brings to mind what Jacob did on the morning after his dream at the place he called Bethel or the House of the Lord:

> And Jacob awaked out of his sleep, and he said, 'Surely the LORD is in this place; and I knew [it] not.' And he was afraid, and said, 'How dreadful [is] this place! This [is] none other but the house of God, and this [is] the gate of heaven.'
>
> And Jacob rose up early in the morning, and took the stone that he had put [as] his pillows, and set it up [as] a pillar, and poured oil upon the top of it.[13]

Unfortunately, we don't know what the cover of the censer or thuribulum that Stukeley mentioned looked like, nor do we know if the vessel to which it belonged once contained oil or charcoal. However, the blunt fact remains that the Church historian Gildas specifically wrote of the 'precepts of Christ' reaching Britain as early as AD 38, so we simply can't rule out the possibility that this strange artefact dated back to this early time.

If we consider that it's inevitable that Jesus would have been drawn the 30 miles or so to Stonehenge from Glastonbury or Priddy, then we have to ask if he'd have prepared himself in some way for a visit to these ruins, regardless of whether he saw them as a Hall of Hewn Stones, the lair of Beelzebub, the Lord of the High Place, or as the House of the Lord and the Gate of Heaven[14] that Jacob saw in his dream. Would he have equipped himself beforehand with a container of oil in preparation for consecrating what was a polluted place, if only on account of the altar being made of hewn stone?

'BLESSED IS HE THAT READETH'

Blessed is he that readeth, and they that hear the words of this prophecy, and keep those things which are written herein: for the time is at hand.

Revelation 1, verse 3

When we bear in mind the isolated setting of the ruins, their unique otherworldly architecture and baleful aura, it's not difficult to see why King James became obsessed with the place. When confronted by the tantalizing engraving of an ancient bladed weapon in the inner sanctum of Stonehenge, a shallow impression in the stone that's physically impossible to grasp, he may've recalled those lines from *Macbeth*, the supernatural thriller written and performed for him by William Shakespeare: 'Is this a dagger which I see before me, the handle toward my hand? Come, let me clutch thee; I have thee not, yet I see thee still.'[15]

There can be little doubt that as far as King James was concerned, Stonehenge reeked of ghosts and death, so why should he of *all* people go to such pains to transport what he'd have seen as a altar to the Devil to a palace in London?

We've already seen how a visitor from the East, such as Jesus, would have been able to view Stonehenge in a number of contradictory ways, and it's clear that exactly the same principle would have applied to King James. So, instead of concentrating on the undoubtedly sinister aspects of Stonehenge, let's try and see if the king could have reasonably viewed the place in an entirely different light, as somewhere with a strong and an exceptionally ancient Christian history.

First of all, we must ask if King James was sufficiently familiar with Biblical matters to come to an informed conclusion; the answer must immediately be a resounding 'yes'. He was a noted scholar of his day and was responsible for commissioning what's now known to us as the King James Bible, one of the great works of English literature and one which we've quoted extensively throughout our investigation. If anyone alive in England at the time was familiar with Biblical stories of heathen temples, gates of heaven, pillars being anointed with oil, hewn stones and altars, then it surely would have been King James. I doubt it was lost on him that Jesus was absent from the record for 18 years, while as a churchman, he'd have also been aware of Gildas's story about the precepts of Christ, as well as the earlier Church councils that affirmed that Christianity had been established in Britain before it had taken root anywhere else.

He'd have certainly been aware of Glastonbury and the ancient Church traditions there; even today, a branch of the Glastonbury Thorn is taken to the queen every year. This thorn tree is said to have originated when Joseph of Arimathea returned to Britain after the crucifixion and thrust his staff into the ground, whereupon it miraculously blossomed. The original tree was cut down and burned by Cromwell's troops during the English Civil Wars, but these traditions endure, and in 1965 Queen Elizabeth II placed a wooden cross at Glastonbury with the following words upon it: 'The cross. The symbol of our faith. The gift of Queen Elizabeth II marks a Christian sanctuary so old that only legend can record its origin.'

Could Stonehenge have been the site of similar ancient Christian traditions? Many of the old illustrations and pictures of it show sheep grazing in and around the ruins, often with shepherds in attendance, and these animals can still be seen there today. As we've seen, Jesus was specifically spoken of as the *Agnus Dei* or 'Lamb of God', so this symbolism may have registered on King James at some point, regardless of the fact that these creatures could be seen in thousands of other locations in England.

Our task is to try to view the ruins as King James saw them, so no detail is too small for our consideration, and our task is made a great deal easier by written records of the time. Inigo Jones's thoughts on Stonehenge were eventually published after his death in 1652 as a book entitled *The Most Notable Antiquity of Great Britain, Vulgarly Called Stone-heng, on Salisbury Plain. Restored*. In brief, he concluded that it was a temple built by the Romans to a sky god named Coelus, an almost identical scenario to that of Jacob's dream, where he saw angels climbing and descending a ladder to heaven. If he had ever mentioned as much to King James, then it's very easy to see how this monarch might have viewed the ruins in a Biblical light as the Gate of Heaven where Jacob anointed a pillar with oil.

Furthermore, Inigo Jones recorded what he described as an altar stone in the centre of Stonehenge and it was this stone that King James took to London. There's another stone called 'the altar stone' at Stonehenge today and it's been there ever since the monument was built, but Inigo Jones described a different stone back in 1620 and this is the one that is missing.

Do we have any record of what King James thought of this stone? Stukeley certainly had something to say about what the Duke of Buckingham and King James got up to, but if anything, it makes matters even more mysterious:

...whether it was the effect of some wretched curiosity or covetousness in searching behind the Altar perhaps for hid treasure, or was it not *a blind act of Christian zeal* to deface this stately monument of antientest [most ancient] superstition? [my italics][16]

Of course, Buckingham and King James may have dug at Stonehenge out of pure curiosity, as many others had done in the surrounding area, but when Stukeley writes of searching behind the altar for treasure, we immediately think of a passage from Pope Gregory's letter to Abbot Mellitus:

> Augustine must smash the idols, but the temples themselves must be sprinkled with holy water and altars set up in them in which relics are to be enclosed. For we ought to take advantage of well-built temples by purifying them from Devil-worship and dedicating them to the service of the true God.[17]

Otherwise, it's curious that Stukeley should say 'was it not a blind act of Christian zeal to deface this stately monument of antientest superstition?' He himself then did something very similar, because he records that on 5 July 1723, 'By Lord Pembroke's direction, I dug on the inside of the altar about the middle: 4 foot along the edge of the stone, 6 foot forward towards the middle of the adytum,'[18] although he later adds that he went nowhere near any of the other stones. It's hard, therefore, to see how Buckingham and James were defacing the monument in the way that Stukeley suggests, because they were clearly searching for something of enormous interest to them and their searches were almost exclusively confined to the area immediately around the altar stone. They'd almost certainly heard of the discovery of the cover for the censer and they may well have found something else that prompted King James to carry the altar stone away to a royal palace in London in 'a blind act of Christian zeal'.

Is there any kind of precedent for a British monarch to remove an altar stone or other sacred stone and take it to London? In 1296, King Edward I, Hammer of the Scots, forcibly removed the Stone of Scone from Scotland and took it to Westminster Abbey, where it was placed into a wooden chair, known as St Edward's Chair. Almost every British monarch since that time,[19] including Queen Elizabeth II, has been crowned while sitting on this 700-year-old chair, but the Stone of Scone was returned to Scotland in 1996 on condition that it could be brought back to London for use in a coronation.

So, what's so important about this undoubtedly ancient stone? Many legends are attached to it, one of which states that it was the travelling altar used by St Columba in Scotland in the sixth century, when he was said to have introduced Christianity to Scotland. However, the stone's also known as the 'Jacob's Pillow Stone' as it's thought to be the very same stone that Jacob used as a pillow when he dreamed of the stairway to heaven, and the same stone that he later anointed with oil as a pillar to mark the spot as Bethel, or the House of the Lord. Wherever it came from, it apparently arrived in Scotland around AD 850 and was used a coronation seat by Scottish kings from that time onwards until it was stolen and taken to London by King Edward I.

Until he became King of England in 1603, King James I of England was known as King James VI of Scotland, so he would certainly have known about this stone and the astonishing legends attached to it, not least because he was crowned while sitting on it. So, what are we to make of the story of him transporting an altar stone from Stonehenge to St James's Palace in London in 1620, especially bearing in mind that the Stone of Scone weighs 336 pounds, whereas if the altar stone that was removed to London was anything like its remaining cousin, it would have weighed something in the region of six tons?

Everything suggests that King James had reason to believe that the altar stone from Stonehenge possessed an even greater significance than 'Jacob's Pillow Stone', which was considered to be the most important stone mentioned in the Bible, despite the fact that the ruins that had once shrouded this primaeval pillar were thought by many to be the work of the Devil himself.

A few years ago, I embarked on a thorough search for Inigo Jones's missing altar stone and I eventually concluded that it stood in full view, in two separate pieces on either side of a lane in the village of Berwick St James, just a mile or so from Stonehenge. The British media developed an interest in this matter and the Stonehenge expert Mike Pitts was invited to look into it, which he did, but his considered opinion was that the stones in question had *not* originally come from Stonehenge.

I'd carried out an extremely detailed investigation into the Berwick St James stones, but the blunt fact is that neither my evidence nor my arguments were compelling enough to persuade any archaeological organization to carry out a more intensive study, so there the matter must rest, and maybe the seventeenth-century stories concerning the stone's removal to St James's Palace are true after all.

If the many legends of Jesus visiting the West Country of England are *also* true, then it's possible that the foundations of the world's first church are concealed beneath the ruins of Glastonbury Abbey and that an altar stone consecrated by Jesus himself now lies hidden somewhere in a royal palace in modern London.

PART III

ISLAND

*'What seest thou else in the dark
backward and abysm of time?'*

William Shakespeare, *The Tempest*

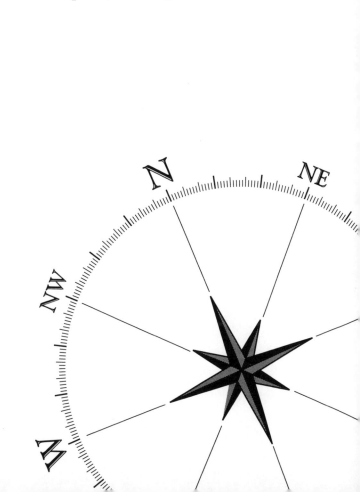

The story of Jesus visiting Britain is often referred to as 'the Holy Legend' and in turn a legend is defined as 'a traditional story sometimes popularly regarded as historical, but unauthenticated; a myth'.[1] The subjects of legends and authentication throw up a number of important questions that can't be avoided if we are to arrive at an informed judgement as to whether or not Jesus once visited Britain.

First, it would be wrong to claim that every legend, tale and myth had some truth at its core. Earlier, for example, we were able to rule out the historical Jesus as having taken part in the creation of the Fonaby Stone in Lincolnshire or in the lengthening of a wooden beam during the building of Christchurch Priory in the New Forest. However, the mere fact that these two strange stories of Jesus exist *at all* shows us that his presence in Britain wasn't unthinkable to people in past ages.

It's a simple fact that Jesus went missing from the Biblical record for 18 years, or over half his entire lifetime, then reappeared in his homeland as a stranger. As such, if there were just one suggestion, credible or otherwise, that he had been seen elsewhere during these 'missing years', we'd be bound to at least *entertain* the notion that the story had some truth to it, especially in the complete absence of any reliable information to the contrary over the 2,000 years or so during which such evidence could have come to light.

For a concrete, up-to-date, scientific and demonstrable example of the way these things are examined, let's look at the relevant procedures of the British police force. As soon as it has been established beyond doubt that someone has gone missing from their usual routine or environment, the police look into their whereabouts, and it's not their practice to dismiss *any* report or sighting out of hand, no matter how seemingly unlikely that sighting might be, until such time as they receive firm or compelling evidence to the contrary. Furthermore, they make every conceivable effort to build up a detailed picture or background of the missing person as far as their disposition, habits, routine, friends, acquaintances, relatives, ability to travel, wealth, health, diet, strengths, weaknesses, skills, interests, fears, hopes, likes and dislikes are concerned; by doing so, they're better able to gain an insight into the character of the person who's missing and they're better able to evaluate the credibility of any sightings that come in.

I doubt that the British police have any interest in investigating a 2,000-year-old missing person's case, however, so perhaps we should look to the archaeologists? I'm one myself and I can't see that this story 'melts away at the touch', yet no archaeologists have seen fit to look into the matter of Jesus visiting Britain.

Could historians authenticate or disprove this legend? Jesus is widely regarded as a historical figure and the period during which he's supposed to have been in Britain isn't a completely closed book, but I'm not aware of any historian who's seriously investigated this matter either. We could perhaps look to folklorists, but the only study I know of, by A. W. Smith, could hardly have been less restricted in scope and as it contains the bald statement that some of Jesus's presumed motives for visiting Britain can be 'dismissed out of hand', it hardly qualifies as an open-minded investigation.

All this leaves us with the Church as the final arbiter, but here we find ourselves running into some serious difficulties. The Roman Catholic Church prides itself on its scholarship, but Pope John Paul II created an inordinate number of saints before his death, far more than any other pope before him had done. It may be that all these beatified individuals were fully deserving of their saintly status, but on the other hand there's the lingering suspicion that their lives weren't examined with the most scrupulous care, in which case we might have some minor reservations as to whether the evidence for Jesus visiting Britain would be examined in an objective fashion.

As for the Church of England, it owns and maintains the remains of Glastonbury Abbey. These ruins are among the most beautiful locations in Britain and they attract visitors from all over the world, who flock to this otherworldly site to experience for themselves the magical atmosphere that pervades the entire locality. The one person most responsible for restoring Glastonbury Abbey as we see it today was Frederick Bligh

Bond, an archaeologist and church architect who lived in the early part of the last century. He had phenomenal success at locating hidden or lost parts of the abbey and he owed a large part of this success, it seems, to his many conversations with the spirits of long-dead monks, who spoke to him and his companions during a series of séances and told them precisely where to dig. When this unorthodox method came to light, the Church took an exceedingly dim view of the whole affair and Bligh Bond found himself banished to the outer darkness. His name was long ago expunged from the 'authorized version' of events.

As the Church authorities have gone to some pains to conceal what they regard as the unpalatable truth behind Bligh Bond's near faultless completion of his brief, it doesn't fill us with confidence that they'd look into the matter of Jesus coming to Britain in an impartial fashion. As Samuel Taylor Coleridge commented, 'He who begins by loving Christianity better than Truth will proceed by loving his own sect or church better than Christianity, and end by loving himself better than all.'[2]

Unfortunately, it's difficult to see how either the Roman Catholic Church or the Church of England could reliably authenticate or disprove the legend of Jesus visiting Britain without being accused of either vested interests or expediency. It seems that we'll have to rely on our own individual judgement and consciences when it comes to forming an opinion, but there are more facts out there that can help us to do so.

CHAPTER TWELVE

'Mine Eyes Have Seen the Glory of the Coming of the Lord'

...Coming events cast their shadow before.
Thomas Campbell, 1777–1844

If the various reports are to be believed, the births of remarkable men throughout history have occasionally been accompanied by striking signs and portents. As Jesus was such an extraordinary and outstanding figure, we'd naturally expect his birth to have been accompanied by such harbingers and sure enough, we read in the Gospel of Matthew that a guiding star led the Magi to Jesus's birthplace.[1] However, in mediaeval times, it was believed that the poet Virgil had foretold the Nativity in one of his poems written some 50 years earlier. The poem is known as 'The Fourth Eclogue' and it contains lines such as:

> ...the majestic roll of circling centuries begins anew: justice returns, returns old Saturn's reign, with a new breed of men sent down from heaven. Only do thou, at the boy's birth in whom the iron shall cease, the golden race arise... whatso tracks remain of our old wickedness, once done away, shall free the earth from never-ceasing fear. He shall receive the life of gods, and see heroes with gods commingling, and

himself be seen of them, and with his father's worth reign o'er a world at peace.

There's more in this vein, so it's easy to see why Virgil was thought to have foretold the birth of Jesus and it's just possible that he did precisely this.

Virgil's prophecy is famous enough, but there was another event 'in ancient time' that's also been interpreted as foretelling the coming of Jesus. It took place during the reign of the Roman emperor Tiberius, who ruled from AD 14 to 37. The Greek historian Plutarch (AD 46 to 120) wrote that an Egyptian sailor named Thamus, who was on board a ship bound for Italy, heard a mysterious voice calling out to him from the island of Paxi, telling him that when he reached the island of Palodes he was to proclaim that the great god Pan was dead; Thamus did this and by way of reply he heard wails and laments coming from the shore. In later times, this episode was thought of as evidence of the triumph of Christianity over paganism, if only because it took place during the reign of Tiberius, which roughly coincided with the life of Jesus.

What's not been so widely reported is that Tiberius himself was fascinated by it, as we can see for ourselves if we examine the precise words written by Plutarch:

Being come to Palodes, there was no wind stirring, and the sea was as smooth as glass. Whereupon Thamus, standing on the deck, with his face towards the land, uttered with a loud voice his message, saying, 'The great Pan is dead.' He had no sooner said this, but they heard a dreadful noise, not only of one, but of several, who, to their thinking, groaned and lamented with a kind of astonishment. And there being many persons in the ship, an account of this was soon spread over Rome, which made Tiberius the Emperor send for Thamus; and he seemed to give such heed to what he told him, that he earnestly enquired who this Pan was; and the learned men about him gave in their judgements...[2]

In addition to these examples and the prophecies of a Messiah in the Old Testament, there may have been other signs of the coming of Jesus that we don't know about, so it's worth asking if the Druids had any foreknowledge of his arrival. Ancient authors such as Cicero and Diodorus Siculus recorded that the Druids were skilled in predicting the future, while Julius Caesar wrote:

> They also hold long discussions about the heavenly bodies and their movements, the size of the universe and of the earth, the physical constitution of the world, and the power and properties of the gods; and they instruct the young men in all these subjects.[3]

Bearing in mind the Druids' obsession with the constellations, they could easily qualify as northern versions of the Magi, who followed the star showing where Jesus had been born. Is there any evidence that they foresaw the coming of Jesus?

THE PILLAR OF THE BOATMEN

In 1711 a stone pillar was discovered beneath the choir of the cathedral of Notre Dame in Paris during renovation work. According to the inscription, it had been dedicated to the Roman god Jupiter by some Parisian sailors during the reign of Tiberius and what's remarkable about it is that on one side this pillar clearly depicts a god named Esus. Furthermore, he's shown as a muscular young man wielding an axe and cutting down a tree, so this carving has naturally been the source of intense interest to many people over the years.

There are other inscriptions mentioning this god by name and, on the face of it, the similarity to Jesus seems inescapable, but what do we actually know of Esus? A great deal has been written on the subject, but it's easy to summarize the few known facts about this god. He was worshipped by the Gauls and in one poem[4] by the Roman poet Lucan, he's mentioned at the same time as the Druids. No one's certain what his name means, although there have been a wide variety of suggestions, including 'master', but it is known that he was part of a trinity of gods, the other two being Taranis and Teutates. Human beings were regularly sacrificed to him and it's likely that he was thought of as a god of war, like the Roman Mars. Lucan describes him as 'horrid Esus with his wild altars',[5] but this is pretty much all that we know about him.

What connection, if any, does all this have with the subject of our study? We know that this stone pillar was erected during the reign of Tiberius, which, as we've already noted, roughly coincided with the life of Jesus. We know that it was erected by sailors and as Paris is in northern France and lies on the River Seine, which ultimately flows into the English Channel, it's impossible to rule out the idea that men who worshipped Esus were in regular contact with Britain and its people.

We know from Lucan's *Pharsalia* that human sacrifice was carried out on altars dedicated to Esus and we know from a number of ancient authors, including Julius Caesar, that the Druids regularly carried out such sacrifices; furthermore, Lucan's poem specifies that they were involved in rituals dedicated to Esus. As for the likelihood of these practices and the reverence for Esus existing in Britain, Caesar recorded: 'The Druidic doctrine is believed to have been found existing in Britain and thence imported into Gaul; even today those who want to make a profound study of it generally go to Britain for the purpose.'[6]

All in all, we're facing the inevitable conclusion that at the same time that Jesus is said to have visited Britain, the Druids and the rest of the populace were aware of a god named Esus whom they thought of as a muscular young man. They depicted him as a carpenter or as someone who felled trees with an axe and may also have thought of him as a god of war. The Britons would therefore certainly have been intrigued by a young man who was said to have been a carpenter and whose name, in Greek, bore such a close resemblance to that of one of their most potent deities. If Jesus had visited them and they had learned that he was thought of in his distant homeland as a Messiah who was destined to free his people from the Roman invaders by force of arms, it would have been extremely surprising if he'd not been welcomed with open arms.

Regardless of whether or not this actually happened, the mere existence of the Pillar of the Sailors shows that conditions were ripe in that precise time and place for the memory of someone named Jesus, Iesos or Esus to survive. In fact, Caesar mentions a whole tribe or possibly a confederation of tribes named the Esuvii or Essuvii, a maritime people who were based near the English Channel in northwestern Gaul and whose name probably meant 'the Followers of Esus'.[7]

However, aside from the pillar and other inscribed stones with the name 'Esus', there are still more physical artefacts for us to consider.

THE DUBUNNI

We've already encountered many apparent coincidences during the course of our investigation, but there's yet another when we come to consider the location that Jesus is said to have lived in while he was in Britain. To be sure, there are tales of him coming ashore at various places in the West Country and working in tin mines in Cornwall, but he is said to have actually resided in or around Glastonbury and to have worked for an unspecified period of time in the Mendip Hills.

In the early first century AD, this was the territory of a British tribe named the Dubunni or Dobunni, who were noted for being craftsmen and farmers. A young Jesus may have been thought of as a Messiah in waiting, but he was likely to have been working at the time as a builder, carpenter or craftsman, so it seems peculiarly fortunate that the later legends should place him in such a perfect setting, among a tribe noted for their peaceful skills. It is extremely unlikely that the people who later passed on the legends of Jesus coming to Britain would have been familiar with the talents of an obscure first-century British tribe who were barely mentioned in ancient texts, so once again we must ask ourselves if there's any significance to this.

There are a number of other curious aspects to what little we know of the Dubunni. If we're to believe the writings of Cassius Dio, they accepted Roman rule or otherwise capitulated to the Romans before the invasion in AD 43. Given the ferocity with which a great many other British tribes fought against the Romans, it seems strange that the Dubunni should ostentatiously throw in the towel before a single Roman soldier had set foot on British soil, but a number of explanations for this spring to mind. The Dubunni could have been well informed enough to realize that they couldn't hope to defeat the Roman legions and their leaders may have already had ties with Rome, but there may have been another reason why they ensured that they wouldn't be involved in an ultimately futile armed conflict with the Romans. There could have been a building on their land that was important to them, and perhaps to other British tribes, that they didn't want to risk being destroyed. It's also possible that, even some decades after Jesus had left their territory, there was someone living among them that they didn't want to risk being killed by the Romans. There's no record in the Bible of Jesus marrying or having children, but if he ever did, it may have happened at some point during his 'missing years'.

The Dubunni were also one of the few British tribes to mint their own coins and stamp them with names prior to the Roman invasion in AD 43. Nonetheless, it still comes as something of a shock to discover that the name 'Eisu' is clearly recorded on Dubunni coins and that whoever this Eisu was, he rose to prominence around AD 30, according to the historians, prehistorians, archaeologists and numismatists who've studied these coins.

Other names such as 'Anted', 'Boduocus', 'Catti', 'Comux', 'Corio' and 'Inam' are also recorded on Dubunni coins and as a result, the professionals have inferred that the territory of the Dubunni was divided into a northern and southern region ruled over by separate kings and that, for example, Eisu was the son of Anted, and so forth. However, these are all informed guesses and no one knows for certain who these people were or what their relationship to each other was.

Nonetheless, there's no doubt that someone called Eisu became sufficiently prominent to have his name recorded on a coin and that this event took place at some time around AD 30, so here we have yet another truly *fantastic* coincidence as far as our investigation is concerned. Jesus is said to have visited Britain and stayed here for a period, which must have been between AD 12 and 30, and all the legends place him in a specific part of Britain. When we look closely at that region, we find that someone with a name closely resembling that of Jesus is commemorated on a coin at precisely that time.

Given how long the legends of Jesus in Britain have been known, we'd suppose that the scholars who compiled the reports on the Dubunni would have made at least some passing comment on this, but there's a resounding silence in all the sources I've studied. In the original Greek of the New Testament, the name of Jesus is rendered as 'Ιησους, which is 'Iesous' in our alphabet, so we can see at a glance the similarities between the two names. The vocative form of Iesous, or the form of the word used when Jesus was addressed directly by someone else, was 'Ιησου, or Iesou,[8] which is even closer to Eisu. We know that Jesus almost certainly spoke Greek during his lifetime, so it follows that the Greek form of his name would have been commonly used by those that knew him, while we also know from Caesar that the Druids used Greek letters.

Furthermore, some of the Dubunni Eisu coins are made of silver and we know that the Romans mined this precious metal in the Mendips soon after their arrival there in AD 43. Given that some of the legends state that Jesus worked as a miner in this area, this raises the possibility, however remote, that he personally mined some of the silver that was later used to make the coins inscribed with the name 'Eisu'. Of course, such an idea might seem truly incredible, but when we recall the number of Biblical prophecies that Jesus fulfilled throughout his life and when we bear in mind that the prophet Malachi foretold of the Messiah 'And he shall sit as a refiner and purifier of silver', the existence of silver coins bearing a name closely resembling that of Jesus seems a truly fantastic coincidence. The odds against them being struck in the same place that Jesus is said to have visited and at the same time that he is said to have been there purely by chance must be astronomical.

Were there two prominent men living in the same area at the same time with very similar names? Or was there just the one and in that case, was it the eastern Iesous or the western Eisu?

We could spend hours examining the minutiae of ancient languages and the resemblance between the names we've been studying, but for now it's worth looking at what we can be certain of and then we can draw our own conclusions:

- The life of Jesus roughly coincided with the reign of Tiberius, the Roman emperor from AD 14 to 37.
- A pillar found in Paris in 1711 was erected during the reign of Tiberius. This pillar commemorates a non-Roman god named Esus, who would have been known to the Britons of the time. Jesus would most likely have been known as Iesous or something similar by those he met.
- On this pillar, Esus is depicted as a muscular young man cutting down a tree with an axe. Jesus may possibly have been a carpenter and if so, then he'd have been known as a 'muscular young man' occasionally wielding an axe during the reign of Tiberius.
- Esus was thought of as a god of war. Jesus was being spoken of as a Messiah, or a warrior mystic who would free his homeland from Roman rule by force.
- The pillar was erected by sailors. There's undeniable evidence that during his missing years, Jesus became a seasoned mariner.
- Aside from being a carpenter, Jesus may have been a skilled worker or builder. The legends place him in the territory of the Dubunni tribe, who were farmers and artisans.
- Dubunni coins record that someone named Eisu rose to prominence in their territory somewhere around AD 30. The later legends speak of Jesus or Iesous being in exactly the same place at exactly the same time.
- Not a single archaeologist, prehistorian, scholar, churchman or academic has so much as commented on this apparent coincidence, despite the legends of Jesus in the West Country being well known and despite the decades-old popularity of William Blake's 'Jerusalem', which virtually spells the matter out.

Most of the Dubunni Eisu coins depict the figure of a horse, but it's not known why this was such a popular motif. The creature may have represented luck or military prowess, but as with so many other aspects of the distant past, archaeologists are uncertain about the precise meaning of this equine symbolism.

It may be unrelated, but just a few miles to the east of the Dubunni territory and just 20 miles north of Stonehenge lies the aforementioned Silbury Hill, a colossal artificial mound that was built roughly 4,500 years ago. Something about this mound was of intense interest to the later Romans, who, as already noted, built a settlement the size of 24 football pitches at its base, and it has continued to intrigue observers and visitors up until the present day.

A persistent legend attached to Silbury Hill is that a legendary King Zil lies buried inside, covered in gold armour and either lying in a golden coffin or seated, life-size, upon a golden horse. William Stukeley discovered a bit from a horse's bridle at the top of Silbury Hill in 1723 and he also recorded the country folk's long-standing tradition of celebrating every Palm Sunday with a fair on top of the hill. These local people could have celebrated any number of Christian or pagan festivals on Silbury Hill, so it strikes me as peculiar that they should choose to commemorate Palm Sunday, the solitary occasion when Jesus was known to have been seated upon a donkey as he made his way as a king into Jerusalem. A donkey isn't a horse, of course, but there's something odd about the combination of the legends placing Jesus nearby, the Eisu coins depicting a horse, Silbury Hill's associations with a golden king on horseback and the fact that for hundreds of years the people of the region chose to celebrate the only time when Jesus rode on a four-legged creature for the specific purpose of fulfilling the prophecy of a king making his way into Jerusalem. Is all this a faint memory of Jesus once visiting Silbury Hill on horseback? Possibly.

For the sake of being thorough, it makes sense for us to ask whether there is any other authenticated depiction of Jesus with a horse, or horses. Indeed there is, and it can be found in the form of a mosaic in what's known as the Tomb of the Julii or the Tomb of Cristo Sole, meaning 'Christ the Sun', in the catacombs beneath St Peter's Basilica in the Vatican City. There are many intriguing aspects to this mosaic, which is believed to have been constructed in the middle of the third century, but the most striking detail is that Jesus is unmistakably shown riding in a chariot pulled by two or possibly more white horses.

The idea of Jesus representing the sun brings to mind the occasion when he underwent a transformation at the top of a mountain and it also resembles one element of a possible visit to Stonehenge. The fact that he's shown riding in a chariot has unmistakable echoes of Britain, because the inhabitants of the island were renowned as being the finest charioteers in the ancient world, as we learn from no less a personage than Julius Caesar, describing the early stages of his attempted invasion of Britain:

In action, therefore, [the British charioteers] combine the mobility of cavalry with the staying power of foot soldiers. Their skill, which is derived from ceaseless training and practice, may be judged by the fact that they can control their horses at full gallop on the steepest incline, check and turn them in a moment, run along the pole, stand on the yoke, and get back again into the chariot as quick as lightning.[9]

TUNIC CROSSES

The pillar depicting Esus as a woodcutter or carpenter and the Dubunni coins inscribed with the name 'Eisu' are baffling enough, but there are other tangible artefacts in the West Country that are said to have a connection with Jesus. As we've already seen, there are stories of stones that he's said to have trodden on or put in place, but there are also the 'tunic crosses', so called because the Christ figures on them are wearing a short tunic, rather than the more usual loincloth. They seem to be of a boy, although given the crude way in which they're carved, it's difficult to tell. There are a number of these crosses in southwestern Cornwall and there's a belief that they were fashioned in this way to commemorate the visits Jesus made to the region when he was a boy.

I've looked into this matter as best I can, but no one seems to be able to speak about the tunic crosses with any degree of certainty. Some say that the crosses show the Jesus figure triumphant, which is markedly different from the forlorn adult figure hanging by nails that we're used to seeing, and they certainly seem to show a figure standing, rather than crucified. I've read that the figures originally represented a pagan god, but if this is the case, it seems strange that when the crosses themselves were carved, they weren't replaced with either a plain stone face or some other form of design or engraving, and it also seems to directly contradict what Pope Gregory had to say about destroying all the idols in Britain. It may be that the figures originally represented a pagan god and the people who later fashioned the stones into crosses simply thought that they were an adequate representation of Jesus on the cross, on the grounds that whatever figure appeared, by definition, simply *had* to be Jesus. It may be that they were originally carved to represent Jesus, but if so, they are unlike any other figures I've seen on crucifixes and we have to wonder why the original masons chose to depict Jesus as a boy dressed in a 'tunic' standing up.

It may be that the legends are accurate and that they *were* originally intended to depict Jesus as a young boy visiting Cornwall. The most informed comment I've been able to find on the matter is this:

> Another curious thing about the Celtic west of England is the presence of its unique 'tunic' crosses. These appear in the greatest number in Cornwall. They show Jesus with his arms outstretched on a cross, but instead of as commonly shown as an adult, stripped and crucified, he is depicted as a young boy wearing a tunic and preaching. A weathered example of such a tunic cross may be found at Marazion.[10]

Whatever the truth of the matter may be, these mysterious representations of a youthful Jesus are yet another tangible archaeological curiosity to be added to the Eisu coins of the West Country and to the carving of the muscular young man named Esus swinging an axe on the Pillar of the Sailors.

CHAPTER THIRTEEN

The Men of The Stones

...My head is bloodied, but unbowed...
'Invictus', W. E. Henley, 1849–1903

During the course of our investigation, we've uncovered some remarkable and thought-provoking facts. Perhaps the most striking are the mentions on coins of someone named Eisu who was a prominent figure in the West Country of England at precisely the same time that Jesus or Iesous was said to have been there. There's also the figure of Esus cutting down a tree on a pillar in Paris, the underground tunnels in the Mendip Hills that may have been the setting for the Harrowing of Hell, King James I's intense interest in a 'pagan' altar stone at Stonehenge and the Biblical confirmation that Joseph of Arimathea was connected with mining or quarrying. To my mind, however, the most persuasive argument in favour of Jesus having visited Britain lies in the precise nature of the location he is said to have lived in. Surprisingly enough, it doesn't concern the Dubunni, those farmers and craftsmen whose territory encompassed Glastonbury and the Mendips, but another Iron Age British tribe, the astonishing Silures, whose domain in south Wales was adjacent to that of the Dubunni and just a short journey by boat across the Severn Estuary.

To discover just who the Silures were and precisely why they're so significant to our study, we must first of all look briefly at how the Iron Age British tribes acquired the names that were recorded by the invading Romans. Judging from what's been left to us, the Romans had little interest in recording these names accurately, as it appears that their scribes simply wrote down the first thing they were told and also 'Romanized' the names to some extent.

A good example of this concerns the Iceni of eastern England, who became famous on account of their leader Boudicca, or Boadicea, who led the Iceni and others in a devastating revolt against the Romans in AD 60. However, when Julius Caesar invaded the east of what's now England over 100 years before, in 54 BC, he made no mention of the Iceni, leaving us instead the name Ceni Magni. There's an obvious similarity between the two titles, but the very fact that they're not exact copies suggests the lack of care that was taken by the Romans over recording these names.

Like the Dubunni, the Iceni were one of the few British tribes to mint their own coinage and to stamp names on them prior to the Roman invasion, so historians have tried to piece together some kind of history of their leaders from the inscriptions on the coins. Curiously, one of these Iceni names or titles is 'Aesu', which immediately reminds us of the Eisu further to the west during the same broad period. What do we know of this Aesu? Very little, other than that he seems to have minted his own coins around AD 45, two years after the Romans landed in his territory. As a result, historians have inferred that he was vehemently opposed to Roman rule and was killed in what appears to have been a civil war among the Iceni in AD 47, fighting on the side of those who wanted the invaders driven from their shores. That's the standard view and there seems to be nothing to object to, but the picture changes slightly if we consider some other possibilities.

If Jesus was in Britain at some point between AD 12 and 30, he'd certainly have been embraced, at least at first, as a Messiah or warrior mystic who was opposed to the Roman occupation of his native land, and he might possibly have been regarded as a manifestation of the war god Esus. If Aesu was issuing his own coins in AD 45 and taking part in a civil war two years later, then it seems reasonable to assume that he was born during the time that Jesus was said to have been in Britain. We've no way of knowing how old Aesu was when he died, but it's not out of the question that he was an impressionable teenager when the famous visitor from the East departed for the final time, presumably to drive the Romans out of his homeland. We don't have any way of knowing who Aesu's father was, but we probably won't be wide of the mark if we assume that he too was an inspirational figure with a warlike aura and no time for the notion of the Romans occupying his homeland.

There will doubtless be those who will maintain that the existence of the Druids' Esus, the Dubunni Eisu and the Iceni Aesu in the same small part of the world during the same narrow time frame in which Jesus is said to have resided in the region is nothing more than pure coincidence, and it may be that these people are correct. There will also be those who will claim that the existence of the name 'Aesu' in the east of England substantially detracts from any significance the name 'Eisu' has in the west of England, especially as far as the presence of Jesus in the area is concerned; again, it may be that these people are right. However, no study of the Eisu coins has so much as remarked on the coincidence between the name they carry and the many legends of a man from the East with an almost identical name who is said to have visited the region in which the coins originated at almost exactly the same time that they were struck. When we look closely at the Iceni Aesu coins, we find a similar scenario that's escaped all mention, presumably because no numismatist, archaeologist or prehistorian believes there's anything *worth* mentioning, but it's our business to look into these matters and to evaluate them for what they may or may not be worth, not to keep them concealed from view.

In 1061 a Saxon noblewoman named Richeldis de Faverches was living in a village called Walsingham in Norfolk, in what had been the very heart of the Iceni territory during the British Iron Age and the subsequent Roman occupation. By the eleventh century Walsingham was an apparently inconsequential village, but for some reason, Richeldis was granted a vision of the Virgin Mary in which she was shown the house in Nazareth in which Jesus had grown up. The Virgin

Mary instructed Richeldis to build an exact replica of this humble wooden abode, which she did, and this was to be no mere mediaeval curiosity, because the Shrine of Our Lady of Walsingham, as it came to be known, went on to become one of the major places of pilgrimage in Britain, on a par with Glastonbury and the shrine of St Thomas à Becket at Canterbury.

The shrine at Walsingham was destroyed during the English Reformation in 1537, but such was its reputation that the place has once again become a notable place of pilgrimage and the official website that is shared by the Anglican and Catholic Churches promotes it as 'England's Nazareth', something that's a highly notable claim by any standards. Furthermore, it strikes me as curious beyond description that in the place where Eisu once lived, Jesus is said to have built a wooden church to the memory of his *mother*, and in the place where Aesu once lived, the mother of Jesus should command a rich widow to build a replica of the wooden house in which her *son* grew up.

Coincidentally no doubt, these instructions were given from one widow to another exactly 1,000 years after another widow, Boadicea, raised her apocalyptic revolt in what is now Norfolk. It seems certain that Boadicea would have known Aesu, whoever he may have been, given that he was powerful and influential enough to have either minted his own coins or have had them minted in his honour. Furthermore, Boadicea was the wife of a prominent Iceni chieftain and her daughters would have been born at roughly the same time that Aesu was killed.

As for the name 'Walsingham', I'm not aware that anyone's examined it in the specific context of any connections the place is believed to have with Mary and Jesus, but *The Oxford Dictionary of English Place-Names* tells us that it derives from an Old English personal name of someone called Waels. However, when we bear in mind the 'wal' in Wales and the 'wall' in Cornwall, both of which refer to a specific group of people, we discover the possibility that Walsingham means 'the homestead of the family or followers of a stranger' or 'the homestead of the family or followers of someone who spoke a strange language'.[1] We must make of all this what we will.

So much for the Iceni; as for other British tribes of this period, the names are generally vague, such as the Cornovii, which probably meant 'the people of the horn', or the Dumnoni, which may have meant 'the people of the land'. The Brigantes were simply 'the people of the goddess Brigantia' and there's nothing really exceptional or noteworthy in the names of other British tribes until we encounter the Silures of south Wales.

TO LEAVE A LIVING NAME BEHIND

The meaning of the name 'Silures' could hardly be clearer, as it derives from the Latin word *silex*, meaning 'stone', 'flint', 'boulder' or possibly 'crag'. As such, Silures means 'the men of the stones', and this has always been taken to refer to the hilly landscape of Gwent, the present-day county in south Wales that was once this tribe's homeland. However, I was born in Gwent and spent the first 18 years of my life there, and in the intervening years I've travelled around Britain a fair bit and studied the various landscapes. Nothing I've ever seen suggests to me that Gwent has a monopoly on either stones or hills, so something else must account for why these people were given this unusually precise name.

The simplest and most obvious explanation is that when the Roman scribes enquired who these people were, they received the immediate reply, 'They're the men of the stones,' and this was recorded, but without the Romans realizing precisely *which* stones were in the minds of the people supplying the information or having any notion of how important those stones were. When *we* ask what stones are being referred to, the answer leaps out at us, because the territory of the Silures bordered on the Preseli Hills, where the famous bluestones for Stonehenge originated.

It seems beyond all possible coincidence that the one tribe in the whole island to be named 'the men of the stones' should be located so closely to the source of the most famous stones in Britain and possibly all Europe. We're told that a tribe named the Demetae lived in the area of the Preseli Mountains at the time of the Roman invasion, but no one can be entirely sure where the ancient boundaries between the British tribes lay, nor how they fluctuated over the centuries. Building stone circles had ceased in Britain long before the arrival of the Romans, but it seems certain that the Silures and others nonetheless retained a clear memory of events some 2,500 years or more before, when people from their region hauled the bluestones from southwest Wales to Salisbury Plain.

It's also possible that the name of the Silures was a fusion of *silex*, meaning 'stone', and *urus*, meaning 'wild ox', which could mean that they were described to the Romans as 'the men of the stones and of the wild ox'. This would also imply that the Silures had exceedingly long memories, because, as we've seen, ox skulls were buried over 5,000 years ago next to the entrances to Stonehenge when it first came into being as an earthwork.

All this is intriguing enough, but if the Silures were indeed known as 'the men of the stones and the wild ox' in the first century AD, it inescapably brings to mind Pope Gregory's order that the temples in Britain should on no account be destroyed and his deep unhappiness about the British slaughtering oxen as sacrifices to the Devil in these places:

And because [the English] are used to slaughter many oxen in sacrifice to Devils, some solemnity must be given them in exchange for this, as that on the day of the dedication, or the nativities of the holy martyrs, whose relics are there deposited, they should build themselves huts of the boughs of trees about those churches which have been turned to that use from being temples, and celebrate the solemnity with religious feasting, and no more offer animals to the Devil...[2]

What we know for sure about the Silures is that while other tribes such as the Dubunni and Iceni were minting coins, weaving textiles and generally exhibiting signs of what we and the Romans might regard as civilization, the Silures were remarkable in that they didn't even make their own pottery. We know little about their society apart from the fact that they were regarded as primitive hunter-gatherers who lived in hill forts, but when we turn our attention to another aspect of them, something quite incredible looms out at us from the mists of history.

ANCESTRAL VOICES PROPHESYING WAR

We've no written records of the Silures before the Roman invasion of AD 43, but the Romans had particularly good cause to record their encounters with these people, and their detailed accounts give us a vivid picture of the tribe.

When the Roman legions landed in Britain in AD 43, their principal adversary was a chieftain or king known as Caractacus or Caratacus, who engaged the invaders in a number of pitched battles but was gradually forced to withdraw to the west. After his defeats in southern and eastern England, where did the man who was trying to be the saviour of his country seek help? Or, more to the point, where did he *find* it?

We know that Caratacus met up with the Silures in what's now southeast Wales and that with their help he continued to fight Aulus Plautius, the Roman general who led the invasion of Britain, and his successor as governor of Britain, Ostorius Scapula. It wasn't until AD 51, eight years after the legions had arrived in Britain, that Ostorius Scapula managed to defeat Caratacus and a combined army of Ordovices and Silures somewhere on the present-day border between England and Wales.

Simple logic suggests that primitive tribesmen or hunter-gatherers who didn't even make their own *pottery* should have effectively become extinct after a defeat by the world's most powerful army, but even after Caratacus had been betrayed by Cartimandua, the queen of the Brigantes, the Silures continued the resistance against the Romans. And they did it in incredible style.

As the Roman historian Tacitus recorded:

Conspicuous above all in stubborn resistance were the Silures... they cut off two of our auxiliary cohorts, the rapacity of whose officers let them make incautious forays; and by liberal gifts of spoil and prisoners to the other tribes, they were luring them too into revolt, when Ostorius, worn out by the burden of his anxieties, died, to the joy of the enemy...[3]

So, far from being exterminated, the primitive Silures actively caused the death of Ostorius Scapula, the governor of Britain. But far worse was to follow for the Romans. The new governor was Aulus Didius Gallus and, as Tacitus records:

Didius, though he quickly arrived, found matters far from prosperous, for the legion under the command of Manlius Valens had meanwhile been defeated... This loss too had been inflicted on us by the Silures, and they were scouring the country far and wide...[4]

It has been little remarked upon, but this loss of the entire legion of Manlius Valens in or around AD 55 was far and away the worst single defeat the Romans had yet suffered in Britain and we should remember that by that time, this most powerful of armies had had 12 years or so to establish themselves on a small island and eradicate the opposition. Furthermore, this disaster was inflicted by a tribe who'd clearly not been remotely subdued by their previous defeat in AD 51.

No one's sure where the destruction of the legion took place, other than it was probably somewhere in the West Country. It may be yet another of the many coincidences that seem to bedevil our study, but if we're to be meticulous about examining all the evidence we should note that just a few miles to the southwest of Stonehenge is the village of Bowerchalke, which in turn isn't far from Bottlebush Down, the home of the phantom Bronze Age horseman we encountered in an earlier chapter. Bowerchalke has long been reputed to be the site of a battle between the Romans and ancient Britons, but I've not been able to establish whether this is true or not. However, if it *is* true, then it could well be where the Silures destroyed the Roman legion led by Manlius Valens.

The echoes of this conflict are supposed to have persisted through the centuries in the form of headless horses rushing around, accompanied by the sounds of battle. I've occasionally visited this gloomy spot over the years, but perhaps it was my imagination that was responsible for the fleeting glimpses I caught of an ancient conflict being re-enacted by moonlight, not far from the baleful temple on the plain that the ancestors of the Silures had laboriously erected over 2,500 years before they defied the Romans.

Tacitus tells us that Didius Gallus later managed to 'disperse' the Silures, but they continued to rebel under the *next* Roman governor, Quintus Veranius, who seems to have suffered a similar fate to Ostorius Scapula. Tacitus tells us that Veranius, after harrying the Silures in a few raids of no great significance, was prevented by death from carrying his arms further.[5] Or, in other words, the Silures comprehensively defeated and killed him, just as they'd done to Ostorius Scapula, the legion of Manlius Valens and many others besides. Little wonder, therefore, that Tacitus added the following observation:

> The Brigantes indeed, when a few who were beginning hostilities had been slain and the rest pardoned, settled down quietly; but on the Silures *neither terror nor mercy had the least effect*; they persisted in war and could be quelled only by legions encamped in their country [my italics].[6]

It should be said that the Brigantes were notoriously warlike and troublesome, to the extent that they bequeathed us the word 'brigand', but compared to the Silures they were conscientious objectors or pacifists. It wasn't until AD 78 under Frontinus that the Silures came close to being subdued, 18 years after the destruction of the Druid stronghold of Mona and the annihilation of Boudicca's confederation of tribes, 23 years after the Silures had wiped out a Roman legion and almost 40 years after the fearsome and otherwise all-conquering Romans had first landed in Britain.

Not only that, but there's even a tantalizing suggestion in the ancient accounts that the Silures had previously been responsible for defeating the legions of Julius Caesar in 55 and 54 BC. When Tacitus described the prelude to what's become known as the Battle of Caer Caradoc in AD 51, where the Romans defeated the Silures, he described how Caratacus tried to rally and inspire his troops for the engagement to come:

> As for Caractacus, he flew hither and thither, protesting that that day and that battle would be the beginning of the recovery of their freedom, or of everlasting bondage. He appealed, *by name, to their forefathers who had driven back the dictator Caesar,* [and] by whose valour they were free from the Roman axe and tribute, and still preserved inviolate the persons of their wives and of their children [my italics].[7]

So, what does all this have to do with any visit that Jesus may have made to Britain?

THE HEART AND STOMACH OF A KING

As we've already seen, the gospels occasionally give us an insight into the character of Jesus. For example, at the age of 12 he went missing for three days in Jerusalem, something that worried his parents a great deal, but when they eventually found him in the temple, he replied with what seems like typical teenage petulance:

> And it came to pass, that after three days they found him in the temple, sitting in the midst of the doctors, both hearing them and asking them questions. And all that heard him were astonished at his understanding and answers.
>
> And when they saw him, they were amazed: and his mother said unto him, 'Son, why hast thou thus dealt with us? Behold, thy father and I have sought thee, sorrowing.'
>
> And he said unto them, 'How is it that ye sought me? Wist ye not that I must be about my Father's business?' And they understood not the saying which he spake unto them.[8]

We've also learned of Jesus exhibiting astonishment, joy, sorrow, anger, defiance, possible humour and even despair, but there's a far more notable aspect of his character, and it's a quality that he patently acquired during the 'missing years'. It's become something of a cliché to refer to him as 'gentle Jesus, meek and mild', but there's unambiguous evidence that while he preached a message of peace, he nonetheless possessed the bearing of a king, nerves of steel and incredible bravery. Furthermore, these admirable qualities would be vital to him if he were to lead by example and fulfil his destiny, because the commandment to love your enemy[9] is naturally all the more potent, impressive and persuasive if it comes from someone who radiates power, authority and kingship, someone you wholeheartedly believe to be perfectly capable of *vanquishing* his enemy if he so chose.

As we've previously learned, Jesus survived an attempt on his life early on in his ministry when he simply walked through a murderous crowd who were trying to throw him off a cliff without batting an eyelid. Then there was the famous occasion when he went into the Temple, overthrew the tables of the moneychangers and the dove sellers and then sharply criticized them;[10] these aren't the actions of someone who lacks conviction or backbone. There are many other examples of his courage and self-belief, but perhaps the most impressive one occurred when this working-class hero was brought before Pontius Pilate, who clearly wouldn't have been *remotely* surprised if Jesus had said, 'Yes, of course,' when Pilate asked if he was King of the Jews.[11]

Jesus must have possessed the tangible demeanour, authority and bearing of a king, because otherwise it's difficult to see why everyone was so troubled by him. As far as the Pharisees were concerned, Jesus was a dangerous subversive and a radical, but in addition to what he had to *say*, his physical presence must have contributed to this impression; or, to put it another way, Jesus could not only 'talk the talk' but he could also very convincingly 'walk the walk'. When we bear in mind the circumstances of his arrest, the agonizing death that awaited him and Pilate's repeated attempts to avoid a travesty of justice, it's accurate to observe that neither terror nor mercy had the least effect upon Jesus, which is of course identical to the description of the Silures that Tacitus bequeathed us.

There's no suggestion in the gospels that Jesus acquired this kingly demeanour during the course of his ministry, so we simply have no choice other than to cast about for where and when he might reasonably have done so. When we follow the evidence that's available to us, we find the domain of the indomitable Silures staring us in the face.

Once again, we can make of this what we will, but we have to wonder at the degree of sheer coincidence involved. Legends, circulated and perpetuated by people who presumably knew next to nothing about Iron Age British tribes, place Jesus in a precise location in the Mendip Hills that would have been of great interest to someone such as Joseph of Arimathea, a man with a demonstrable Biblical pedigree for mining or quarrying, and a man in a realistic position to transport his young nephew to a distant island. This location, among the Dubunni people, could hardly have been better suited to someone who was a carpenter, builder or a craftsman, while it also directly bordered the domain of some of the most ferocious warriors on Earth, men who were implacably opposed to the Romans and who may well have been culturally primed to expect a Messiah or warrior mystic named Esus who was a carpenter. The astonishing stone temple with which they were intimately associated lay just 30 miles to the east of where Jesus is said to have lived, and this temple, Stonehenge, may well have been a symbol for national resistance at the time.

All this is extraordinary enough, but Jesus had still other affinities with the Silures.

A COUNTENANCE OF MANY COLOURS

Throughout the western world, Jesus has been depicted for centuries as tall, often blond and Caucasian, despite the fact that no contemporary description of him survives. However, as he was of Mediterranean stock, he was almost certainly olive-coloured, a view shared by Professor Vincent Wimbush of California's Claremont Graduate University, an expert on ethnic interpretations of the Bible, and by New Testament scholar Dr Mark Goodacre of the University of Birmingham, who was an advisor to a BBC production entitled *The Son of God* in 2001.[12]

In addition to these learned opinions, there are the Hadith or oral traditions of Islam, several of which mention Jesus, or Isa as he's known to Muslims. For example:

Narrated Abdullah: 'The Prophet mentioned... "While sleeping near the Kaaba last night, I saw in my dream a man of brown colour, the best one can see amongst brown colour, and his hair was [so] long that it fell between his shoulders. His hair was lank and water was dribbling from his head and he was placing his hands on the shoulders of two men while circumambulating the Kaaba. I asked, "Who is this?" They replied, "This is Jesus, son of Mary."'[13]

Another Hadith reads:

Narrated Salim from his father: 'No, by Allah, the Prophet did not tell that Jesus was of red complexion but said, "While I was asleep circumambulating the Kaaba (in my dream), suddenly I saw a man of brown complexion and lank hair walking between two men, and water was dropping from his head. I asked, "Who is this?" The people said, "He is the son of Mary."'[14]

If further confirmation is needed, we can look to early Roman mosaics, which also show Jesus as dark-skinned, or the fact that Jesus was named Top Black Icon of 2004 by the *New Nation* magazine, but simple logic tells us that if Jesus came from the Mediterranean, he'd have been the same colour as the other people of that region.

And what does all this have to do with the Silures? Well, they were the only British tribe who warranted a detailed physical description by Tacitus, who wrote:

The dark complexion of the Silures, their usually curly hair and the fact that Spain is on the opposite shore to them, are evidence that

Iberians of a former date crossed over and occupied these parts.[15]

Tacitus got his geography wrong, because Spain isn't on the opposite shore to south Wales, but this is unimportant because he was doing his best to offer us a group of people with whom we could compare the Silures. He chose Spaniards, a Mediterranean nation, so regardless of whether we describe them as olive-skinned, swarthy or dark, it's clear that Jesus was exactly the same colour as the people of this warlike tribe.

Again, this doesn't prove that Jesus visited the west of England, but if the Silures had heard of a young visitor making an impression on the locals on account of his name, his trade and the idea that he was some kind of Messiah in waiting, then discovered that this mysterious newcomer shared their skin colour, which was unique on the island at the time, it's not difficult to imagine the reception he'd have been afforded. Nor is it hard to see that over the course of time he'd have acquired some of the extremely tough characteristics of the Silures and that the memory of such a remarkable visitor would have persisted.

So, apart from having seemingly inherited the Silures' complete immunity to terror or mercy, is there any suggestion that Jesus ever visited south Wales?

MARY AND THE KINGDOM OF HEAVEN

The stories of Joseph of Arimathea and Jesus visiting England may seem incredible at first, but when we look further into the matter, the likelihood of these events having taken place veers sharply from a near impossibility to a virtual certainty. Nonetheless, it's still stupefying to learn of a story that places Mary, the mother of Jesus, in the same area at roughly the same time.

Wales has a profusion of holy wells, but by far the most noteworthy is Ffynnon Fair, in the parish of Kidwelly in Carmarthenshire in south-west Wales. Mary is said to have travelled by sea to Kidwelly and the tone and unambiguous content of the tale make clear that the event occurred 'in ancient time' – in other words, it's not a story of the Virgin Mary appearing as a supernatural figure many centuries after her time on Earth, but of an historical event.

Quite simply, Mary is said to have asked one of the people living in the area to show her the way back to her ship, but whoever it was refused, then killed her. This horrendous deed is said to have taken place in a field named Arvell Meade and a well or spring appeared on the spot where Mary fell.[16]

Now, we have no way of knowing if there's any truth to this remarkable and apparently unlikely story, but as we're studying every scrap of information in our investigation, it's worth asking ourselves a few questions about why the mother of Jesus is thought to have visited southwest Wales 'in ancient time'.

What would she have been doing in this precise part of the world? The most obvious answer, even though the detail is not supplied in the legend, is that she went there after the crucifixion of her son because she wanted to see with her own eyes some of the places he'd visited during his absence from his homeland. This would satisfactorily account for her being there, but the legend states that she asked someone to guide her back to her ship, which implies that she'd wandered a considerable distance away from the port or harbour in which it was moored, so we have to ask if there was anything in the region that she might have been particularly interested in that was somehow linked with her son's earlier travels.

The most notable aspect of the landscape would have been the Preseli Hills, lying just 20 miles or so to the northwest of the site where Mary is said to have been slain. As we've learned, these hills are where the famous bluestones from Stonehenge originated, but why would Jesus have visited them?

The meaning of the name of the Silures leads us to the conclusion that they and others retained a clear memory of the bluestones having been taken from south Wales to Salisbury Plain in prehistory. Some of the surviving bluestones at Stonehenge still possess joints, which tell us that, like the larger sarsens, they once formed a complex structure, either at Stonehenge or possibly on a mountaintop in Wales. When we also bear in mind that the stones at Stonehenge are the only known example of dressed stones in Britain from prehistoric times, then it's understandable that a Biblically attested 'cutter of stone' such as Joseph of Arimathea would have developed an interest in the monument, then travelled to see the quarry or holy mountain from which the stones came, taking his young nephew with him.

Alternatively, there are many references in the gospels to the Kingdom of Heaven, and Joseph of Arimathea himself is described as a man who was waiting for the Kingdom of God, so we can easily picture an exchange between Jesus and one of the ancient Britons he encountered, perhaps a senior Druid. If Jesus was ever asked the perfectly reasonable question, 'What are you seeking?' and he replied, 'The Kingdom of Heaven,' then, to his undoubted surprise, he may well have been immediately pointed towards a physical location.[17]

But what does this have to do with the Preseli Mountains? One of the most notable characteristics of the bluestone, which was also known as 'holy stone' in the west of England, is its appearance when freshly quarried. White flecks show up against a blue background and when you gaze at it, it's as if you're staring at the stars or the Milky Way encapsulated in stone. Nor is this a fanciful idea, because it's been put forward by Professor Timothy Darvill of Bournemouth University, an authority on Stonehenge,[18] who also suggests that the Preseli Hills were once the 'abode of the gods', which sounds very much like a 'Kingdom of the Heavens'. I also have it on good authority that the late Sir Arthur C. Clarke, when writing *2001: A Space Odyssey*, based his memorable concept of a monolith filled with stars on the Stonehenge bluestones.

Jesus certainly had a spiritual realm in mind when he spoke of the Kingdom of Heaven, but it's not difficult to see how a misunderstanding could have arisen that resulted in him travelling to a remote mountaintop in southwest Wales. If he was highly regarded by the Silures, then there's also every chance that he'd have visited their capital at some point, a place that the Greek geographer Ptolemy later called Bullaeum and which is now present-day Usk, while an earlier capital may have been the hill fort or 'high place' at Llanmelin.

Admittedly, this is all informed speculation that doesn't prove that

Jesus ever visited what's now Wales, although we've already noted one occurrence of the Holy Legend that placed him in Caerleon and we should also perhaps bear in mind the prehistoric iron ore mines at Clearwell, in what was once apparently the territory of the Dubunni but which is now Gloucestershire, just six miles away from Monmouth. However, this *does* show that even a legend as seemingly incredible as Mary visiting the region can make perfect sense if we place her son there some years beforehand. It makes even more sense if we take into account what we know of the Silures, the Biblical evidence for Joseph of Arimathea working in stone, his nephew's revered status and a simple misunderstanding between men from different countries concerning the precise meaning of the Kingdom of Heaven.

DÉJÀ VU?

If we're to be satisfied that we've conducted our investigation as thoroughly as possible, there's another question we must ask ourselves: is there any reference in the New Testament to Stonehenge? While examining this, we should bear in mind that there's a distinct difference between simply posing a question and actively trying to find something that may not be there. The New Testament is rich in imagery and there are frequent references to rocks, stones, high places and the like, but it would serve no useful purpose to try to see something that simply didn't exist. However, when we consider that the legends place Jesus within a day's walk of Stonehenge, far and away one of the most remarkable structures in the ancient world and one that was drawing people from across the continent as far back as 2300 BC, then it seems slightly *less* unlikely that the gospels could contain a veiled reference to the monument.

We can be virtually certain that the outer ring of sarsens and lintels was undamaged at the time that Jesus is said to have been in England, with the possible exception of a stone or two at the southwest, while the five huge trilithons inside were certainly standing. The ruins we see now have suffered an extra 2,000 years of weathering and vandalism, much of which has been recorded, so as far as Stonehenge's structural integrity is concerned, an observer at the time of Jesus would have seen a fairly intact monument. It's also worth bearing in mind that no one has ever discovered anything quite like it elsewhere; it's certainly unique, but it must remain a matter of personal opinion as to whether this suspended ring of elegantly dressed and curved stone atop the uprights could be described as beautiful.

What function would it have performed at the time of Jesus? We've already seen that it was virtually identical to the Cretan Labyrinth, that it also qualified as a Hall of Hewn Stones and that there's no question that it was intimately associated with death. It lies at the centre of a vast barrow cemetery, a huge amount of human remains have already been recovered from inside the monument itself and there may be still more in the unexcavated sections. Mediaeval accounts make it clear that great quantities of bone, some human, some animal, were found when early treasure-hunters dug there, so there are numerous convincing reasons for regarding it as a tomb, a sepulchre or a place of the dead. For many people, the ruins still possess a baleful aura and, as we saw earlier, if any place on Earth was ever haunted, it was Stonehenge, so it's hard to avoid the conclusion that it would have been perceived as a dark forbidding place, infested with evil spirits and other supernatural entities.

Do we have any idea about the physical appearance of Stonehenge in the early years of the first century, other than the fact that it was largely intact? Well, the oldest known name for Britain is Albion and we've already seen that the Land of the Albiones was known to seamen from the Mediterranean in or around 525 BC.[19] It seems beyond doubt that the name meant 'white', making Albion 'the Land of the White Ones', while around the time of Jesus, we read of Druids wearing white, especially when gathering an important plant called selago and when cutting mistletoe (a white plant) from an oak tree and dropping it into a white cloak before sacrificing white bulls beneath the white light of the moon.[20] If the stones of Stonehenge were ever decorated or painted for rare or important occasions, then the most obvious colour would have been white, and as Salisbury Plain is made up almost entirely of chalk, there would have been a limitless supply of material with which to make a primitive whitewash.

On the balance of probability, an inquisitive visitor to Stonehenge in the early first century AD would have seen an impressive circular monument that may well have been pleasing to the eye and there's a chance that it would have been coated in white. On closer inspection, it would have been apparent that it was a structure associated with the dead, if only on account of the many burial mounds surrounding it. It was certainly full of the bones of humans and animals from ages past, although more recent remains might have been in view, as opposed to being buried. If Jesus ever saw the place, the hewn stones that comprised the monument may have marked it out as unclean or polluted,[21] and the malignant heathen aura of spirits would have reinforced this notion.

Is there anything in the New Testament that remotely fits this description? One example immediately leaps to mind and it's an occasion when Jesus was taking the scribes and Pharisees to task for being hypocrites, on the grounds that they were 'like unto whited sepulchres, which indeed appear beautiful outward, but are within full of dead [men's] bones, and of all uncleanness'.[22]

It's certainly a colourful of turn of phrase that conveys a powerful message, but is there anything unusual about it? Or is it simply an observation based on an everyday sight in the Holy Land of the time?

Jesus refers to 'sepulchres' in the plural, so we must decide whether we regard the complex arrangements of stones at Stonehenge as one structure or many, while the original Greek, ταφοις κεκονιαμενοις (taphois kekoniamenois), translates as 'whitewashed sepulchres'. The implication seems to be that these places are full of the bones of dead men, but the original Greek doesn't specify this, because the words γεμουσιν 'οστεων νεκρων (gemousin osteon nekron) literally translate as 'filled with bones of the dead', which presumably means that the bones could belong to humans or animals or possibly both.

The customs of the times are something of a minefield because there seem to have been so many views of what was unclean, but it seems strange that Jesus should speak so forcefully of beautiful whitewashed sepulchres filled with 'all uncleanness' when he was singularly unconcerned by such base things, not least because he'd raised the dead, healed lepers and expelled a host of unclean spirits and demons from the man named Legion who lived among the tombs.[23] '*All* uncleanness' brings to mind a mesmerizing picture of a place where every last one of the Biblical abominations was practised, from unnatural congress with beasts to murder, allowing witches to live, raising the spirits of the dead and polluting stones by dressing them with chisels or hammers, all of which sounds far less like an ordinary tomb in the Holy Land and far more like a heathen structure purpose-built for Devil worship in some far-flung country at the edge of the world.

If nothing else, the 'whited sepulchres' expression is a vivid and highly memorable one, and it's just one example among many that demonstrates the phenomenal powers of oratory that Jesus possessed. We must ask ourselves if he acquired this fantastic skill while working as a carpenter for 30 years in Nazareth, or if it gradually came to him as a result of travelling and working among those famed for their oratory during those years of his life on which the Bible is apparently silent.

CHAPTER FOURTEEN

O Brave New World

*The Church says that the Earth is flat, but I know that
it is round, for I have seen the shadow on the Moon,
and I have more faith in a shadow than in the Church.*
Attributed to Ferdinand Magellan, 1480–1521

It's surely obvious that the so-called 'missing years' of Jesus constitute a vast, undiscovered country and we've barely scratched the surface of the subject. For example, Jesus is the second most revered prophet in Islam, yet we've only managed a glimpse of him as far as these venerable traditions are concerned, while the landscape and gaping swallets of Priddy remain largely unexplored, as do the tin mines of Cornwall.

We've examined the Druids in some depth, but even so, it's certain that a detailed study of these people could throw a great deal more light on the subject. In his *History of the English-Speaking Peoples*, Winston Churchill wrote:

The unnatural principle of human sacrifice was carried by the British Druids to a ruthless pitch. The mysterious priesthoods of the forests bound themselves and their votaries together by the most deadly sacrament than man can take. Here, perhaps, upon these wooden altars of a sullen island, there lay one of the secrets, awful, inflaming, unifying, of the tribes of Gaul.[1]

The idea that the Druids possessed a secret with the potency to lead whole nations in uprisings against the Roman invader would probably be laughed out of court were it not for this sombre and insightful observation by Winston Churchill, though the notion that it's perfectly possible to discover what this secret actually *was* is strictly taboo as far as the establishment of present-day scholars and archaeologists is concerned. Could an examination of the Druids and their conflict with Rome shed some further light on Jesus in Britain?

THE END OF THE DRUIDS?

Many archaeologists and scholars exhibit an almost pathological dislike of the British Druids, probably because when we look closely at the lives of these remarkable men and women, we experience the uneasy realization that they did indeed possess some highly potent secret, as Winston Churchill observed. Their existence and achievements hang like an impenetrable veil over great periods of British history and prehistory. There's also the uncomfortable fact that they were to all intents and purposes the Al-Qaeda of their time, inasmuch as they were an influential group motivated by religious ideals who took on a military superpower.

Regardless of whether or not that's a legitimate comparison, according to all standard histories the Druids were virtually exterminated by the Romans in AD 60 and any survivors merely eked out an existence as fortune tellers and magicians until the cult eventually faded into oblivion. However, given what we've uncovered so far, it's certainly worth looking at the apparent demise of the Druids more closely.

Julius Caesar described Britain as the place where Druidism originated and we know that the Druids' heartland was the Island of Mona, or present-day Anglesey, in northwest Wales. The legends place Jesus close to the domain of the Silures and it seems fair to assume that these people were followers of the Druids, and possibly of the war god Esus. A body of later legends states that Joseph of Arimathea returned to Glastonbury after the crucifixion of Jesus, but we've not examined these particular tales because our primary purpose has been to investigate any possible visit made to these shores by Jesus some years before. However, as all these visits are said to have been to specific locations close to the Druid heartlands, it seems perverse to assume that the Druids and their followers would have been anything other than well disposed towards Jesus, most likely because they were all in roughly the same business of opposing the Romans invading their lands. Whatever Joseph of Arimathea had to say about love and forgiveness or any other Christian practices when he eventually returned to Britain for good, it's not hard to picture the Druids and others being incensed to learn that the young man they'd revered and had had such high hopes for had been crucified by the Romans before he'd been able to fulfil his promise.

Does this shed any light on the apocalyptic battle fought between the Romans and the Druids on the Isle of Mona in AD 60? Let us look at what Tacitus has to tell us about this awesome confrontation:

> On the shore stood the opposing army with its dense array of armed warriors, while between the ranks dashed women in black attire like the Furies, with hair dishevelled, waving brands. All around, the Druids, lifting up their hands to heaven and pouring forth dreadful imprecations, scared our soldiers by the unfamiliar sight, so that, as if their limbs were paralysed, they stood motionless and exposed to wounds. Then urged by their general's appeal and mutual encouragements not to quail before a troupe of frenzied women, they bore the standards onwards, smote down all resistance and wrapped the foe in the flames of his own brands. A force was next set over the conquered, and their groves, devoted to inhuman superstitions, were destroyed. They deemed it, indeed, a duty to cover their altars with the blood of captives and to consult their deities through human entrails.[2]

It's something of an understatement to point out that there was obviously a great deal of ill-feeling on both sides here, not least because the Druids played a prominent role in the battle and because, whatever their 'dreadful imprecations' were, they were clearly giving vent to some extremely strong views. It's just possible that they bitterly resented the Romans having crucified one of their own, as they may have perceived Jesus, but it's unlikely we'll ever know. However, there may be slightly more to the matter, because around three to four years after the Romans annihilated the Druids, the emperor Nero launched his infamous attack on the Christian community in Rome. We learn some details of what the Christians suffered from Tacitus:

> Nero fastened the guilt and inflicted the most exquisite tortures on a class hated for their abominations, called Christians by the populace. Christus, from whom the name had its origin, suffered the extreme penalty during the reign of Tiberius at the hands of one of our procurators, Pontius Pilatus, and a most mischievous superstition, thus checked for the moment, again broke out not only in Judaea, the first source of the evil, but even in Rome, where all things hideous and shameful from every part of the world find their centre and become popular. Accordingly, an arrest was first made of all who pleaded guilty; then, upon their information, an immense multitude was convicted, not so much of the crime of firing the city as of hatred against mankind. Mockery of every sort was added to their deaths. Covered with the skins of beasts, they were torn by dogs and perished, or were nailed to crosses, or were doomed to the flames and burnt, to serve as a nightly illumination, when daylight had expired.[3]

The standard view is that Nero blamed the Christians for causing a huge fire in Rome, but Suetonius, another historian of the time, simply says, 'Punishment was inflicted on the Christians, a class of men given to a new and mischievous superstition,'[4] without so much as mentioning the fire. So, there's a good chance that both the Christians and the Druids were being punished by Nero simply on account of who they were, i.e. men and women belonging to a cult deemed to be dangerous to Rome. Their fates were similar, because Tacitus tells that when the Roman army defeated the Druids, they 'wrapped the foe in the flames of his own brands', and he goes into painful detail about the Christians being 'doomed to the flames and burned'.[5]

When we look more closely at the Druids and the early Christians, other coincidences emerge. As well as being cults that were savagely suppressed in a similar way by the same emperor just a few years apart, we learn from the Roman historian Pliny that '...it was in the time of the Emperor Tiberius that a decree was issued against their Druids and the whole tribe of diviners and physicians. But why mention all this about a practice that has even crossed the ocean and penetrated to the utmost parts of the earth?'[6] This business of a cult penetrating to the 'utmost parts of the Earth' sounds very similar to the matter of the apostles being ordered to spread the gospels to 'all nations'.[7]

Pliny also wrote, 'Therefore we cannot too highly appreciate our debt to the Romans for having put an end to this monstrous cult, whereby to murder a man was an act of the greatest devoutness, and to eat his flesh most beneficial.'[8] No one else ever accused the Druids of cannibalism and this specific act of ritually eating human flesh being thought of as greatly devout inevitably brings to mind the Last Supper and the occasion when Jesus said, 'Take, eat; this is My body which is broken for you; do this in remembrance of Me.'[9]

The Druids were also accused of devoting their groves to 'inhuman superstitions', while the Christians, at precisely the same time, were accused of practising 'abominations', two charges that sound suspiciously similar. Winston Churchill deliberately chose to describe the Druid practices as a 'sacrament', a word with obvious Christian associations.

In addition, there's the matter of the Druids claiming descent from a single heavenly father, the lack of worship of idols and all the other subjects we examined earlier. With all this in mind, it doesn't seem entirely out of the question that the Druids who resisted the Romans on the Isle of Mona in AD 60 or 61 had some links with or else possessed a memory of Jesus. It certainly strikes me as strange that the Druids of Mona, whose practices were so similar to early Christianity, should engage the Romans in a British version of Armageddon and that the other conflicts of a comparable ferocity during this time occurred between the Romans and the Silures in the region where the Eisu coins were found and between the Romans and the Iceni where the Aesu coins originated.

If the notion that a foreign priesthood such as the Druids could have had any form of secret allegiance to Jesus seems unthinkable, then we only have to look to the Biblical examples of Joseph of Arimathea and perhaps Nicodemus, who managed to conceal their allegiance far closer to home for a number of years. Given the horrors they'd survived, any Druids from Mona would have been extremely unlikely to broadcast their existence, let alone their religious secrets, to later Roman historians, but we must make of this what we will.

JESUS CHRIST IN WALES... AGAIN?

If there's any uncertainty about Jesus visiting the West Country and south Wales in the early years of the first century AD, there's no doubt whatsoever that someone of the same name was there, albeit briefly, some 1900 years later, and that his father was an Arch Druid.

In brief, Dr William Price was born in 1800 in Rudry in mid-Glamorgan, in south Wales. He was by any standards a truly extraordinary character who used to wander the hills of Wales naked in his youth, although in later years, when he styled himself an Arch Druid, he wore a foxskin as a headdress and took part in the failed Chartist Uprising of 1839. Despite these and other noted characteristics, such as being a vegetarian and going barefoot for his entire life, he was a highly accomplished and skilful doctor of medicine, but he's perhaps most famous for being the person responsible for making cremation legal in Britain.

This came about when, at the age of 83, Price fathered a son with his housekeeper, Gwenllian Llewellyn, who was aged 27. Sadly, the child died at the age of five months, at which point Price decided to cremate the infant rather than bury him, but he was prevented from doing so by a furious mob, who rescued the remains from the fire and repeatedly tried to lynch Price. He was described by one newspaper headline at the time as a 'pagan monster', then put on trial at Cardiff Assizes, but he successfully argued that there was nothing in law to prevent him cremating his son. After this ruling, cremation was practised in Britain for the first time in millennia, which is remarkable enough in itself, but for the purposes of our investigation, Price was responsible for something even more astonishing.

Price was fascinated by stone circles, antiquities, the history of Wales and Druidism; at his trial in Cardiff in 1884, he refused to swear on the Bible when he gave evidence, stating that he was 'under the protection of older gods'. He styled himself an Arch Druid and named his baby son Iesu Grist Ap Rhys, which is Welsh for 'Jesus Christ Price', because he believed that when the child grew to adulthood, he would reign over the Earth and restore the ancient Druidical system;[10] he also believed that the Biblical patriarch Abraham had been a cannibal, which is a curious observation in light of what we recently learned from Pliny about the Druids eating human flesh.

It may be that Dr William Price was deluded or insane, but his convictions were profound and there was certainly a great deal more to this unique man than the deeds that inspired the lurid headlines of the time. He was a fluent Welsh speaker and steeped in the lore of the old country, and his justification for naming his son Jesus Christ was that in ancient times the Druids chose whoever was to be the governor or king and called this person Mab Daw, 'the Son of God'. He claimed a Druidical descent that entitled him to name his son Jesus Christ, though the fact that his father was the Reverend William Price makes this lineage somewhat suspect and I must confess that I've found the greatest difficulty in following his reasoning from the material available. Nonetheless, it's curious that this remarkable man from south Wales should choose the name of Jesus Christ, of *all* names, to bestow upon his son, in the belief that doing this would ultimately reveal the lost wisdom of the Druids, not least because no apparent connection was made between Jesus and the Druids during the time that Dr Price was alive, even though William Stukeley had seen the cult as being a forerunner or cousin of Christianity.

Bearing in mind what we've seen about the original Jesus and a possible connection he may have had with horses, it's also odd to read what Gwenllian, the child's mother, had to say about her dead son:

There was on his back a most curious representation of a man on horseback, the horse being seen at full gallop. Even the reins and saddle could be plainly discerned. The mark first appeared when the child was about three weeks old.[11]

It's difficult to know exactly what to make of this bizarre episode, because while Dr William Price undoubtedly equated Jesus with the Druids, I've not been able to find any evidence that he was aware of a tradition placing Jesus in Britain 'in ancient time' other than in William Blake's poem. Nonetheless, when we cast around elsewhere in the same era, we find tantalizing suggestions of this apparent visit. We've already seen a part of the poem 'Stonehenge', written in 1823 by Thomas Stokes Salmon, that speaks of 'How, at midnight, by the moon's chill glance, unearthly forms prolong the formless dance...', but it continues:

> On wings of light Hope's angel form appears,
> Smiles on the past, and points to happier years;
> Points, with uplifted hand, and raptur'd eye,
> To yon pure dawn that floods the opening sky;
> And views, at length, the Sun of Judah pour
> One cloudless noon o'er Albion's rescued shore.

The renowned expert on Stonehenge Christopher Chippindale points out that the narrative of how 'the Christian dawn drives paganism away' in such verse is absolutely conventional.[12] This may well be so, but nonetheless, it's strange to read of such a notion in a verse entitled 'Stonehenge', which furthermore specifically describes a haunting in the ruins of Stonehenge.

The link between Christianity and Stonehenge is echoed in an 1842 painting by J. R. Herbert entitled 'The First Preaching of Christianity in Britain', where, as we might guess, a tonsured monk is accompanied by a young boy wielding a wooden cross as various heathen warriors and Druids kneel to receive communion or a blessing. These images are not so surprising, but this memorable event is unmistakably depicted as taking place directly beneath the lintels of Stonehenge, which begs the question why the artist should have thought that Stonehenge was *the very first place* in Britain where Christianity was taught.

A painting by Charles West Cope, another Victorian artist, carries an identical title and depicts a very similar scene, but on this occasion a group of Celtic warriors and Druids are seen struggling to plant a rough wooden cross in the ground where a hole has been dug specifically for the purpose. Nailed to the top of the cross is a sign reading *Iesus Hominum Salvator*, which is Latin for 'Jesus, the Saviour of Mankind', while a less than accurate but nonetheless perfectly recognizable Stonehenge sits atop a hill close by.

Why should both these artists have depicted the first preaching of Christianity as taking place at such a unique and instantly recognizable landmark? Although the latter painting depicts Stonehenge in an imaginary landscape next to the sea, a pit has been dug in the ground and two figures are sitting on what appears to be a large stone. Is there anything comparable in the real Stonehenge landscape?

In August 2007 I watched as archaeologists from the Stonehenge Riverside Project carefully excavated the area around the Cuckoo Stone, so called because it's a lone out-of-place megalith on a gently sloping hill just a mile or so northeast of Stonehenge itself. The archaeologists discovered Bronze Age artefacts there, but it was also clear that at some point during the Roman era, the place had come to be regarded as a kind of shrine on account of the coins that were found there. The way these coins were dispersed suggested that they'd been deliberately offered up for ceremonial religious reasons rather than being accidentally dropped or concealed as part of a hoard that had become scattered by later ploughing. A number of them were engraved in honour of Emperor Constantine, who's best known as the first Roman emperor to convert to Christianity and was proclaimed emperor while he was in Britain in AD 306. We can add these coins from the Stonehenge landscape to all the other intriguing legends, artefacts and places connected with early Christianity in Britain and consider them for what they're worth, but I doubt they'll be the last such discoveries to see the light of day.

CHAPTER FIFTEEN

I Am Legend

I am the master of my fate:
I am the captain of my soul.
'Invictus', W. E. Henley

Let us now look back at what we've learned so far, from the most obvious facts to those which perhaps weren't so immediately apparent.

Jesus is the most famous human being ever to have lived. He's the central figure in Christianity and the second most important prophet in Islam, so his influence simply cannot be overstated. In addition, there must be many millions of people the world over who think of themselves as 'cultural Christians', people who may not subscribe to the tenets of Christianity yet who enjoy attending carol concerts and nativity plays, not to mention harvest festivals and other occasions. With all this in mind, I find it shocking that no concerted attempt has been made to investigate the 'missing years' of Jesus, a period that surely constitutes the greatest enigma in human history.

There's no shortage of material indicating that Jesus visited Britain and we must ask if it provides us with a credible history that fits perfectly with the other known details of his life. It's also worth bearing in mind that everything we've discovered lies squarely in the public domain, not in some mysterious archive accessible only to initiates or a chosen few.

It'll simplify matters if we regard this evidence from a legal perspective, or from the point of view of a modern police officer diligently investigating a missing person's case. We'll examine any motive, means and opportunity that Jesus had for visiting Britain, we'll consider a possible alibi and the existence of an 'accomplice' and then we'll see if there are any signs of his passing in the area concerned. We'll also study what we know of his later life to see if anything in the New Testament suggests that he spent some time in the west of England in the early years of the first century AD.

MOTIVE

According to the Bible, Mary and Joseph fled to Egypt to safeguard their baby son from being murdered by King Herod. The appearance of a guiding star and the coming of the Magi had foretold that a baby had been born who would become the King of the Jews, so Herod eradicated any potential opposition by murdering all the young males in the region of Bethlehem in what came to be known as the Slaughter of the Innocents.[1]

Jesus came to prominence when he was 12 on account of his command of the scriptures, so even though the murderous Herod had died many years before, he would have come to the attention of others who had good reason to cut short the career of a potential Messiah, or King of the Jews. The most obvious candidates were the Romans, but as Jesus frequently came into conflict with the Sanhedrin, who ultimately caused his death, then it's unavoidable that as he got older he would have been viewed with increasing suspicion and resentment, not only by the occupiers of his land but also by others of his own kind. The most prudent course would have been for him to leave his homeland by slipping away on a ship from Tyre or Sidon. It matters little if he decided on this himself or if it was suggested and planned by others; either way, in the flight to Egypt there was an established precedent for him going to another country to escape persecution.

It's one thing for circumstances to have pressured Jesus into leaving his homeland to go elsewhere, but why would he have specifically chosen Britain?

There are likely to have been several reasons for this. The island's inhabitants would have been figures of admiration to nations who'd been subjugated by Romans, as the Britons had twice repelled invasions by Julius Caesar, in 55 and 54 BC. Caesar claimed to have conquered the British tribes he encountered and suggested that he'd have taken over the entire island had it not been for the fact that unrest in Gaul drew him away, but it's highly doubtful that this is how other people of the time would have viewed matters.

In the thriving ports of Tyre and Sidon, many other captivating mariners' tales of Britain and its inhabitants would have been circulating. The British priesthood of the Druids had been known of for centuries before Jesus was born and we have to ask what effect stories of these white-clad priests would have had on him, bearing in mind his intimate familiarity with the scriptures. The Druids claimed descent from a single heavenly father, they abhorred idols, they had great powers of oratory, they commanded respect, they were capable of halting armed conflicts between warring tribes, and much else besides, so these aspects and the fact that they were behind the successful resistance to the Roman invaders would have made them appealing and intriguing figures to a young man from Nazareth.

We've already looked at the links between the Phoenicians and the tin mines in Cornwall, which led Sir Edward Creasy to write that 'the British mines mainly supplied the glorious adornment of Solomon's Temple'.[2] If it's true that Hiram of Tyre created his stunning treasures of bronze for the Temple of Solomon with British tin, and if that was known, or even rumoured, in Jesus's time, then it could hardly have failed to have made a profound impact on him.

Many archaeologists maintain that Silbury Hill and Stonehenge were ignored by people in the early first century, but the Romans who arrived in Britain shortly after the time of Jesus had such an intense interest in the only British pyramid that they constructed a town the size of 24 football pitches at its base. Mary and Joseph had fled to Egypt, the land of pyramids, with their baby son to escape Herod, so if Jesus had heard tales of an artificial mountain or pyramid in Britain, then simple logic tells us that it would have intrigued him and made a favourable impression on him.

Excavations in early 2008 at Stonehenge uncovered Roman artefacts at the lowest levels of some of the pits dug there, indicating that the Romans altered the structure of the ruins, which also shows that they had more than a passing interest in the place. We know that people were drawn from continental Europe to Stonehenge as far back as 2300 BC, so it becomes impossible to avoid the conclusion that the fame of these mysterious ruins was widespread in distance and enduring in time. Whether Jesus heard Stonehenge described as a Druid meeting place, a symbol for national resistance against the Romans, a 'Hall of Hewn Stones', a temple of kings that drew down starlight, and/or a miracle of ancient engineering, it's certain to have caught his attention.

Another unique and accessible place that would have become known to a scriptural prodigy who was intimately familiar with the many Biblical laws concerning ritual bathing would have been the hot springs at Bath. These were the only such springs in Britain and the invading Romans transformed them shortly after their arrival, so it seems likely that the young Jesus would have heard of them too.

We've seen archaeological evidence that the earthworks at Priddy were in use at the time of Jesus, inasmuch as human remains were found buried at the entrance to at least one of the strange swallets, or entrances to the underworld. We know from the Roman historian Pomponius Mela that the Druids carried out ceremonies in caves, which makes it unavoidable that the British priesthood of the time was engaged in rituals in this area, most likely with the intention of contacting the dead, as they were said to believe that there was 'another life in the infernal regions'.[3] Did word of these activities ever reach the ears of Jesus, along with other stories of the strange island to the north? Given the sheer size of the Priddy Circles, the antiquity of the rituals carried out there and the prominence of the Druids at the time, it again seems far more likely than not.

The Romans commandeered the silver and lead mines in the Mendips just a few years after the invasion of AD 43, so we must ask if mariners' tales of these many physical wonders would have reached the eastern Mediterranean in the early years of the first century and the answer must surely be 'yes'. Silbury Hill, the mines in the Mendips, the Priddy Circles, Stonehenge and the hot springs at Bath were all in the same small area of a small island, just up the coast from the prized Cornish mines, so it seems inescapable that a young Jesus would have been fascinated not just by Britain as a whole, but by the specific area in which the later legends place him.

When we examined the probable career that Jesus followed, we discovered from the word τέκτων, or *tekton*, that he'd have been a stonemason, carpenter or general builder. The mines in the Mendips were in the territory of the Dubunni, an Iron Age tribe noted for their abilities as farmers and as craftsmen, so this is something else that an enterprising young man wanting to make a living as a carpenter or builder would have noted.

In ancient times, the Straits of Gibraltar were known as the Pillars of Hercules, but there's every possibility that someone of Jesus's background would have viewed these titanic landmarks from a Biblical perspective, as physical manifestations of the twin pillars sent by the Lord to guide the Jews out of exile and into the Promised Land. We've already seen a long list of aspects of Britain that would have made it appealing to Jesus, but the idea that this 'Promised Land' could be reached via twin pillars of smoke and flame is a compelling one.

Prophecies and their fulfilment played an important part throughout the life and ministry of Jesus, so Malachi's prophecy of the Messiah being a 'refiner of metals' may be yet another factor that influenced his decision to visit a land that provided the all-important tin. The second part of the Book of Isaiah speaks of isles afar off [4], the ends of the Earth trembling and a Messiah who was 'raised in the East',[5] while Isaiah also says of this Messiah, 'I have raised up one from the North and he shall come…'[6]

From the requirements of finding employment to admiring an island whose inhabitants had uniquely defied Julius Caesar to fulfilling one or more Biblical prophecies, there were so many alluring aspects to Britain that it's hard to see how Jesus could have *avoided* visiting the place.

MEANS

Jesus lived close to the eastern shore of the Mediterranean, whose northern region was known as Phoenicia. Five hundred years before he was born, a Phoenician mariner named Himilco sailed into the north Atlantic past Britain and probably into the North Sea, while at the same time, another Phoenician, named Hanno, sailed around Africa.[7] The port of Tyre and its supremely skilled mariners were so famous that the prophet Ezekiel devoted two whole books to complaining about how its inhabitants had mastered the seas everywhere, including the remark, 'When thy wares went forth out of the seas, thou filledst many people; thou didst enrich the kings of the earth with the multitude of thy riches and of thy merchandise.'[8] We know that Jesus visited Tyre at least once during his ministry[9] and also Sidon,[10] further to the north, so the means to travel to Britain by ship were readily available to him.

OPPORTUNITY

The opportunity for Jesus to visit Britain was available to him throughout his life up until the age of 30, so we have no fewer than 18 years, or nearly two decades, during which he could have found passage on a boat sailing for Britain.

LACK OF ALIBI

Jesus was absent from his homeland for so long that he eventually returned as a stranger, unrecognizable to many of those who should have known him best; at the same time, numerous legends and traditions place him in specific locations in the west of England, a place to which he would have been drawn and which he had both the means and opportunity of visiting.

If we were considering anyone else's whereabouts and weighing up a complete lack of evidence for them being in Location A against numerous credible reports of them being in Location B, we would conclude they were in Location B without a second thought. However, we've been culturally conditioned over millennia into visualizing the most famous person in history spending his entire life in the Middle East, despite the glaring lack of evidence for this scenario. The blunt fact is that Jesus disappears completely from the Middle East to reappear on the map and in the traditions of the west of England at precisely the same time that the Bible falls silent.

SIGNS OF HIS PASSING

Numerous legends place Jesus in the West Country, from the southernmost tip of Cornwall up to the Mendips and Glastonbury, and if there's any truth whatsoever behind the bizarre story of his mother being murdered in south Wales, he may also have visited the Preseli Mountains or 'the Kingdom of Heaven' in southwest Wales, as well as the settlements of the Silures tribe in present-day Usk and Llanmelin.

However, in addition to these stories of Jesus stepping ashore, visiting wells and mines and so forth, there are persistent and tantalizing suggestions of physical signs of his passing 'that yet survive, stamped in these lifeless things'.[11] Miners in the West Country spoke of the prehistoric artefacts they discovered in old mine shafts, while modern archaeologists believe the Priddy Circles could have been 'used for "hidden" ceremonies and/or deposition of artefacts'.[12] The remnants of the church that Jesus is said to have built to the memory of his mother Mary in Glastonbury supposedly survived for centuries and were believed to have originally been built by the 'hands of Christ himself',[13] which shows a strong belief that Jesus stayed in the region and constructed a place of worship that was largely intact and venerated long after he'd left.

Something intangible yet undeniably real is the atmosphere of serenity in the field adjoining Nine Barrows Lane in Priddy, which I suspect may be 'the Lord's Walk' mentioned by writers in the last century. We could argue that an unseen thing cannot constitute any kind of proof, but then we'd also have to deny the existence of the world-famous aura around Glastonbury and the mesmerizing quality that draws around one million people a year to visit Stonehenge.

There's also the famous edict against destroying British temples and the other writings mentioning the precepts of Christ being seen in Britain, which we might consider to be circumstantial evidence, along with the decisions of the four mediaeval Church councils which repeatedly ruled on the great antiquity of the British Church.

There are the legends of the second visit to Glastonbury by Joseph of Arimathea, stories which we've barely touched upon but which nonetheless carry the unavoidable inference that he was revisiting a location where he'd once spent time with Jesus.

The 'eternally to be lamented' loss of an inscribed tablet of tin discovered at Stonehenge during the reign of King Henry VIII might be relevant, given the proximity of these ruins to the places where Jesus is said to have stayed and the recurring link between Joseph of Arimathea and the tin trade. The Stonehenge landscape might yet yield other tangible suggestions that Jesus once visited the monument, but in the meantime we must consider the strange matter of King James I removing an altar stone from the ruins and we must ask ourselves why such a noted Christian scholar should take a relic from a place supposedly associated with the Devil to one of his palaces in London.

There are also the mysterious tunic crosses in Cornwall depicting what appears to be a young Jesus standing upright and wearing a tunic of sorts. The covers of some mediaeval Bibles are adorned with similar figures that might be described as ungainly in appearance, and while the Cornish crosses may have originally depicted a pagan god or gods, it's still curious that Cornwall should also be home to so many traditions of Jesus visiting the region when he was a young man.

Other remarkable artefacts are the Dubunni Eisu coins. The name on them is unmistakably reminiscent of Jesus, especially the Greek form of his name, Iesou, the form by which he was addressed. Could these coins have been minted in his honour? It's astonishing that someone by the name of Eisu should rise to prominence around AD 30 and that this Eisu should be living in the Mendips at precisely the same time that Jesus is said to have been there. I've not encountered a solitary archaeological or numismatic report that's so much as noted this stunning coincidence, because, like the matter of the hauntings at Stonehenge, the subject of Eisu in the Mendips in the early years of the first century AD is one that 'dare not speak its name'.

In addition to these physical signs that may indicate the passing of Jesus, we have numerous historical events to weigh up. One of these concerns the Silures, the primitive tribe who resisted the Romans with unbending ferocity for almost 40 years and whose territory was in such close proximity to the places where Jesus is said to have lived. Does this resistance indicate that they remained loyal to the memory of a revered visitor to their realm, someone they believed was the embodiment of armed resistance against the Romans? And does the premature capitulation of the Dubunni tribe indicate that there were notable individuals and structures in their territory that they wished to protect from the ravages of warfare against the Romans?

A similar train of thought occurs to us when we consider the Druids, the British priesthood that was never known to oppose Christianity. They conducted rituals in and around the strange underground chambers at Priddy, where the belief that Jesus once visited the place was so strong that it was enshrined in the saying 'As sure as Our Lord walked in Priddy'. What we know of the practices and customs of the Druids has much in common with Christianity and we have tangible evidence from the Pillar of the Sailors in Paris that they revered a young muscular carpenter named Esus. Rather than bow the knee to the Roman invader, the Druids and their loyal followers fought a war in which they faced annihilation on account of their apparently abominable beliefs, while the Romans meted out an almost identical punishment to the Christians in Rome shortly afterwards on the same grounds.

JOSEPH OF ARIMATHEA – AN 'ACCOMPLICE'

The role played by Joseph of Arimathea in facilitating Jesus's visit to Britain could hardly be clearer and we needn't look to any more exotic source than the New Testament for all the information we need. The gospels contain a mere 411 words in total on Joseph, so let's remind ourselves of the facts the ancient authors bequeathed to us:

When the even was come, there came a rich man of Arimathaea, named Joseph, who also himself was Jesus's disciple: He went to Pilate, and begged the body of Jesus. Then Pilate commanded the body to be delivered. And when Joseph had taken the body, he wrapped it in a clean linen cloth, and laid it in his own new tomb, which he had hewn out in the rock: and he rolled a great stone to the door of the sepulchre, and departed.[14]

Joseph of Arimathaea, an honourable counsellor, which also waited for the kingdom of God, came, and went in boldly unto Pilate, and craved the body of Jesus. And Pilate marvelled if he were already dead: and calling [unto him] the centurion, he asked him whether he had been any while dead. And when he knew [it] of the centurion, he gave the body to Joseph. And he bought fine linen, and took him down, and wrapped him in the linen, and laid him in a sepulchre which was hewn out of a rock, and rolled a stone unto the door of the sepulchre.[15]

And, behold, [there was] a man named Joseph, a counsellor; [and he was] a good man, and a just: (The same had not consented to the counsel and deed of them;) [he was] of Arimathaea, a city of the Jews: who also himself waited for the kingdom of God. This [man] went unto Pilate, and begged the body of Jesus. And he took it down, and wrapped it in linen, and laid it in a sepulchre that was hewn in stone, wherein never man before was laid.[16]

And after this Joseph of Arimathaea, being a disciple of Jesus, but secretly for fear of the Jews, besought Pilate that he might take away the body of Jesus: and Pilate gave [him] leave. He came therefore, and took the body of Jesus. And there came also Nicodemus, which at the first came to Jesus by night, and brought a mixture of myrrh and aloes, about an hundred pound [weight]. Then took they the body of Jesus, and wound it in linen clothes with the spices, as the manner of the Jews is to bury. Now in the place where he was crucified there was a garden; and in the garden a new sepulchre, wherein was never man yet laid. There laid they Jesus therefore because of the Jews' preparation [day]; for the sepulchre was nigh at hand.[17]

The first thing that leaps out at us is the fact that Joseph is a rich man, something spelled out by Matthew but also strongly inferred by Mark, Luke and John when they tell us about the purchase of the spices and fine cloths. Jesus made it clear that it was easier for a camel to pass through the eye of a needle than for a rich man to enter the Kingdom of Heaven, yet Joseph of Arimathea was described as someone waiting for the Kingdom of God. The obvious conclusion is that Joseph of Arimathea's wealth, or the means by which he acquired it, was of paramount importance to Jesus's life or ministry, so Joseph was exempt from the otherwise stern prohibition. Something about the nature of this wealth meant he could function perfectly well as a follower of Jesus for years yet not have to *relinquish* his wealth – at least, not during Jesus's lifetime or ministry.

Matthew tells us that Joseph of Arimathea excavated his own tomb, or else cut, quarried or mined the rock, which strongly suggests that his riches were derived from mining. The other gospels tell us that Joseph laid the body of Jesus in a new tomb, or one that hadn't been used, while John implies that Jesus was buried in this particular tomb because it was close at hand. Whichever way we look at it, Joseph of Arimathea must have *owned* this tomb, because if anyone else had done so, they would hardly have been best pleased to find their new sepulchre occupied by the body of a condemned criminal.

We asked earlier why Joseph of Arimathea went 'boldly' to Pilate, and concluded that this apparent audacity was borne of personal familiarity. We learned that Pilate's seat of residence was the thriving port of Caesarea Maritima and we reasoned that this was where Joseph and Pilate most likely became acquainted, thereby placing this wealthy man, whose riches were acquired through quarrying or mining, at a harbour on a coast famous for its connections with Britain in centuries past.

To this we can add the extreme likelihood that Joseph of Arimathea was a close relative of Jesus, on account of the fact that he was allowed to claim his body from the cross. Most traditions suggest that he was Mary's brother, so it comes as a shock to learn of a Church tradition that Saint Anne, Mary's mother (and, by inference, Joseph of Arimathea's mother as well) is the patron saint of miners.

John tells us that Joseph of Arimathea was a secret disciple of Jesus who feared the Jews, but why should he fear the Jews in general when he was one himself? This apparent fear didn't stop him from either voting against or abstaining from convicting Jesus. It didn't stop him from publicly asking Pilate for the body of a condemned criminal or collecting it from the cross and laying it to rest in a rich tomb.

Nothing suggests that Joseph of Arimathea was remotely frightened of the Jews, so the obvious solution is that he was engaged in some form of activity that the Jews wouldn't countenance. The one thing that the Jews of this period feared and loathed more than anything else was the possibility of their religion being contaminated by an outside source, so this suggests that Joseph of Arimathea was engaged in a pursuit that could be viewed as contaminating the Jewish beliefs by importing some kind of foreign element.

And what of the name 'Arimathea'? Luke describes it as a city of the Jews, while the only other reliable thing we know about it is that it may have been 'Ramata, where the pupils of the prophets reside',[18] which would make it a perfectly appropriate place for Joseph to be located in his capacity of a secret disciple of Jesus. Arimathea may possibly have been the 'Rama' where Rachel mourned her children,[19] but it's mistaken to automatically assume that Joseph was actually *born* there; for proof, we need look no further than the example of Jesus himself, who's invariably described as Jesus of Nazareth, despite the fact that he was actually born in Bethlehem.

Can we ascertain any other realistic translation or definition for Arimathea? Consulting *A Dictionary of the Names of Towns and Villages in Lebanon*, we immediately find that there's a consistent and unmistakable meaning to *ram* or *rum*, the basic root of the word 'Arimathea':

- *Rum* comes from *Rawma* (in Syriac), and means 'the elevated high place'.
- *Rumyana* means 'high elevation'.
- *Rumine* means 'plateau', 'elevated land'.
- *Rumyi* means 'hills', 'high places'.[20]

In Aramaic and Hebrew, Rama comes from *ram* and means 'high place', according to *Harper's Bible Dictionary*.[21] In the Lamsa Bible,[22] we read that 'there was a man named Joseph the counsellor of Ramatha, a city of Judea, a good and righteous man',[23] and this name too points towards Joseph of Arimathea being associated with a high place or places, and not necessarily one where he was born.

Perhaps the most interesting piece of information is to be found when we look at the ancient Phoenician language, bearing in mind the long association these ancient mariners had with the west of Britain and its tin mines. Here, too, *ram* or *rum* means 'high place',[24] so as Joseph of Arimathea became a rich man in the locality of a number of Phoenician ports, it's at least reasonable to consider his name as being a reference to a Phoenician high place, or a high place or places that the Phoenicians may once have travelled to.

We already know that the New Testament is littered with references to Jesus fulfilling all manner of Biblical prophecies and we're left to wonder if his life involved fulfilling *other* predictions, such as the Messiah being a 'refiner of metals' as mentioned by Malachi and the strange geographical locations that Isaiah spoke of, or if they were somehow deemed unimportant and left unfulfilled. If they were thought to be of any value, then it's not difficult to see how Joseph of Arimathea, a man described as a secret disciple in a gospel specifically pointing out that 'there were many other things that Jesus did', could have been instrumental in taking Jesus, one who was 'raised in the east' to the 'isles afar-off' where he could also have become 'a refiner of metals' and one who would go on to be 'raised from the north'.

Everything we know of Joseph of Arimathea tells us that he was involved in something that could have been interpreted as bringing an unwanted foreign influence into the Jewish religion. Whatever the precise nature of this business was, it was known to the author of the Book of John, who took pains to point out that Jesus had done a great many other things in addition to those mentioned in the New Testament.

Once Joseph of Arimathea had taken his nephew's body down from the cross and buried it in a tomb he'd personally dug, he vanished from the Biblical account, and it seems that he used his wealth to flee the anger of the Sanhedrin by sailing for one of the far-off isles to the north with which he was familiar. In so doing, he helped spread the word to 'all nations' and in giving up his home and wealth, he was able to see the Kingdom of Heaven.

WAS JESUS 'RAISED FROM THE NORTH'?

Remembering Dr Joseph Bell's dictum to be mindful of 'the vast importance of little distinctions and the endless significance of trifles', let's examine some of Jesus's characteristics to see if there's the remotest suggestion that he spent some time on an island in the north Atlantic.

State of Preparedness
From the beginning of Jesus's ministry right through until his death, he's consistently sure of his ground; there's no occasion when he has to retreat because he is mistaken, and his ministry has all the hallmarks of someone who's thoroughly prepared themselves for what's to come. His miracles are performed effortlessly, his speeches and parables are delivered with conviction, his judgements are sound and he's always ready to forcefully argue his point with even his most vociferous detractors. He returns to his homeland as a stranger, which suggests that he's spent a considerable time preparing his ministry in a country that is

sympathetic to him and conducive to such preparations, and there's no doubt that there was every reason for him to be welcomed and to feel at home in the West Country of Britain in the early years of the first century.

Command of Greek

It's virtually certain that Jesus spoke Greek, which was the common tongue in his homeland while he was alive; furthermore, the gospels, which were written in Greek, pointedly refer to the few occasions when Jesus lapsed into Western Aramaic. Caesar tells us that the Druids wrote using Greek letters, so it's hardly out of the question that the British priests of the time were able to speak Greek also. There were many other countries in which Jesus could have kept his knowledge of Greek alive, but the one place that he's consistently located in during his missing years is Britain.

Association with Women

Few would deny that a world in which Jesus's views on tolerance, brotherly love and forgiveness were observed would be a desirable place in which to live, but his treatment of women as equals, worthy of reverence and respect, was so revolutionary at the time that its repercussions have echoed down the centuries to the present day, causing controversy and heated debate the world over.

Perhaps the most striking example of how Jesus treated women can be found in the Gospel of Luke, where he healed a woman who'd suffered from infirmity for 18 years in a synagogue on the Sabbath day. The chief of the synagogue was outraged, but Jesus faced him down, rebuked him and shamed him, causing everyone else present to rejoice.[25] Not only that, but Jesus accepted women as full disciples, because a number of them travelled with him and his 12 male disciples during his ministry.[26]

As his behaviour toward women was considered so remarkable at the time, it's reasonable to assume that Jesus developed this reverence for women in a country other than his own, and it's also reasonable to assume that this took place at some point during his missing years. A number of ancient writers tell us how women held equal status to men in Britain of the first century and there's every chance that the Druids accepted women into their ranks, as we saw in Tacitus's description of the Roman assault on the Isle of Anglesey in AD 60.

At the same time, a British queen named Cartimandua ruled the warlike Brigantes tribe, while Boadicea or Boudicca roused the Iceni and other tribes in an apocalyptic revolt against Roman rule, and the reason for this insurrection was the inhuman treatment meted out to Boadicea and her two daughters by the Romans. The women in Britain were far removed from the cowed and servile creatures in the New Testament, so their status would have made an enormous impression upon a young man from the East. This doesn't prove that Jesus visited Britain and adopted the natives' reverence for their womenfolk, but he's unaccounted for in his homeland during the formative years of his life and a mass of other evidence places him firmly in Britain in the first century, when Cartimandua and Boadicea were held in such esteem by their people.[27]

Oratory

Luke's gospel tells us that Jesus's parents found him in the temple in Jerusalem and that 'all that heard him were astonished at his understanding and answers',[28] but there's a great difference between a young boy discoursing in a learned fashion in a temple and a grown man addressing 'great multitudes'[29] in the open air. A powerful physique would help when projecting one's voice to such a gathering and it's not hard to imagine that Jesus could have acquired such a frame if he had worked as a carpenter; if he had been engaged in other strenuous work such as mining, then the chances are that his build would have been even more powerful.

However, a skilled orator not only possesses the capacity to make themselves heard, but also the ability to deliver a lengthy speech that will keep an audience engaged. The Koran tells us that Jesus was able to speak as a baby,[30] but the ability of a baby to speak is still not the same as the ability of a grown man to address great multitudes and make himself heard and understood.

No ancient author specifically tells us that the Druids were orators, but Caesar records that they habitually spent 20 years memorizing verse, officiated at the worship of gods and regulated public sacrifices,[31] so it's fair to assume that they could deliver speeches to large crowds. Cicero, Strabo and Pomponius Mela suggest the same thing, while Tacitus puts lengthy speeches into the mouths of Caratacus, Boadicea and Calgacus as they rallied their troops before doing battle with the Romans. Whether or not these leaders delivered the precise words later attributed to them is by the way, but it at least shows that they were capable of delivering such speeches to huge armies.

The existence of skilled orators in first-century Britain doesn't prove that Jesus visited the place, because he could have acquired this ability elsewhere, but it does appear that at some point between the ages of 12 and 30 he acquired formidable skill as a public speaker and the only place in which he's consistently located during this time is Britain.

Exercise of Judgement

Throughout Jesus's ministry, he was constantly faced with religious problems and moral dilemmas, but he was never once caught out, nor is there any record that he ever had to retreat to think matters through after being found wanting.

Again, it's one thing for a 12-year-old prodigy to amaze everyone with his understanding of holy texts, but quite another for an adult to be confronted with situations involving heated passions, deeply held beliefs or prejudices and large groups of hostile people, often in positions of power. It's next to impossible to learn how to deal successfully with such scenarios from a textbook, should one even exist, so it stands to reason that Jesus became a seasoned and learned judge of these things during his missing years.

Again, when we look to the Druids, we're struck by the unambiguous and glowing references to their ability to pass judgment. For example:

The Druids officiate at the worship of the gods, regulate public and private sacrifices, and give rulings on all religious questions. Large

221

> numbers of young men flock to them for instruction, and they are held in great honour by the people. They act as judges in practically all disputes, whether between tribes or between individuals; when any crime is committed, or a murder takes place, or a dispute arises about an inheritance or a boundary, it is they who adjudicate the matter and appoint the compensation to be paid and received by the parties concerned.[32]

> The Druids are considered the most just of men, and on this account they are entrusted with the decision, not only of the private disputes, but of the public disputes as well...[33]

I've read a great deal of speculation that Jesus went to Britain in search of 'Druid wisdom', but unless we know what this wisdom was, it's difficult to have an informed opinion. We can think of wisdom as common sense or we can think of it as a repository of knowledge concerning language, mathematics, medicine or some other subject. Jesus was clearly not short of skilled teachers in his own land, so it's hard to see that he would have gone to Britain to learn *anything*, although he may have been intrigued by precisely how the Druids held such powerful sway over their people. However, once he was there, he'd have found himself in the company of highly respected men and women who were able to arbitrate on passionate disputes that arose among some extremely warlike people, so it's difficult to imagine a better environment in which he could hone his skills as a judge.

Melting Unharmed through Crowds

Jesus possessed a striking ability to make his way through teeming crowds without difficulty, such as when a hostile gathering tried to hurl him from a cliff early in his ministry.[34] Diodorus Siculus and Strabo tell us that the Druids could walk between tribes drawn up on the field of battle and stop the combatants from fighting;[35] this may not be exactly the same thing that Jesus was capable of doing, but it's close enough.

The Romans took over 40 years to subdue the British tribes, so the Druids must have possessed some very special qualities to be able to intersperse themselves between fired-up groups of proud warriors without coming to harm. Diodorus Siculus[36] adds the fascinating detail that the opposing armies were sometimes held 'spellbound', a term that brings to mind the supernatural ability Jesus had to have possessed in order to pass quietly, unscathed and unnoticed, through the very people who'd just dragged him out of a synagogue and up a hill to throw him off a cliff. Of course, it's possible that Jesus may have acquired this ability elsewhere, but again the only country he is reliably placed in during his missing years is Britain and it seems certain that British Druids would have possessed the same abilities as those of their counterparts in Gaul.[37]

Association with High Places

Jesus displayed a marked preference for going to high places for the purposes of prayer, solitude, finding repose or performing miracles such as the Transfiguration. The Gospel of John tells us that he attended a high place prior to performing three miracles, which were the feeding of the 5,000, walking on water and calming a storm.[38] Jesus's only secret disciple, Joseph of Arimathea, is inextricably linked with high places by virtue of his name, while Jesus was openly accused at the beginning of his ministry of being in league with Beelzebub, the Lord of the High Place.[39]

There are many regions where Jesus may have acquired his preference for visiting high places during his missing years, but again, the only country in which he is consistently located during this time is Britain. Furthermore, he is located at some prominent high places there, such as Glastonbury, Priddy and the Mendip Hills, while the other notable high places of Silbury Hill, Stonehenge and the Preseli Mountains were within very easy reach.[40]

The Harrowing of Hell

The Bible is extremely vague about what's become a Christian myth of Jesus descending to hell, but numerous legends place him in Priddy in the early years of the first century AD. The curious limestone shafts around the earthworks at Priddy were in use as ceremonial entrances to the underworld from the Bronze Age right through to the time of the Roman occupation of Britain, and the ability of these shafts to suddenly open up without warning bears a marked resemblance to what Jesus would have learned about Sheol, the Jewish underworld. In the ancient world, many locations were thought of as entrances to the underworld, but once again, the only place where Jesus is consistently located during his 'missing years' is the west of England, where Priddy lies.

Healing

The ability to cure a wide variety of ailments, including leprosy, blindness, infirmity, withered hands and others, was another notable aspect of Jesus's ministry. I must confess that I don't have the faintest idea how someone can acquire an ability such as this, but as there's no mention of Jesus healing prior to the age of 12, then we must assume that he either acquired or was granted this gift at some point during his missing years.

In early 2008, the BBC and the Smithsonian Museum funded an excavation of Stonehenge, concentrating on a story that Geoffrey of Monmouth had told in the twelfth century, namely that the stones that went into building the monument had once possessed healing properties. A short distance to the northwest of Stonehenge, Bath was renowned for the curative powers of its waters, while south Wales in particular had many healing wells and springs.

Banishing Unclean Spirits

Jesus's ability to heal was impressive enough, but there's no doubt that he was the greatest exorcist the world has ever known. There are many examples of him driving out unclean spirits, perhaps the most famous one involving the man who gave his name as Legion,[41] while there are also numerous accounts of unclean spirits appearing to him.[42] Jesus seems to know a great deal about them, because he tells his disciples that unclean spirits or demons specifically seek waterless places for rest once they have been driven out of their human hosts.[43]

As Pomponius Mela informs us, the Druids believed in another life in the infernal regions, and we have the physical remains and the contents of the swallets in the Mendip Hills to attest to this, as well as the disturbing noises that emanate from these fearsome shafts into the underworld.

As for other prehistoric hauntings that would have infested the land-scape at the time of Jesus's visit, we have the monstrous barrow guardian that terrified the man who saw it at the Hangley Cleave barrows in Somerset in 1908. We also have the hostile Bronze Age horseman at Bottlebush Down who was sighted by an eminent archaeologist who had excavated at Stonehenge in the first part of the last century.

Dartmoor in Devon, not that far away, is a huge elemental wilder-ness covered with the remains of prehistoric structures such as Chaw Gully, an ancient tin mine that's also known as 'the Roman mine'. This foreboding abyss cutting through a prehistoric stone avenue has long been regarded as cursed, but the whole of Dartmoor possesses a savagery and a reputation for malevolent hauntings such as the Wild Hunt, where phantom horsemen or demonic figures scour the land for victims. The leader of the Wild Hunt was often thought to be the pre-Roman god Cernunnos, meaning 'the Great Horned One', whose image and name can be seen on the Pillar of the Boatmen along with that of the axe-wielding Esus.

This Wild Hunt was also known as Herod's Hunt in France in mediaeval times,[44] as Herod was supposed to be in search of 'Holy Innocents' or male children who might become King of the Jews. There's a strong suggestion that it was also known as Herod's Hunt in the West Country,[45] while in Cornwall, where there are so many stories of Jesus as a young man, we learn that Holy Innocents' Day was considered particularly unlucky by mothers.[46] The explanation given for this is that monstrous characters such as Herod had been cursed by their sins and were doomed to repeat their evil acts until the Day of Judgement. And yet it's still curious to find a king from the ancient Middle East who'd driven Jesus and his family into exile in another country reappearing in northern Europe, another region where Jesus is said to have travelled as a young man.

There are many other inimical hauntings in the west of England, some of which would have been active during the first century. It's as well to bear in mind the haunted Bronze Age barrow at Wick Moor, whose malevolent reputation was so potent that the builders of a modern nuclear power station, Hinkley Point B, fenced it off and left it alone rather than destroy it and risk disaster in 1967. Glastonbury, where legends locate Jesus, has long been thought of as an entrance to the underworld, but the most demon- and ghost-infested location of them all in the early first century has to be Stonehenge. It's apparent that any resident supernatural entity there would have held the title of 'Lord of the High Place' and Jesus was accused of being in league with just such an entity at the beginning of his ministry.

So, Jesus may have been divinely granted the ability to drive out unclean spirits or it may have been a skill he acquired over time. There's no mention of it up until the age of 12, but as his mastery over these supernatural entities was a striking aspect of the early days of his ministry, it stands to reason that he somehow acquired the power to drive out unclean spirits during his missing years, and it's hard to find a better place where he could have exercised this ability than in the west of England, which is where the legends consistently locate him.

A Seasoned Mariner

The New Testament tells us about Jesus's familiarity with boats, water, fishermen and the people who lived in the region of Tyre and Sidon. The most striking example of Jesus as a seasoned mariner has to be the fact that he could actually *sleep* through a storm that terrified everyone else on board to the extent that they thought they were going to die,[47] and these were men who were presumably familiar with the rough conditions. We have to ask how Jesus could have become so comfortable on water; the obvious answer is that he'd spent a considerable time aboard a ship in far worse weather than that which he encountered on a lake in his homeland.

There are many voyages he could have embarked upon, but the fact remains that there are numerous legends of him arriving by boat in the west of England. This voyage had been successfully accomplished by Phoenician sailors at least 500 years before he was born, so the notion is a perfectly feasible one and it would furthermore explain his familiarity with extremely hostile weather conditions on board a seafaring vessel.

As we have seen, a curious tradition says that his mother Mary was killed in south Wales and her most prominent official title is *Stella Maris*, 'Star of the Sea', someone who protected and guided mariners through inhospitable or unfamiliar waters.[48]

The Bearing of a King

Jesus was proclaimed as a king by the Magi, but the gospels don't record any sign or intimation of him possessing a kingly bearing by the age of 12. He preached a message of love and forgiveness throughout his ministry, something that's reinforced our image of 'gentle Jesus, meek and mild', yet when he met Pontius Pilate and the Roman governor asked him if he was a king, the tone of the gospels makes clear that Pilate wouldn't have been remotely surprised if Jesus had given an affirmative reply, while a sign was posted above him on the cross spelling out that he was the King of the Jews.[49]

Jesus's bearing at his trial is identical to Tacitus's description of the Silures tribe of south Wales, a people upon whom 'neither terror nor mercy had the least effect'.[50] The legends about Jesus in Britain place him on land directly adjoining that of the Silures and just a short boat ride away from it, and also within a mere 30 miles or so of Stonehenge, the monument that was partly built with stone that came from or passed through the domain of this fearsome tribe. However, there's yet another possible link between Jesus and the Silures that could have contributed to Jesus's perceived status as a royal.

In or around 350 BC, the Greek mariner Pytheas of Massilia became the first person we know of to visit Britain and leave a written record of his time there. His account now only exists in fragments, but he spoke of seeing an unusual and remarkable temple, and what he had to say is worth reproducing in full:

> And there is also on the island both a magnificent sacred precinct of Apollo and a notable temple decorated with many offerings... spherical in shape [and] a city is there which is sacred to this god...

> and the kings of this city and the supervisors of the sacred precinct
> are called Boreades, since they are descendants of Boreas...[51]

This is a subject that I've looked into in great detail elsewhere[52] and it long ago became clear that no other structure of the time comes close to fitting the description that Pytheas gave, although Stonehenge does so in every respect. One reason for this is because Pytheas speaks of a city which, by clear implication, lies close to this remarkable temple and the word he used was πολις, or *polis*, which can describe anything from a small settlement to a large city such as Athens or Rome. The Iron Age hill fort now known to us as Vespasian's Camp fits the description perfectly, because we know that it was occupied during the time of Pytheas's visit, and no other structure remotely resembling 'a notable temple... spherical in shape' has anything like a city of the times nearby.

It's satisfying enough to be able to point to the location of a lost city and, furthermore, one in the vicinity of Stonehenge, but Pytheas's account contains something of even greater interest. He says, 'The kings of this city and the supervisors of the sacred precinct are called Boreades, since they are descendants of Boreas...'[53] Boreas was the Greek god of the North Wind, but when we look into the matter further, we find that he's described as being dark and baleful with shaggy hair, of great physical strength and possessing a violent temper, characteristics that tally with what we know of the Silures. It seems at least possible that the kings of Stonehenge who were supposed to be descendants of Boreas were men of the Silures, and the link is strengthened by the fact that the Stonehenge bluestones originated so close to their territory.

When we ponder the characteristics that Jesus may have acquired during a stay in Britain, each one is food for thought, or a talking point. When we consider them as a whole, they constitute a formidable body of evidence, and when we also consider Jesus's powerful motives for visiting Britain, his ready means, his gaping window of opportunity, his well-placed 'accomplice' and the abundant signs of his passing, it becomes increasingly futile to cast around for a remotely credible alternative to the notion that William Blake was accurate to a fantastic degree and that the most famous human being who has ever lived spent his formative years in what's now the west of England and south Wales.

There's no doubt that when William Blake wrote of 'dark, satanic mills', he was referring to Stonehenge, because the poem for which 'Jerusalem' was written as a preface contains several pictures of trilithons and megaliths in amongst references to 'starry Mills of Satan' and the like. Blake also created illustrations for the Book of Job and, in one, a Stonehenge trilithon replaces a cathedral and the figure of Satan is seen swooping over this unique structure. As if this weren't enough, Blake also wrote about Stonehenge in the poem *Milton*, mentioning 'unhewn demonstrations in labyrinthine arches'. As far as I'm aware, he is the only person ever to describe Stonehenge as 'labyrinthine' apart from Professor Richard Atkinson, who implied as much in his book on the ruins.

This still isn't the end of the matter, though, because Blake also described two of the sarsens at Stonehenge as 'frowning', something that no one else had ever done, which is truly remarkable when we consider the discovery in 1999 of what's been described as a 'frowning face' on one of the sarsen uprights. If Professor Terence Meaden, who first noticed this face, is correct, then this countenance had gone unnoticed by anyone for around 1,000 years, with the possible exception of William Blake.

The implications of all this are astonishing, but before we examine them we must address what are apparently two extremely tough questions, the trump cards played by those who dismiss the notion that Jesus once visited Britain.

CHAPTER SIXTEEN

The Sound of Silence?

The best lack all conviction, while the worst
are full of passionate intensity.
W. B. Yeats, 'The Second Coming'

The first question is this: if the belief existed in mediaeval times that Jesus had visited Britain and Glastonbury, why didn't the supposedly mercenary monks at Glastonbury announce it to the four winds? Or, in the words of the British historian and author Geoffrey Ashe, 'What is morally certain is that if the belief had existed in the Middle Ages... Glastonbury's monks would have exploited such a stupendous claim. They never even hint at it.'[1]

Very well, let's see if this categorical statement is as incontestable as it appears. In 1184, a great fire destroyed the buildings at Glastonbury and many of the books there were lost,[2] so any written account of a visit by Jesus or Joseph of Arimathea is likely to have gone up in smoke, but this catastrophe alone can't explain why the monks of Glastonbury never spoke of Jesus visiting the place in which they resided. So, let's try to visualize the outcome if one of their number *had* done so.

It's very hard to see how any one of them could have stood to gain from voicing the claim that Jesus had once stayed in Glastonbury, although there were plenty of suggestions from earlier Church writers that something like this had happened. During what we'll broadly call the Middle Ages (AD 500–1500), the gospels had been in existence for centuries and despite the glaring omission of 18 years of Jesus's life, there seems to have been no ecclesiastical desire to find out where he'd been. It must have been obvious to anyone with an ounce of sense, however, that there was ample opportunity and ready means for him to have visited Britain.

It's perfectly reasonable to accept that Jesus could have been drawn to Britain to find sanctuary from the Roman threat and a sympathetic environment in which he could formulate his ministry and hone his skills in oratory, judgement, healing and exorcism before returning home to fulfil his destiny; after all, his cousin John the Baptist had done something very similar by disappearing into an unspecified wilderness at around the same time. However, the subtleties of this would certainly have been lost on any senior mediaeval churchman. If Jesus *had* visited Glastonbury, the reasoning would have gone, there would be a clear record of it in the Bible and his mere presence would have converted the whole island. As for any suggestion that Jesus could have *learned* anything from the Britons, no less a personage than Pope Gregory the Great had made it abundantly clear that Britain was a literally God-forsaken hell-hole at the tail end of the known world whose primitive inhabitants had become heathen idolaters and Devil worshippers to a man.

The Middle Ages weren't conspicuous for their tolerance as far as matters of religion were concerned, one particularly brutal example being the Albigensian Crusade that began in 1209, lasted for around 20 years and was responsible for the deaths of around one million unfortunate souls in the south of France. During this time, the Fifth Crusade (1217–21) was launched with the aim of retaking Jerusalem, so we have to ask what the Albigensians had said or done to merit being ranked alongside the Saracens of the Holy Land and singled out for extermination. The heretics in question were Cathars, whose most sacred text was the Gospel of John, and one of their unforgiveable sins was to regard Jesus as a physical manifestation of a divine spirit. This seems reasonable enough given the nature of his birth and pronouncements such as 'I am the light of the world',[3] but fine theological distinctions were lost on the Church authorities, who waged a truly merciless war on the Cathars.

With this cautionary example in mind, it would have taken a very brave or incredibly stupid person to stand up and profess that Jesus had once visited Britain, then argue the case that he'd not only lived in harmony with the barbaric natives but had actually learned a thing or two from them and had otherwise benefited from his stay in the back of beyond before departing for home without having apparently converted a single ancient Briton.

Apart from this, are we to suppose that the monks at Glastonbury were utterly mercenary? It's impossible to measure the atmosphere that a location possesses, but Glastonbury is undeniably endowed with an aura of mystical serenity. It's long been said to be the Isle of Avalon, where King Arthur was taken to recover from his wounds, so it's a fair guess that it has possessed 'the beauties of nature', as St Augustine described it in the sixth century, for a very long time indeed, and it's perfectly possible that any monks at Glastonbury who were in on the secret considered themselves truly blessed and chose to luxuriate in the uniqueness of their surroundings rather than risk ruining their idyll by being accused of heresy.

As we have already learned, the four Church councils of Pisa in 1409, Constance in 1417, Sienna in 1424 and Basle in 1434 all agreed that the Church of Britain was founded by Joseph of Arimathea immediately after the passion of Christ. With this resounding vote of confidence behind them, why even bother to tempt Fate and try to go one better by claiming that Jesus had actually *visited* Glastonbury? Around 1240, the Glastonbury monks were openly saying that Joseph of Arimathea had settled there with 12 disciples in AD 63 and had built the old church,[4] which was a prestigious claim by *any* standards and more than enough to keep everyone happy.

We might suppose that Glastonbury sought to emulate its 'founding father' by becoming rich, as it undoubtedly was, but the other most notable aspect of Joseph of Arimathea was that he was Jesus's only secret disciple (Nicodemus possibly being one by inference). The original

Greek word used to describe Joseph of Arimathea's secret status was κεκρυμμενος, or *kekrummenos*, which could mean that Joseph chose to conceal himself or that others concealed him, but either way, the principal element is one of secrecy or concealment. The Glastonbury monks were not 'Arimatheans' in the sense that other orders such as the Franciscans, Cistercians and even Templars strove to adhere to the guiding principles of their respective founders, but if they were likely to follow *any* guiding principle, simple logic tells us that it would have been secrecy, particularly as far as their links with Jesus were concerned. Joseph of Arimathea never so much as hinted at his secret links with Jesus, so we shouldn't realistically expect the Christian monks of Glastonbury to have done so either.

Otherwise, we might well think it 'morally certain' that the author of the Gospel of John would've provided us with at least a hint of the many other things that Jesus did, but he didn't, so if he felt precluded from speaking out on this subject, then it's perfectly understandable if the Glastonbury monks followed his example.

THE TELL-TALE HEART

What I give form to in daylight is only one per cent of what I have seen in darkness.

M. C. Escher

Finally, we might well think it 'morally certain' that if a distinguished professor of archaeology were charged with excavating the most mysterious prehistoric monument on Earth, he would conclude his investigations in a blaze of glory and would be proud to present every last detail he had discovered to a global audience yearning for an insight into the ruins, but this was very far from being the case.

Professor Richard Atkinson began digging at Stonehenge in 1950 and continued until 1964:

And yet over all those years Atkinson analyzed and published but a bare fraction of what he dug up. When you excavate a 4,000-year-old deposit, you destroy it. It is as if you have an old manuscript, of which only one copy survives. As you read the pages, you rip them up. If you don't quickly pass on the story, your memory becomes the only record. Then you find another manuscript, read and rip up; and another, and another, until the plot of one mixes with the argument of the next. You lose it. What's more, Atkinson made it difficult for students to access records of excavations [at Stonehenge] in the 1920s by William Hawley, also not fully published, that were far larger and more important than his own...[5]

In 1995, English Heritage published a history of the excavations at Stonehenge during the twentieth century[6] and this colossal volume included the information that had been provided by Atkinson's excavations. One reviewer noted that the book's authors had been 'careful not to be judgmental', but added, 'We on the other hand are perhaps entitled to make judgements... in addition to "scandalous", the adjectives "incompetent" and even "immoral" spring to mind.'[7] In addition, Atkinson and his former colleague Stuart Piggott tried to interfere with the successful completion of the English Heritage history of excavations at Stonehenge, so this sorry tale is as good an example as any of how moral certainty can unhappily end in an accusation of immorality instead.

It's sorely tempting to join the growing chorus of condemnation of Atkinson, but in all fairness, I've personally witnessed far worse neglect of Stonehenge-related information and artefacts by senior archaeologists long after Atkinson's shortcomings were exposed, yet those responsible for these shameful practices have been allowed to continue on their merry way with utter impunity. Be that as it may, it's worth looking at Atkinson's behaviour, because our attempts to trace the footsteps of Jesus strongly suggest that this young man from the East once visited the very same ruins on Salisbury Plain in which the profoundly religious Professor Atkinson immersed himself 2,000 years later.

Whatever faults Atkinson possessed, he wasn't stupid. He was frequently filmed at Stonehenge and at Silbury Hill, another unique prehistoric monument that he excavated in 1968 with ultimately unhappy results, so he was fully aware of the intense worldwide interest in the monuments he was investigating. He must have realized with stark clarity that his failure to record and pass on the irreplaceable information he'd acquired would one day result in the loss of his professional reputation; nonetheless, he persisted in his chosen course and took whatever secrets he'd gleaned from Stonehenge to the grave with him. Why? Why on Earth should such a man embark on such a seemingly futile, irrational and destructive course of action?

Atkinson was a Quaker of such religious conviction that he possessed the moral courage to be a conscientious objector during World War II, a principled stance that often met with ridicule, contempt and hostility from others. He was in the privileged position of being allowed to excavate at Stonehenge for 15 years and he wrote a book on the ruins in 1956 that has been reprinted several times over the years, the later editions not being notably different from the original.[8] The book contains much detail, including the passing observation about the Labyrinth we noted earlier, although nowhere near as much as it could have done.

One of Atkinson's colleagues was Professor Stuart Piggott, author of a highly regarded book on the Druids,[9] so it's certain that the well-educated Atkinson was extremely familiar with these ancient British priests and their methods, and he may well have been aware of Winston Churchill's observation about some terrible secret they possessed. If, by some miracle, the ancient British Druids weren't quietly discussed over the course of 15 years spent digging at Stonehenge with Stuart Piggott, then the regular presence of latter-day Druid orders at the ruins simply cannot fail to have concentrated Atkinson's mind on the matter.

Why did Atkinson keep silent about what he'd seen at Stonehenge? Logic suggests it was because he'd found something that he coveted, hated or feared. Given that he had written a manual for field archaeologists, we can rule out the idea that he may have thought his information was of no worth to anyone.

I've read an explanation for Atkinson's shortcomings that suggests he was overworked, on the grounds that an excavator of his time was expected to 'produce unassisted, in his own time, the results of his work'.[10] This idea's patently nonsense, because Atkinson was in charge of the excavations throughout, so it was entirely down to him to keep pace with the digging and to record the results. An archaeologist's job isn't just to dig holes, something that hundreds of thousands of gardeners and unskilled labourers the world over do every day, but to methodically record what they find as soon as is humanly possible. We might reasonably think that if Atkinson was lagging behind after the first season's digging, he'd have caught up before starting again, but he didn't.

If Atkinson found something that he coveted, he may have reburied it at a later date, because he was seen digging holes around Stonehenge as late as 1978.[11] If the thought of a respected archaeologist 'accidentally' removing finds from Stonehenge, of all places, sounds wildly unlikely, then I'd simply point out that a mass of relics from Stonehenge that were 'collected' by William Hawley in 1921 appeared for sale on eBay in 2006 and I know of other Stonehenge-related artefacts that have mysteriously 'gone missing' or been similarly mistreated far more recently than 1921. Atkinson wouldn't have been the first archaeologist to appropriate something that had caught his eye and he certainly won't be the last. If he did remove something from Stonehenge and later reburied it, then there's a good chance it's still there.

The idea that Atkinson hated something he saw or discerned at Stonehenge might seem inappropriate or just plain wrong, but there's firm evidence that this was precisely the case. In 1958, during restoration work at Stonehenge, Atkinson was nearly killed by a stone when a crane's safety mechanism malfunctioned,[12] something that's hardly likely to have endeared the place to him. He was also constantly asked what the monument was and why it was built, but he was unable to supply a definitive answer. I've personally worked with archaeologists who are intensely irritated by Stonehenge for the same reason: it's arguably the best-known prehistoric monument in the world and people are endlessly fascinated by it, but most archaeologists are simply unable to satisfy this curiosity.

We may therefore reasonably infer that Atkinson had an intense dislike of the place and of the people who built it. In fact this hatred has been recorded in unambiguous form. In 1963, the late astronomer Gerald Hawkins had a paper published in the journal *Nature* in which he presented evidence that led him to believe that Stonehenge was a Neolithic computer and astronomical observatory.[13] Hawkins was one of many dignitaries of the time to speak of the builders of Stonehenge in an enlightened fashion, praising their abilities, observational skills, craftsmanship and other advanced qualities. When asked about this, Atkinson responded that Hawkins's work was 'tendentious, arrogant, slipshod, and unconvincing, and does little to advance our understanding of Stonehenge', an observation he could've equally well applied to his own work there, but worse was to come.

Atkinson was interviewed in 1964 at Stonehenge by the renowned American reporter Alexander Kendrick for a CBS documentary. Kendrick put it to him that other professionals were developing a high opinion of the original builders of Stonehenge and he asked Atkinson for his opinion, receiving the outraged response that these people were 'practically savages – howling barbarians', which virtually echoed Pope Gregory's scathing opinion of the Britons some 1,500 years earlier. I've watched this segment hundreds of times and there's no mistaking Atkinson's genuine loathing of the men and women who laboriously constructed the monument behind him. But why did he hate them so?

Atkinson's dates for the construction of Stonehenge have long been revised, but it was clear to him in the 1960s that whatever Stonehenge was, it had remained in use for millennia, presumably because it worked to the satisfaction of the people who performed observances and ceremonies there. As Atkinson made clear in his book, he was in little doubt that some of these ceremonies involved human sacrifice, and he suggested that some 'calamity' must have overtaken the people of the time to cause them to place chips of bluestone in the pits 'to ward off evil' then to abandon the monument overnight. His use of the word 'evil' leaves little doubt that he viewed it as a place where magical rites of a highly sinister nature had long been successfully performed, something that naturally went against his religious views, so to hear these same people lauded as scientists and astronomers with the respect that accompanies these achievements was too much for him to bear, hence his passionate outburst.

As for Atkinson fearing something he discerned in the shadows and broken columns at Stonehenge, the evidence is similarly clear. I can't prove that he suspected that Jesus had once visited the place, but to anyone who has chosen to familiarize themselves with the legends of Jesus visiting the West Country, the simple fact that Stonehenge is around 30 miles away from a site where Jesus is said to have lived for years cannot help but leap out at you. Numerous studies of the legends were published in the 1930s, so it would be truly amazing if someone of Atkinson's religious convictions had never heard of them, nor wondered where Jesus had disappeared to during his missing years. It's similarly unthinkable that Atkinson had never sung or heard Blake's 'Jerusalem', or wondered about its content, and if he had any view of Stonehenge, it was surely as a 'dark, satanic mill'.

MONSTROUS DARK DELUSIONS

Great God! I'd rather be a Pagan suckled in a creed outworn...
William Wordsworth, 1770–1850

Why should Atkinson have feared something he saw or discerned at Stonehenge? It was clear to him that Stonehenge had functioned for gloomy centuries as a place where heathen ceremonies were performed successfully and to the complete satisfaction of the participants, and I don't doubt that over the course of 15 years he also become aware of the curious phenomenon of the ruins somehow 'drawing down starlight'. Latter-day Druid ceremonies had been taking place there in a well-organized fashion and on an impressive scale since the start of the century and there's a photo of Winston Churchill, later the wartime leader of Britain, being accepted into the Albion Lodge of the Ancient Order of Druids at Blenheim Palace on 15 August 1908.[14] These Druids had been burying the ashes of their dead at Stonehenge since at least

1905,[15] but by 1963 Stonehenge had become such a popular place to visit for the growing counter-culture of the time that Atkinson was employed to fill in the holes left by the excavations and cover the surface inside the ruins with gravel[16] to prevent it from being destroyed by the feet of the thousands of visitors, who included Druids.

The 1960s was also the time when the open practice of witchcraft became prominent in Britain, on account of the widely-publicized 'King and Queen of the Witches', Maxine and Alex Sanders, who founded the Alexandrian covens to enormous interest from the press at the time. This is hardly something that can have met with Atkinson's approval, but perhaps the last straw came in 1968 when the world-famous Rolling Stones chose Stonehenge as the setting in which they wished to be photographed for the cover of their album *Their Satanic Majesties Request*. In 2006, pagans in Greece were granted the right by a court to resume their worship of the Olympian gods, which led to them being described by a senior Greek churchman as 'miserable resuscitators of a degenerate dead religion who wish to return to the monstrous dark delusions of the past',[17] an observation that was surely an exact echo of Atkinson's private thoughts in the 1960s.

Atkinson died in 1994, so he had seen a growing global fascination with Stonehenge and ever-growing visitors' numbers to the site, while huge touring rock bands such as Black Sabbath and Led Zeppelin helped to imprint the unique image of the iconic ruins by featuring reconstructions of Stonehenge as part of their stage sets. He'd also have been aware of the increasingly violent confrontations between riot police and those wishing to spend the solstice among the stones of this dark, satanic mill, people who, it's fair to say, weren't marching under a Christian banner.

We can be sure that this would have disturbed the deeply religious Atkinson and in addition, his intellect had made the connection between the axe hieroglyphs at Stonehenge and the idea of the Labyrinth, something he recorded in print. He'd have known that the Labyrinth was also a dance floor and that Stonehenge had been described as 'the Giants' Dance', so when he heard 'Lord of the Dance' in the 1960s, composed by his fellow Quaker and conscientious objector Sydney

Carter, it's inevitable that the idea of Jesus visiting Stonehenge would have occurred to him. It's also possible that he came across evidence to support this idea during the 15 years he spent scouring the ruins. With all this in mind, it's hardly surprising that he chose to conceal what he knew of the workings of this astonishing and to his mind infernal prehistoric mechanism. It's unthinkable that he'd have wished to add to its baleful pagan allure, and the fact that to the end of his days he tried to interfere with the compilation of the history of excavations at Stonehenge during the twentieth century makes the whole matter pretty much final.[18]

THE MEMORY OF THE STONES

'Say, from whence you owe this strange intelligence?'
William Shakespeare, *Macbeth*

And so we come to the final objection, that an oral history or spoken tradition of Jesus's visit couldn't have survived for 2,000 years. Leaving aside the way in which William Blake encapsulated the idea as far back as 1805, three men notably collected the legends of Jesus in the West Country and published their findings in the early twentieth century: Lionel Smithett Lewis, who was the vicar of St John's at Glastonbury for over 20 years, H. A. Lewis of Talland in Cornwall and the Rev C. C. Dobson, vicar of St Mary in the Castle, Hastings. These men have been accused of wishful thinking, but when we look at H. A. Lewis's *Christ in Cornwall*, for example, we find the following:

Before I proceed to show that the legend did actually exist in Cornwall, and still survives in parts, I throw out a word of warning to casual searchers. It is no use tackling all and sundry with a bald question 'Did you ever hear...?' The probability is that you would get a negative answer in almost every case. The Cornish folk are not fond of talking about their old legends and traditions to us 'foreigners'. They are very sensitive to ridicule, and ridicule has, alas, nearly killed the Holy Legend. Once suggest that a tradition is 'rubbish', and no oyster can ever be closer than the Cornish man or woman. For the same reason, the younger generation has not often heard of it, because the parents have feared that their sophisticated children would laugh at them.[19]

He proceeds to tell of hearing examples of the Holy Legend, and the unadorned simplicity of these accounts suggests that the people who spoke to him were sincere in their beliefs.

Be that as it may, we're looking for verification that an accurate oral tradition of a far-distant event can survive, so we'd like to be able to examine a tradition from the West Country directly connected with one of the subjects we've studied, ideally with undeniable proof that the tradition has existed in unwritten form for at least 2,000 years. Fortunately, we have something that fits the bill in every respect.

Geoffrey of Monmouth was a monk who lived from around 1100 to 1155 and he's most famous for having written the *Historia Regum Britanniae*, or 'History of the Kings of Britain', in about 1135. The book has been belittled as a worthless pseudo-history and Geoffrey himself has been vilified as a fantasist and as an out-and-out liar, accusations that remind us of the thinly disguised allegations levelled against the three clergymen who compiled the legends of Jesus. It may be that none of these men is without fault; all the same, Geoffrey of Monmouth's much-derided work contains a fascinating account of the construction of Stonehenge, which is roughly as follows.

In the fifth century AD, after the Romans had left Britain, the Saxons invaded the island and their leader Hengist went to war with the British King Vortigern, who'd usurped the British throne from Constantine II. The Saxons treacherously killed 460 British nobles during the course of a truce, then Aurelius Ambrosius, the rightful heir to the British throne, accompanied by his brother Uther Pendragon, returned from exile in Brittany and killed Vortigern. The brothers captured Hengist, who was later executed, but Aurelius wished to raise a monument to the memory of the murdered British nobles. He consulted Merlin, the personal wizard to the late Vortigern, who said:

If thou be fain to grace the burial place of these men with a work that shall endure forever, send for the Dance of the Giants that is in Killaraus, a mountain in Ireland. For a structure of stones is there that none of this age could arise save his wit were strong enough to carry his art. For the stones be big, nor is there stone anywhere of more virtue, and, so they be set up round this plot in a circle, even as they be now there set up, here shall they stand forever... for in these stones is a mystery, and a healing virtue against many ailments. Giants of old did carry them from the furthest ends of Africa and did set them up in Ireland what time they did inhabit therein. And unto this end they did it, that they might make them baths whensoever they ailed of any malady, for they did wash the stones and pour forth the water into the baths, whereby they that were sick were made whole.[20]

Aurelius sent his brother Uther with an army to Ireland, where they defeated the native army, but Uther's men couldn't move the stones. Merlin helped to transport them to the coast, where they were loaded onto ships, then brought to Salisbury Plain and reassembled.

It's a clear, colourful and detailed story, so let's compare it with what we know of Stonehenge's origin. The stone monument wasn't erected in the fifth century AD and the bluestones came from south Wales, not from Ireland. Neither Merlin nor Aurelius, if they ever were historical characters, had any part in setting the stones in place, and no one's yet found 460 British nobles from the same period. Geoffrey tells us that Aurelius was buried at Stonehenge, as was Uther, who became king after him, but no one's found either of them there, so the story seems to be pure fantasy.

However, when we remove the dates and names from Geoffrey's account, it becomes indistinguishable from the facts we've established today, and all this from someone with no knowledge of geology or archaeology who's furthermore been accused of being a self-serving liar. The bluestones weren't brought from Ireland, but they *were* brought from a land to the west of England across a large expanse of water; furthermore, the precise spot from which they came was under the dominion of Irish royalty from around AD 360 onwards and throughout the Arthurian period that Geoffrey was describing. The stones came from the top of a mountain, exactly as Geoffrey specified, and Professors Darvill and Wainwright have maintained that they were believed to have possessed healing or curative properties while they were in their Welsh setting.

Geoffrey also tells us that the temple was intact when it was found, dismantled, then reassembled on Salisbury Plain. We know from surviving joints and other features on some of the bluestones that they once formed trilithons like the later sarsens did, so there's a good chance that a standing temple made of dressed and interlocking stone once existed in the Preseli Mountains, in which case they'd have been dismantled, brought to Salisbury Plain then re-erected – again, *exactly* as Geoffrey described.

In May 2002, as already related, the remains of the 'King' and the 'Prince' of Stonehenge were discovered. A study of their bones showed that these two men were closely related and analysis of their tooth enamel showed that the king had been raised in continental Europe, so here we have tangible echoes of Aurelius and Uther, the two royal brothers who were responsible for building Stonehenge, arriving in Britain after a period of exile abroad.

Geoffrey makes clear on no fewer than seven occasions that Stonehenge was to be built as a memorial to the British nobles who were slain during a truce. The remains of approximately 240 people have been found at Stonehenge, although there may have been many more,[21] and these remains date to a time before their 'memorial in stone' was erected; furthermore, a recent analysis of them has led a number of senior archaeologists, such as Professor Mike Parker-Pearson, to conclude that these people belonged to a royal dynasty, something that seems a fair description of 'nobles'.

We could continue a while yet, as there are other intriguing similarities between Geoffrey's account and the facts that we know today. It's just possible that Geoffrey invented the whole thing and that he turned out to be right against truly astronomical odds, but simple logic tells us that in AD 1135 he was recounting a stunningly accurate version of the building of Stonehenge, an event that had taken place over 3,500 years before his time and quite possibly many centuries earlier than that. Geoffrey tells us that he acquired his information from an ancient book lent to him by his friend Walter, the Archbishop of Oxford; however, we don't know when this book was compiled or even if it existed at all. What we *can* be sure of is that the much-maligned Geoffrey of Monmouth was recounting an oral tradition of the building of Stonehenge that had survived for over 3,000 years in the west of England. When we bear in mind the huge timescales involved and the fact that the event in question happened long before the advent of writing, it makes the survival of an account of Jesus visiting the West Country in the early years of the first century seem mundane, predictable and completely unremarkable by comparison.

ALL YOU NEED IS LOVE

The previously untold story of Jesus tells of a young man being compelled by cultural and scriptural considerations to visit the British Isles, while his uncle, Joseph of Arimathea, made available the means of transport and provided employment for his nephew.

I think that Jesus found the west of England to be an environment in which he could 'grow in favour with God and with men' while remaining faithful to his own religious upbringing. He may have initially been an object of curiosity to the native Britons when they became aware of the similarity between his name and that of one of their gods, and I think that the Silures in particular would have taken an interest in the young man who shared their skin colouring. He'd have grown in stature as his individuality became apparent and as he began to exercise his abilities in the areas of healing and banishing unclean spirits. In the complete absence of any other candidates, I feel that the descent to the underworld or Harrowing of Hell took place in the Mendip Hills, if it physically took place anywhere, and I think it certain that Jesus acquired his fondness for high places in the west of England and in south Wales.

I don't believe that Jesus came to Britain in search of 'Druid wisdom', but it seems perfectly reasonable to suppose that he would have improved his natural abilities as an orator and as a judge or arbiter of disputes among a priesthood famed for these characteristics, while he'd have been impressed and influenced by the revered status of women among the Britons.

I think that he'd have been captivated by almost every aspect of the small island on which he found himself and he would have found common cause with a people who prided themselves on having twice repelled the legions of Caesar in the not-too-distant past. He may well have wondered at the similarity between his own beliefs and the beliefs of the Druids, but disillusionment would have quickly set in when he went to view the 'Kingdom of Heaven' in the Preseli Hills, only to discover that it was a sacred and enchanting landscape of rocks rather than the glorious spiritual realm he had in mind. Nonetheless, his time in Britain would have provided a perfect and highly suitable retreat in which he could grow to an adult while carefully preparing and formulating his famous ministry.

The narrative that emerges is in complete accord with everything we know of the west of England in the early years of the first century, as well as with the later legends. Not only does it dovetail perfectly with the Biblical accounts, but it also fulfils various prophecies of Isaiah and Malachi, it offers a credible explanation for why Jesus was accused, early in his ministry, of being in league with the Lord of the High Place, and it explains how he returned to his homeland as a stranger endowed with all manner of striking abilities and characteristics.

Three further points are worth examining, the first of which is where and when Jesus's famous ministry came to be formulated. It hadn't come into being by the time he was 12, so simple logic tells us that Jesus actively prepared his message and how he would deliver it during his missing years. If this is true, and there seems precious little reason to consider otherwise, it appears that the world's largest religion ultimately originated in the 'mountains green' and 'pleasant pastures' of a small region in the west of England and south Wales at some point between around AD 12 and 30.

Secondly, Britain has a number of islands that are regarded as holy. The two that spring most readily to mind are Iona and Lindisfarne. Anglesey was regarded as holy by the ancient Druids and many people view the Isle of Lundy, off the north coast of Devon, as a holy island on account of its serene atmosphere and the presence of an early Christian cemetery there. Glastonbury, or the Isle of Avalon, obviously qualifies as a holy island as far as both Christians and pagans are concerned and there are official moves afoot to twin it with the holy island of Patmos, where St John is said to have written his Book of Revelation.[22] I'd say that the existence and persistence of what's now known as 'the Holy Legend' is enough to qualify the relevant parts of the west of England and south Wales as a Holy Land.

Finally, we could well argue that the single most striking thought that Jesus ever presented to the world was 'Love thine enemies.'[23] As Timothy Freke and Peter Gandy observed, 'These beautiful and profound teachings are usually seen as a revolution in spirituality, replacing the old Jewish law of "an eye for an eye". They were indeed a radical departure from such Jewish sentiments...',[24] yet the idea was not completely new in the ancient world. But whether Jesus originated or adopted such a sentiment is unimportant. What matters is that while he was formulating his ministry, he broke away from and dismissed any idea of becoming a Messiah in the sense of one who would lead an armed rebellion against the Roman occupiers of his homeland, choosing instead to preach a message of peace. I can't say if this came about as a result of divine inspiration or if it was a considered response to a moral problem of how to act as far as the Roman occupation of his homeland was concerned. He would certainly have known that the Romans weren't invincible, but whether or not he ever seriously entertained the idea that he could succeed in physically driving them from his homeland, it's self-evident that he adopted a higher ambition than becoming a military leader. This consisted of not only taking on the Romans *and* the Jewish establishment of the time, but of changing the world, and I'd argue that this decision was the single most momentous event in human history, even if later followers of Christianity have often failed abysmally in living up to its lofty ideals.

The decision to preach the commandment 'Love thine enemies' may have been the natural and obvious philosophical option for such a radical thinker, decided upon in a cool and rational manner. It may have been an option that came to mind, after much soul-searching, to someone wrestling with the natural anguish, humiliation and sense of injustice that all oppressed peoples feel, because we're told that Jesus came to Earth to experience what it was like to be human. Alternatively, it may have been formulated in the aftermath of a real, symbolic or imagined confrontation with a malevolent supernatural entity, in which case we may picture the making of this decision as a revelation, a banishing of an unclean spirit or a Biblical 'temptation', but however it came into being, the conscious adoption of this philosophy must have happened at a particular time and at a particular place. Everything suggests that this took place when Jesus was between the ages of 12 and 30, which in turn points to the west of England or south Wales as being the setting. More specifically, it's likely to have happened on one of the high places that Jesus so pointedly favoured for contemplation, such as the one where in later years he prepared himself for the miracles of feeding the 5,000, calming the storm and walking on water, or where his remarkable transfiguration and conversation with the phantoms of Moses and Elijah took place. We have a number of candidates, but standing head and shoulders above the competition is the ancient place of kings, the abode of the Lord of the High Place, the Hall of Hewn Stones, the ruins that 'drew down starlight' and were so closely linked with the warlike Silures or Men of the Stones, a whited sepulchre, filled with bones and all uncleanness, or what was later known to us as a 'dark, satanic mill' – Stonehenge.

WILLIAM BLAKE, MASTER OF REALITY

There's no doubt that the celebrated visionary and mystic William Blake knew of the legend of Jesus coming to Britain and that he described this ancient visit to perfection in the first verse of his poem 'Jerusalem', just as Geoffrey of Monmouth somehow knew precise details of the building of Stonehenge over 3,000 years after the event took place. There's some debate over whether or not 'Jerusalem' qualifies as a hymn in the strict sense of the term, but Blake's creation, with music by Hubert Parry, has long since been Britain's most popular patriotic song. Any attempt to analyze precisely why this should be is probably futile, but the idea that there was once a paradise or heaven on Earth for *all* men in ancient Britain is an enchanting and uplifting one, as is the idea that it might one day be recreated in England's green and pleasant land.

A farmer in Somerset named Michael Eavis has come as close to anyone to making this vision of 'New Jerusalem' a reality by staging the Glastonbury Festival, a hugely successful event that attracts visitors and artists from around the world. The proceeds from this 'rock' festival are given to charitable causes, while this city of tents, stages and a pyramid is set among the very fields and hills in which Jesus is said to have wandered. However, in terms of sheer scale, it's been dwarfed by a ceremony staged on another continent.

On the evening of Sunday 24 August 2008, the Beijing Olympic Games drew to a close and as part of the handover ceremony to London in 2012 the British put on a performance that was intended to represent the best of what Britain had to offer. As part of this presentation, the Director of Music, Philip Shepherd, staged a rendition of 'God Save the Queen' which was sung by members of the UK's National Youth Theatre. This version was based on a seventeenth-century arrangement and, in keeping with the Olympic ideal of a peaceful and better world, it featured a seldom-used verse which asked 'That men should brothers be, and form one family, The wide world o'er.'

However, at the beginning of the British contribution and in perfect keeping with the occasion, an audience of billions the world over was treated to the hauntingly evocative melody of the opening lines of 'Jerusalem', by way of setting the tone for what was to follow.

William Blake would have *loved* it.

Conclusion

*Science is a way of thinking much more
than it is a body of knowledge.
When you make the finding yourself –
even if you're the last person on Earth to see the light
– you'll never forget it.*
Carl Sagan, 1934–96

In the last few years, works by Leonardo da Vinci and Archimedes have miraculously come to light, as has an account of the trial of the Knights Templar from the depths of the Vatican archives, so I don't doubt that still more information relevant to the stories of Jesus visiting Britain will surface one day, whether it's in the form of literary or archaeological evidence.

In the meantime, it seems to me that we can just completely ignore all the evidence, as the founder of Opus Dei did when he spoke confidently of Jesus working as a carpenter in Nazareth for 30 years,[1] or else we can give it some serious consideration and try to piece together a coherent and credible narrative from the information available to us. This may require a leap of faith, but I would argue that this is well worth making. At this point, I imagine that many intelligent and discerning men and women will accuse *me* of making a huge leap of faith by piecing together what seem to me to be the main events in the 'missing years' of Jesus. I'd say this is a perfectly valid point, but I'd respond by quoting Carl Sagan and pointing out that 'Imagination takes us to worlds that never were, but without it, we go nowhere.'

There are some men in our time, such as Richard Dawkins and James Randi, doubtless honourable, who scorn supernatural or religious explanations in favour of answers arrived at via the scientific method, which is all well and good until we remember that scientists once calculated that if a train carriage travelled at more than 21 mph, all the air would be sucked out and the passengers would suffocate.

However, there's a far more serious point to be made when it comes to discussing what truly qualifies as a leap of faith. According to the scientists, our solar system is surrounded by a cloud of unimaginable proportions that's the home of the comets that sometimes grace our skies. Known as the Oort Cloud after the Dutch astronomer who developed the idea, this structure is made up of trillions of tons of rock and ice, and by some calculations it's as much as two light years in diameter. Whatever the current estimates for the size of this 'cloud', Carl Sagan once wrote, 'These numbers are so staggering that they invite disbelief,'[2] and I'm quoting this famous astronomer not just because he was in his time an authority on such matters, but also because he was profoundly sceptical about matters of religion and the supernatural.

My point is that scientists are inviting us to believe in the physical existence of a structure so vast that it defies comprehension, but to quote Carl Sagan once more:

To account for the handful of new comets that appear in our skies each year, a vast, mind-numbing multitude of invisible comets, living far beyond the orbit of Pluto, is postulated. The idea explains what we know about comets in an elegant way that no other theory even approaches. The trillions of comets are now widely accepted by astronomers all over the world and they are called, properly, the Oort Cloud. Many scientific papers are written each year about the Oort Cloud – its properties, its origin, its evolution. Yet there is not a shred of direct observational evidence for its existence. No spacecraft has voyaged to the Oort Cloud to count the comets there. No measurements by ground-based or space-borne telescopes have detected a cloud, nor, so far as we can see, can the cloud be detected, at least with present instruments.[3]

In the view of people such as Richard Dawkins, and probably many others, religious faith qualifies as a delusion or a fixed false belief, but with the best will in the world, it's very difficult to see the difference between how some people infer the existence of God and the method by which scientists postulate the existence of the infamous Oort Cloud.

How is all this relevant as far as the subject of this book is concerned? Well, scientists are inviting us to believe in the existence of a truly vast but invisible physical structure on the basis of some passing fires in the sky, a set of arcane calculations that only a tiny fraction of the Earth's population can understand and, it's fair to say, some degree of speculation and imagination. On the other hand, I'm merely asking those of you reading this book to contemplate the possibility that a visionary young man who lived close to one of the most famous ports in the ancient world once travelled to Britain, an island that had been known to the people of the eastern Mediterranean for centuries, and inviting you to consider that the experiences he had on that island went some way towards forming the person he would become in later life. Rather than offer up complex mathematical formulae, I've provided all manner of literary, historical, ecclesiastical, Biblical, linguistic and archaeological evidence to support this simple supposition, as well as suggesting that you experience for yourself the captivating atmosphere in certain places in the West Country.

We must each make of the evidence what we will, but for me, the Biblical passage that made the single biggest impression was the warning from the Book of Matthew where Jesus said, 'For there shall arise false Christs, and false prophets, and shall shew great signs and wonders; insomuch that, if it were possible, they shall deceive the very elect.'[4] Why? Well, it's a rare thing to be able to experience true wonderment, something money can rarely buy, but I've been fortunate enough to have known this sensation throughout the writing of this book.

Few would deny that some places on Earth are imbued with an atmosphere which, regardless of its cause, is almost tangible, be it one of evil or of beauty. One of these places is the aforementioned Nine Barrows Lane near Priddy, which I described earlier, but there's one location that's of great relevance to the subject of this book that I've deliberately left out, simply because some of you may wish to experience the sheer exhilaration of finding it for yourselves, then basking in the uplifting silence and serenity that permeate this spot like an indelible blessing.

Some years ago, I happened to encounter an old man on a dusty path somewhere in the regions I've described in this book and we fell into conversation. After a while, this man volunteered the information that he'd spent most of his life working for the Forestry Commission and when I expressed an interest in the various features of the countryside around us, he immediately pointed out one particular site that he was certain I'd enjoy visiting, adding that this place possessed an atmosphere of almost supernatural peacefulness and tranquillity that was so potent that it had to be experienced to be believed.

The location he pointed out was within easy reach, so when we eventually went our separate ways, I investigated the place for myself and I was astounded by what I can only describe as the 'magic in the air', although I've never been able to decide whether this breathtaking, otherworldly beauty is due to a combination of natural features or a more mystical cause.

I'm not aware of any legends or tales linking this site with Jesus, but if the other stories are true, then simple logic suggests that this too was one of the places where the feet of one of mankind's truly great visionaries, revolutionaries and prophets once walked 'in ancient time', and it shouldn't be difficult to find it for yourselves, if you wish. If you do, then you can decide for yourselves whether or not a visit by this astonishing man 2,000 years ago left a deep-seated impression, but in any event, it's a place to make the heart sing and the spirit soar, regardless of whether your heart and head incline you towards faith, science or something in between.

'Somewhere, something wonderful is waiting to be discovered.'

NOTES AND REFERENCES

Introduction

1. Luke 2, verse 52

2. The question of whether or not supposedly spurious ancient accounts have any value as guides or pointers to factual events or real locations is one of the foremost themes of this book. As the reader will discover, I've considered a wide range of Biblical writings and stories from Greek and Roman antiquity, as well as mediaeval literature, legends, obscure folklore and other sources, then I've done my best to see if there's any supporting evidence to be found for them, but the reader will have to judge for themselves whether or not this exercise was worthwhile. When summarizing the results of a lengthy and detailed investigation during the 1960s into the reality of King Arthur's Britain, Geoffrey Ashe wrote, '...objective research has not borne out either the credulous romantics or the ultra-sceptical professional scholars. But, as at Troy and elsewhere, it has shown that the credulous were slightly less wrong than the extremists of the destructive party... The naive believers have no right to claim that they have been vindicated. They have not. Excavation shows that we go wrong if we take the legends literally. But it also shows that we go more wrong if we refuse to take them seriously. This is the same lesson that follows from the work of Schliemann and his successors...' (*The Quest for King Arthur's Britain*, ed. Geoffrey Ashe, Book Club Associates, 1972, pages 201–2). My view is this: if it was good enough for Heinrich Schliemann, it's most certainly good enough for me.

PART I

Chapter 2: Stranger in a Strange Land

1. The original Greek text names this coin as a drachma.

2. The English translation describes this levy as a 'temple tax', but the

money in this case was for the upkeep of the synagogue at Capernaum. In Judaism, there was only one Temple, which was at Jerusalem, with the single exception of a temple ruin on the island of Elephantine in the Upper Nile in Egypt. Some archaeologists believe that this temple housed the Ark of the Covenant.

3.   The original Greek word is 'αλλοτριων or *allotrion*, meaning 'others', which conveys the same sense as the word 'foreigners', especially in this context. The same 'al' prefix exists in Latin, so we have words such as 'al-ter ego', 'al-ien', 'all-egory' and so forth, all of which still convey an unmistakable sense of 'otherness'.

4.   Here the Greek text substitutes the word 'stater'. A stater varied in value in the ancient world, but was commonly worth two drachma.

Chapter 3: Behold the Man

1.   Matthew 14, verses 22–3
2.   Ibid., verse 13
3.   Matthew 17, verses 1–2
4.   Ibid., verses 2–3
5.   Mark 1, verses 35–6
6.   Mark 3, verses 13–14
7.   Luke 6, verses 12–13
8.   Luke 8, verses 32–3
9.   The Sea of Galilee is in fact a large freshwater lake and the various settlements on its shores are referred to in the New Testament as 'the lakeside towns'. It is called a sea through tradition on account of its sheer size.
10. John 6, verse 3
11. John 8, verse 1
12. Matthew 5, verses 1–12
13. Matthew 4, verses 8–10
14. Luke 1, verses 6–14
15. Luke 8, verses 53–6
16. Herod had previously had John beheaded; see Mark 6, verses 27–9.
17. Luke 9, verses 7–8
18. Matthew 16, verses 13–14
19. Luke 1, verse 80
20. Matthew 3, verses 1–5
21. Matthew 24, verses 23–6
22. Luke 4, verses 28–30
23. Matthew 4, verses 12–14

24. Ibid., verses 19–20
25. Matthew 14, verse 13
26. Mark 7, verse 24
27. Matthew 15, verses 21–2
28. Luke 5, verses 4–8
29. Luke 6, verses 17–18
30. John 6, verses 16–21
31. Matthew 8, verses 23–7
32. Mark 4, verses 35–41
33. Luke 8, verses 22–5

Chapter 4: A Siren Song

1. Matthew 27, verses 46–7
2. Ibid., verse 50
3. Luke 23, verse 46
4. John 19, verse 28
5. Ibid., verse 30
6. Matthew 27, verses 57–8
7. Mark 17, verses 43–4
8. Luke 23, verses 50–52
9. John 19, verses 38–9
10. 1 Samuel, verse 1
11. The *Targum Yerushalmi*
12. Luke 23, verse 51. Judea was a province of the historical land of Israel.
13. On 14 July 2006, the Culture Secretary Tessa Jowell announced that the mining landscape of Cornwall and west Devon had become a World Heritage Site, as the World Heritage Committee had recognized that the area had supplied much of the world's tin for the previous 4,000 years.
14. 1 Kings 7, verses 13–51
15. Matthew 27, verses 57–60
16. The original Greek is και 'εθηκεν 'αυτον 'εν τω καινω 'αυτο μνημειω 'ο 'ελατομησεν 'εν τη πετρα... The crucial part is 'ο 'ελατομησεν, or *ho elatomesen*, which literally means 'which *he* had quarried' (my italics).
17. Mark 15, verses 43–6, Luke 23, verses 50–53, and John 19, verses 38–42
18. Mark 16, verses 3–5
19. Ibid., verses 5–7
20. Luke 24, verses 5–6
21. Ibid., verses 10–11
22. Mark 16, verses 1–5

23. John 19, verse 39
24. Matthew 27, verses 62–8
25. Mark 15, verses 43–4
26. John 19, verses 38–9
27. Flavius Josephus, *Antiquities of the Jews*, Chapter 18, pages 55–9
28. Mark 15, verse 43
29. The Sanhedrin was an assembly of judges who would meet in the Hall of Hewn Stones in the Temple of Jerusalem prior to its destruction in AD 70 by the Roman general Titus.
30. Matthew 19, verses 16–26
31. The original Greek word is προσδεχομενος, which literally means 'was towards receiving' or anticipating.
32. Matthew 19, verse 29
33. Matthew 19, verse 30
34. Matthew 26, verses 20–25
35. Isaiah 53, verses 8–9
36. John 21, verses 24–5
37. See the relevant section of the official website of the Archbishop of Canterbury at www.archbishopofcanterbury.org.
38. Ibid.
39. See Luke 2, verses 47–8: 'And all that heard him were astonished at his understanding and answers.'
40. Matthew 27, verse 60
41. Mark 15, verses 43–5
42. The original Greek word is a participle deriving from τολμαο, or *tolmao*, meaning broadly 'I dare'.
43. John 3, verses 1–3
44. Matthew 27, verses 11–14
45. John 27, verses 12–14
46. Ibid., verses 15–19
47. Ibid., verse 25
48. This inscribed limestone block was discovered in 1961 and is currently housed in the Israel Museum in Jerusalem.
49. 1 Kings 7, verses 13–51
50. Pliny the Elder wrote that a Carthaginian named Himilco explored the outer coasts of Europe, i.e. those countries bordering the Atlantic Ocean, the English Channel and the North Sea (*Natural History*, 2.169a).
51. William J. Watson, *The Celtic Place Names of Scotland*, Birlinn Limited, 1993

52. In ancient Greek, this was translated as χϱιστος, or *Christos*, from which we derive our word 'Christ'.
53. Tacitus, *Annals*, Book XII, page 33
54. Leviticus 15; *see also* Numbers 19.
55. Herodotus, *History*, Book 4
56. Julius Caesar, *De Bello Gallico* (The Conquest of Gaul), trans. S. A. Handford, Penguin Books, 1960
57. Ibid.
58. Ibid.
59. Exodus 20, verses 3–5; *see also* Deuteronomy 5, verses 7–9.
60. Exodus 32, verse 4
61. Judges 16, verse 23
62. Diodorus Siculus, *Histories*, Book 5
63. Matthew 5, verse 9
64. Pliny the Elder, *Natural History*, Book 16
65. 1 Kings 8, verse 63
66. Caesar, op. cit.
67. Mark 5, verse 41
68. Mark 15, verse 34
69. John 1, verse 42
70. An idea first proposed by William Serfaty in 1997.
71. Exodus 13, verses 21–2
72. Matthew 2, verse 13

Chapter 5: 'And There's Another Country I've Heard of Long Ago'

1. Winston Churchill, *A History of the English-Speaking Peoples*, Volume 1, Cassell & Company, 1974, page 3
2. The first revolt was known as the Great Revolt or the first Jewish–Roman War. It lasted from AD 66 to 73. The next was the Kitos War of 115–17 and the third was Bar Kokhba's Revolt from 132 to 135.
3. Matthew 10, verse 34
4. By complete coincidence, there is a bright green mineral of hydrous copper carbonate named malachite which takes a high polish and was used in antiquity for the ornamentation of beads and pots.
5. Malachi 3, verses 1–3
6. Mike Pitts, *British Archaeology* 91, 42–7
7. See Rev. Lionel Smithett Lewis, MA, *Glastonbury: Her Saints*, page 66, and *Guide to Penzance*, Ward, Locke & Co.
8. http://www.cornwalls.co.uk/Marazion/
9. Diodorus Siculus, *Histories*, Book V, page 22

10. Collected by Ruth Tongue in her 'Folklore of Somerset', *County Folklore* 8.

11. *Popular Romances of the West of England*, collected and edited by Robert Hunt, 1903

12. Sabine Baring-Gould, *Cornwall*, 1910, page 57

13. Raymond E. Capt, *The Traditions of Glastonbury*, Artisan Sales, 1983, page 34

14. Tongue, op. cit., also Crowcombe and Holford, *Oral Tradition and Collection*, 1901–55, also heard locally by the author in the first part of the twentieth century.

15. Capt, op. cit., page 33

16. This stone, from Place Manor church at St Anthony-in-Roseland in Cornwall, is now lost, according to A. W. Smith, 'And did those feet? The "legend" of Christ's visit to Britain', *Folklore* 100, no. 1, 1989.

17. Ibid.

18. Ibid.

19. Ibid.

20. Submitted by T. L. H. Honey of Fowey under the heading 'Christ in Cornwall?' *See also* A. W. Smith, op. cit.

21. This lengthy article was entitled 'Was Christ in Cornwall? "Joseph was in the tin trade" – Voyage by own ship to St. Michael's Mount by Henry Jenner of Hayle'.

22. This is the exact text of what the foreman reportedly said, but Jenner made clear that he was reporting the details and not quoting the foreman word for word. See A. W. Smith, op. cit.

23. The pleadings at the Council of Constance appeared in a rare quarto entitled *Disputatio super Dignitatem Angliae et Galliae in Concilio Constantiono* by Theodore Martin, Lovan, 1517, cited in Cressy's *Church History of Britain*, Lib. II, p.20, and reproduced in Lionel Smithett Lewis, *St Joseph of Arimathea at Glastonbury*, The Lutterworth Press, Cambridge, 2004, page 18.

24. William of Malmesbury, *De Antiquitate Glastoniensis Ecclesiae*, trans. H. F. Scott Stokes, Thomas Hearne, p.25

25. See extensive footnotes on pages 24 and 25 of Rev. C. C. Dobson, *Did Our Lord Visit Britain as They Say in Cornwall and Somerset?*, Avalon Press, Glastonbury, 1947.

26. Gildas, *De Excidio Britanniae* (On the Ruin of Britain), Section 8, page 25

Chapter 6: The Harrowing of Hell

1. Rev. C. C. Dobson, *Did Our Lord Visit Britain as They Say in Cornwall and Somerset?*, Avalon Press, Glastonbury, 1947, pages 6–7

2. See L.V. Grinsell, *The Ancient Burial Mounds of England*, 1953, page 141.

3. All the following archaeological information on Priddy, unless otherwise stated, comes from Jodie Lewis, 'Monuments, ritual and regionality: The Neolithic of northern Somerset', *British Archaeological Reports*, Archaeopress, Oxford, 2005, and from references contained in this report.

4. Ibid.

5. Clement of Alexandria, *Stromata*, Book I

6. Jodie Lewis, 'Upwards at 45 degrees: The use of vertical caves during the Neolithic and Early Bronze Age on Mendip, Somerset'.

7. The Reverend Skinner was active in his antiquarian pursuits in the early part of the nineteenth century.

8. Lucan, *Pharsalia*, Book 1, pages 450–58

9. Pliny the Elder, *Natural History*, Book 16

10. Tacitus, *Annals*, page 14

11. Pomponius Mela, *De Situ Orbis*, Book III

12. Julius Caesar, *De Bello Gallico* (The Conquest of Gaul), Book VI, trans. S. A. Handford, Penguin Books, 1960

13. 2 Chronicles 28, verse 3; *see also* 2 Kings 23, verse 10.

14. See Deuteronomy 32, verse 22, Genesis 37, verse 35 and Psalm 86, verse 13.

15. Numbers 16, verses 28–34. In a footnote to these verses, the Jerusalem Bible describes Sheol as indicating the deepest parts of the Earth; the dead 'go down' to it.

16. 1 Peter 3, verse 18

17. 1 Peter 4, verse 6

18. See, for example, 2 Corinthians 2, verse 14, also Ephesians 4, verses 8–10, which contains the question: 'Now that he ascended, what is it but that he also descended first into the lower parts of the earth?' As for the prophet Zecharia, he states, 'As for thee also, by the blood of thy covenant, I have sent forth thy prisoners out of the pit wherein is no water.'

19. Matthew 17, verses 2–3

20. Carew, 'Survey of Cornwall', Appendix AA, in *Popular Romances of the West of England*, collected and edited by Robert Hunt, 1903

21. Jodie Lewis, 'Monuments, ritual and regionality: The Neolithic of northern Somerset', *British Archaeological Reports*, Archaeopress, Oxford, 2005

Chapter 7: Stonehenge

1. For more detailed information, see the relevant entries on my Eternal Idol website, www.eternalidol.com.
2. *Stonehenge in its Landscape*, English Heritage, 1996
3. John North, *Stonehenge, Neolithic Man and the Cosmos*, HarperCollins, 1997, page 544
4. Mike Pitts, *Hengeworld*, Arrow Books, 2001, page 121
5. *Stonehenge in its Landscape*, op. cit.
6. Aubrey Burl, *The Stonehenge People: Life and Death at the World's Greatest Stone Circle*, J. M. Dent & Sons Ltd, 1987, pages 214, 215
7. Ibid., page 154

PART II

Chapter 8: The Man, the Monster and the Maze

1. According to the *Oxford Classical Dictionary*, some later writers situated the Labyrinth at a quarry near Gortyn, rather than at Knossos itself.
2. *The Fragments of Sophocles*, edited with additional notes from the papers of Sir R. C. Jebb and Dr W. G. Headlam by A. C. Pearson, III, 141, fr.1030, 1917. Also discussed in Karl Kerenyi and Ralph Manheim, *Dionysus: Archetypal Image of an Indestructible Life*, Princeton University Press, 1996, page 94.
3. Homer, *The Iliad*, Book 18, line 590; *see also* Phrynichos, *Praeparatio Sophistica*, s.v 'Achanes' (in Greek lettering in the original DP – 'αχανης) in Bekker, *Anecdota Graeca*, I, 28, 27–8: 'At Knossos, a roofless dancing ground was spoken of as a "labyrinth".'
4. Homer, *The Odyssey*, Book 8, line 260
5. See Plutarch's *Life of Theseus*, 21, also relevant entry in *The Oxford Classical Dictionary*.
6. Picture available.
7. R. J. C. Atkinson, *Stonehenge*, 1956; revised edition, Penguin Books, 1990
8. Quoted in L. Sprague de Camp and Catherine de Camp, *Citadels of Mystery*, Fontana Books, 1973, page 46.

Chapter 9: Lord of the High Place

1. Coincidentally, Coleridge wrote 'The Rime of the Ancient Mariner' while staying at Watchet in Somerset, one of the ports Jesus is said to have visited, and the poem is often seen as a Christian allegory.

2. Jodie Lewis, 'Monuments, ritual and regionality: The Neolithic of northern Somerset', *British Archaeological Reports*, Archaeopress, Oxford, 2005

3. R. J. C. Atkinson, *Stonehenge*, first published 1956, 3rd edition 1979, pages 83–4

4. The full passage reads as follows: '...a fragment or two of bluestone (almost always rhyolite) at the very bottom [i.e. in the primary fill]... and perhaps if it is not too fanciful to see them as propitiatory token offerings, made as symbolic substitutes for the bluestones themselves, to ward off any evil consequences that might result, so to speak, from depriving the gaping holes of their rightful and expected contents.' Ibid., page 84

5. Robert Graves, 'Preface', *True Ghosts and Spooky Incidents*, ed. Vikas Khatri, Pustak Mahal, 2008

6. See Ian Kidd and Robin Wakefield, *Essays by Plutarch*, Penguin Classics, 1992, pages 277–8, also Thucydides, I.132–4, and Daniel Ogden, *Magic, Witchcraft and Ghosts in the Roman and Greek Worlds*, Oxford University Press US, 2002, page 29.

7. Pliny the Younger, *Epistles*, vii, 27

8. Lucan, *Pharsalia*, Book III, verse 470

9. Tacitus, *Annals*, Book XIV, Chapter 32

10. Quoted in the *Sunday Times*.

11. Quoted in Janet and Colin Bord, *The Secret Country*, Granada Publishing Ltd, 1978, page 184.

12. Anthony D. Hippisley Coxe, *Haunted Britain*, McGraw-Hill Book Company, 1973, pages 52, 54 and 55

13. Reverend F. Warre, *Proceedings*, Somerset 5, I, 30ff. 1854; *see also* Janet and Colin Bord, op. cit., page 202.

14. L. V. Grinsell, *The Archaeology of Wessex*, Methuen, 1958, page 57

15. Aubrey Burl, *The Stonehenge People: Life and Death at the World's Greatest Stone Circle*, J. M. Dent & Sons Ltd, 1987, pages 221–2

16. Thomas Stokes Salmon, 'Stonehenge', winner of the Newdigate Poetry Prize at Oxford in 1823, cited in Christopher Chippindale, *Stonehenge Complete*, Thames & Hudson 2004, page 150

17. The hare, and later the rabbit, have long been closely linked with Easter and with the Resurrection.

18. Mark 3, verse 11

19. Mark 3, verse 12

20. Mark 3, verses 13–15

21. Mark 3, verse 22

22. Mike Pitts, *Hengeworld*, Arrow Books, 2001, page 125

23. 1 Samuel 28, verses 3–25

Chapter 10: The Doors of Perception

1. Matthew 2, verse 9
2. John North, *Stonehenge, Neolithic Man and the Cosmos*, HarperCollins, 1997, page 526
3. Marcus Aurelius, *Meditations*, iii, 11.17
4. Matthew 13, verse 55, and Mark 6, verse 3
5. Luke 2, verses 46–7
6. Judges, verses 21–30
7. Quoted in Aubrey Burl and Neil Mortimer, *Stukeley's Stonehenge, an unpublished manuscript 1721–1724*, Yale University, 2005.
8. Genesis 28, verses 10–19
9. Matthew 17, verses 1–3
10. John 8, verse 12
11. Gildas, *De Excidio Britanniae* (On the Ruin of Britain), Section 8
12. Exodus 20, verse 25
13. Matthew 16, verse 18
14. Doublethink is 'the power of holding two contradictory beliefs in one's mind simultaneously, and accepting both of them ... To tell deliberate lies while genuinely believing in them, to forget any fact that has become inconvenient, and then, when it becomes necessary again, to draw it back from oblivion for just so long as it is needed, to deny the existence of objective reality and all the while to take account of the reality which one denies ... Even in using the word doublethink it is necessary to exercise doublethink. For by using the word one admits that one is tampering with reality; by a fresh act of doublethink one erases this knowledge; and so on indefinitely, with the lie always one leap ahead of the truth.' (George Orwell, *Nineteen Eighty-Four*, Martin Secker & Warburg Ltd, 1949, page 220)
15. Christopher Chippindale, *Stonehenge Complete*, Thames & Hudson, 2004, note, page 22.
16. Sydney Carter, *Green Print for Song*, Stainer & Bell, 1974
17. 2 Samuel 6, verse 14: 'And David danced before the LORD with all his might; and David was girded with an ephod [a religious and ceremonial Jewish garment].'
18. Sydney Carter, *Lord of the Dance and other Songs and Poems*, Stainer & Bell, 2002

Chapter 11: The Pillars of Creation

1. Quoted in Bede's *Ecclesiastical History of England*, a revised translation with introduction, life and notes by A. M. Sellar, late vice-principal of Lady Margaret Hall, Oxford, George Bell and Sons, London, 1907.
2. Quoted in William of Malmesbury, *De Antiquitate Glastoniensis Ecclesiae*, trans. H. F. Scott Stokes, Thomas Hearne, p.25
3. Bede, op. cit.
4. Quoted in Maev Kennedy, 'Stonehenge was "Lourdes of prehistoric Europe", claim archaeologists', *Guardian*, 22 September 2008
5. Quoted Bede, op. cit.
6. William Stukeley, *Stonehenge: A Temple Restor'd to the British Druids*, 1740, Chapter VI
7. Job 19, verses 23–4
8. Christopher Chippindale, *Stonehenge Complete*, 2004, pages 47–8
9. Ibid.
10. Anon., 'The Description of Stonehenge', *Holborn-Drollery*, 1673
11. Stukeley, op. cit.
12. Henry of Huntingdon, *Historia Anglorum*, 1135
13. Genesis 28, verses 17–18
14. We've already seen how Henry of Huntingdon viewed the great stones as doorways, or portals, or gates.
15. William Shakespeare, *Macbeth*, II, i, 33–5
16. William Stukeley, *Stonehenge: A Temple Restor'd to the British Druids*, 1740, Chapter VI
17. Quoted in Bede's *Ecclesiastical History of England*, a revised translation with introduction, life and notes by A. M. Sellar, late vice-principal of Lady Margaret Hall, Oxford, George Bell and Sons, London, 1907.
18. Stukeley, op. cit.
19. The sole exception was Queen Mary II.

PART II

1. *The Concise Oxford Dictionary*, 1992
2. Samuel Taylor Coleridge, *Aids to Reflection; Moral and Religious Aphorisms*, XXV

Chapter 12: 'Mine Eyes Have Seen the Glory of the Coming of the Lord'

1. Matthew 2, verse 2
2. Plutarch, Moralia

3. Julius Caesar, *De Bello Gallico* (The Conquest of Gaul), trans. S. A. Handford, Penguin Books, 1960
4. Lucan, *Pharsalia*, Book I
5. Ibid.
6. Caesar, op. cit.
7. Ibid., Chapter 3, section 1, page 95
8. See, for example, Mark 1, verse 24, where he is addressed by name.
9. Caesar, op. cit.
10. Paul D. J. Arblaster, *Celtic Christianity Yesterday, Today and for the Future: Gleaning Wisdom from the Primitive Protestants*, Virtualbookworm Publishing, 2002, page 112

Chapter 13: The Men of the Stones

1. Private correspondence with Michael Goormachtigh of http://www.proto-english.org.
2. Quoted in Bede's *Ecclesiastical History of England*, a revised translation with introduction, life and notes by A. M. Sellar, late vice-principal of Lady Margaret Hall, Oxford, George Bell and Sons, London, 1907.
3. Tacitus, *Annals*, Book 12, XXXIX
4. Ibid., XL
5. Ibid., Book 14, XXIX
6. Ibid., Book 12, XXXII
7. Ibid., Book 12, XXXIV
8. Luke 2, verses 46–50
9. Matthew 5, verse 44
10. Matthew 21, verse 12
11. Luke 23, verse 3
12. From a BBC report of 27 October 2004.
13. Bukhari 4:55:649. (Bukhari is a collection of Muslim sayings related to the Koran collected by someone of the same name.)
14. Ibid., 4:55:650
15. Tacitus, *Life of Agricola*, Section 11
16. All these details are from a talk given to the Llanelli Art Society on 3 February 1971 by Kemmis Buckley, MBE, DL, MA, and have since appeared in print elsewhere.
17. The original Greek words are βασιλειαν των 'ουρανων, or *Basileian ton ouranon*, which literally means 'the Kingdom of the Heavens', although it doesn't really matter if the last word's plural or singular.
18. Timothy Darvill, 'Message in the stones', *Current Archaeology*, August 2005

19. Recorded by Avienus in the fourth century AD.
20. Pliny the Elder, *Natural History*
21. Exodus 20, verse 25: 'And if thou wilt make me an altar of stone, thou shalt not build it of hewn stone: for if thou lift up thy tool upon it, thou hast polluted it.'
22. Matthew 23, verse 27
23. Mark 5, verse 9; Luke 8, verse 30

Chapter 14: O Brave New World

1. Winston Churchill, *A History of the English-Speaking Peoples*, Volume 1, Cassell & Company, 1974, page 3
2. Tacitus, *Annals*, Book XIV, page 30
3. Ibid., XV, page 44
4. Suetonius, *The Lives of the Twelve Caesars*, Chapter 16
5. Tacitus, op. cit.
6. Pliny the Elder, *Natural History*, Book 30, page 13
7. Matthew 28, verses 18–20
8. Pliny, op. cit.
9. Matthew 26, verse 26, Mark 14, verse 22, and Corinthians 11, verse 24
10. See *Doctor William Price – Saint or Sinner?* Carreg Gwalch Publishers, 1997.
11. Gwenllian Price, interviewed in May 1888, apparently by the *Cardiff Times & South Wales Weekly News*, quoted ibid.
12. Christopher Chippindale, *Stonehenge Complete*, Thames & Hudson, 2004, page 151

Chapter 15: I am Legend

1. Matthew 2, verse 16
2. Sir Edward Creasy, *The History of England*, 1869
3. Pomponius Mela, *De Situ Orbis*, Book III
4. Isaiah 41, verse 2
5. Ibid., verse 25
6. See the poem *Ora Maritima* by Avienus, a Roman writer who lived in the fourth century AD.
7. These mentions of 'isles afar off' and a Messiah coming from the north inescapably bring to mind the ancient description of Britain as Hyperborea, or the Land beyond the North Wind, that was said to be an island, no smaller than Sicily, off the coast of Gaul.
8. Ezekiel 27, verse 23
9. Matthew 15, verse 21

10. Mark 7, verse 31
11. Percy Bysshe Shelley, 'Ozymandias'
12. Jodie Lewis, 'Monuments, ritual and regionality: The Neolithic of northern Somerset', *British Archaeological Reports*, Archaeopress, Oxford, 2005
13. See A. W. Smith, 'And did those feet? The "legend" of Christ's visit to Britain', *Folklore* 100, no. 1, 1989; also Rev. C. C. Dobson, *Did Our Lord Visit Britain as They Say in Cornwall and Somerset?*, Avalon Press, Glastonbury,1947, pages 24 and 25.
14. Matthew 27, verses 57–60
15. Mark 15, verses 43–6
16. Luke 23, verses 50 –53
17. John 17, verses 38–42
18. According to an Aramaic translation of the Hebrew Bible known as the *Targum Yerushalmi*.
19. Matthew 2, verse 18
20. Freyha Anis, *A Dictionary of the Names of Towns and Villages in Lebanon*, Beirut, 1956, pages 80–81
21. Paul J. Achtemeir *et al.*, *Harper's Bible Dictionary*, The Society of Biblical Literature, New York, 1985, page 852
22. The English translation of the Aramaic Peshitta Bible.
23. Luke 23, verse 50
24. Mark McMenamin, *A Concise Phoenician–English, English–Phoenician Dictionary*, South Sadley, Massachusetts, 1997, page 15
25. Luke 13, verses 10–17
26. Luke 8, verses 1–3
27. Interestingly, the British Women's Institute website states that composer Sir Hubert Parry put Blake's words to music in 1916 for the Fight of the Right movement and in 1918 it was sung at the Royal Albert Hall to celebrate the granting of votes for women. The words have since been sung and recorded by Emerson, Lake and Palmer, Billy Bragg and Bruce Dickinson, singer for Iron Maiden.
28. Luke 2, verse 47
29. See, for example, Luke 6, verse 17.
30. The Koran, Chapter 19, 27–30
31. Julius Caesar, *De Bello Gallico*, (The Conquest of Gaul), Book VI, trans. S. A. Handford, Penguin Books, 1960, page 13
32. Ibid.
33. Strabo, *Geography*, Book IV
34. Luke 4, verses 28–30

35. Strabo, op. cit: '...they even arbitrated cases of war and made the opponents stop when they were about to line up for battle.'

36. Diodorus Siculus, *Histories*, Book 5

37. Caesar wrote: 'The Druidic doctrine is believed to have been found existing in Britain and thence imported into Gaul; even today those who want to make a profound study of it generally go to Britain for the purpose.'

38. John 6, verses 3–21

39. Mark 3, verse 22, but *see also* Matthew 12, verse 24.

40. Professor John North examines the nature and importance of high places on pages 536–9 of his superb *Stonehenge, Neolithic Man and the Cosmos*, HarperCollins, 1997.

41. Luke 8, verses 29–30

42. For example, see Mark 3, verse 11.

43. Luke 11, verse 24

44. M. Oldfield Howey, *The Horse in Magic and Myth*, Courier Dover Publications, 2002, page 51; also H. A. Guerber, *Myths of Northern Lands*, Kessinger Publishing, 2003, page 32

45. See, for example, Anthony D. Hippisley Cox, *Haunted Britain*, page 30.

46. Clement A. Miles, *Christmas in Ritual and Tradition*, 1912, Chapter XIV

47. Luke 8, verses 22–5

48. St Jerome (AD 347–420) was the first to describe Mary in such terms, but it's long been an official Roman Catholic epithet for her.

49. Luke 23, verse 38

50. Tacitus, *Annals*, Book 12, XXXII

51. Quoted in Diodorus Siculus, *Histories*, 2.47, pages 2–3, 6

52. See the numerous entries on my Eternal Idol website, www.eternalidol.com.

53. Quoted Diodorus Siculus, op. cit.

Chapter 16: Sound of Silence?

1. Geoffrey Ashe, *Avalonian Quest*, Methuen, 1982, pages 96–7

2. Adam de Domerham, *Historia de rebus glastoniensibus*, Oxford, 1727, page 344

3. John 8, verse 12

4. Richard Cavendish, *King Arthur and the Grail; The Arthurian Legends and their Meaning*, Butler and Tanner Ltd, 1978, page 180

5. Mike Pitts, *Hengeworld*, Arrow Books, 2001

6. *Stonehenge in its Landscape*, English Heritage, 1996

7. Anthony Harding, *The Archaeological Journal* 153, 1996, 359–63,

reproduced in Pitts, op. cit., note 5, page 346

8. Ibid., note 1
9. Stuart Piggott, *The Druids*, Thames & Hudson, 1970
10. Roger Mercer, *Antiquaries Journal* 77, 1997, 407–12, reproduced ibid., note 2
11. Mike Pitts, op. cit., page 2
12. See Christopher Chippindale, *Stonehenge Complete*, Thames & Hudson, 2004, page 206.
13. Gerald Hawkins, *Nature*, 1963
14. Reproduced in Piggott, op. cit.
15. Chippindale, op. cit., page 174
16. Ibid., page 261
17. See the article in the *Guardian* newspaper and other reports of 5 May 2006.
18. In an interview with Robin McKie of the Guardian, 24 July 2005, Dr David Miles, the chief archaeology adviser to English Heritage, said, in a classic example of extreme understatement, 'Stonehenge has not been well served by archaeology... Even in the 20th century, archaeological work, although carried out by professionals, was generally poor.'
19. H. A. Lewis, *Christ in Cornwall*, J. H. Lake, 1900
20. Geoffrey of Monmouth, *History of the Kings of Britain*, trans. Lewis Thorpe, Penguin Books, 1973
21. Mike Pitts, *Hengeworld*, Arrow Books, 2001, page 121
22. See the official town council and community website of Glastonbury, Somerset: www.glastonbury.gov.uk.
23. Matthew 5, verse 44
24. Timothy Freke and Peter Gandy, *The Jesus Mysteries*, HarperCollins, 1999, pages 83, 84. *See also* note 40, page 333, and Plato's *Crito*, 49b–e.

Conclusion

1. José María Escrivá de Balaguer, *Conversations with Monsignor Escrivá de Balaguer*, Ecclesia Press, Dublin, 1977
2. Carl Sagan and Ann Druyan, *Comet*, Book Club Associates, 1985, page 170
3. Ibid., page 175
4. Matthew 24, verse 24

INDEX